Chinese Music and Musical Instruments

By Xi Qiang
with China National Orchestra

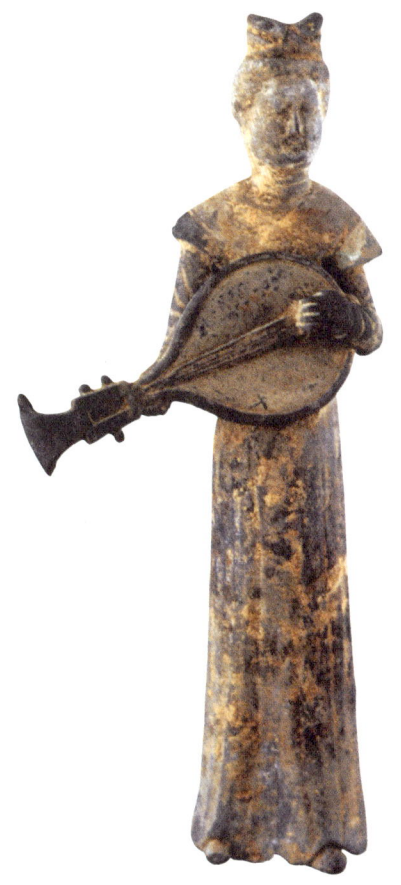

Better Link Press

Copyright © 2011 Shanghai Press and Publishing Development Company

All rights reserved. Unauthorized reproduction, in any manner, is prohibited.

This book is edited and designed by the Editorial Committee of *Cultural China* series

Managing Directors: Wang Youbu, Xu Naiqing
Editorial Director: Wu Ying
Editors: Yang Xiaohe, Greg Tantala
Translator: Qiu Maoru

By Xi Qiang with China National Orchestra
Photographs: Niu Jiandang

Cover Design: Wang Wei
Interior Design: Yuan Yinchang, Li Jing, Xia Wei
Cover Image: Quanjing

ISBN: 978-1-60220-105-7

Address any comments about *Chinese Music and Musical Instruments* to:
Better Link Press
99 Park Ave
New York, NY 10016
USA

or

Shanghai Press and Publishing Development Company
F 7 Donghu Road, Shanghai, China (200031)
Email: comments_betterlinkpress@hotmail.com

Printed in China by Shanghai Donnelley Printing Co., Ltd.

1 3 5 7 9 10 8 6 4 2

Contents

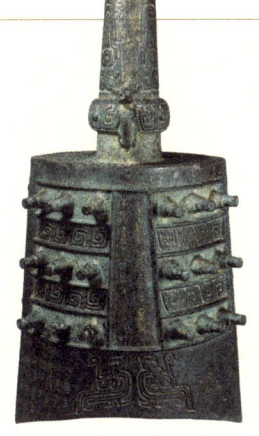

Preface ... 7

Chapter One Present-day Chinese Folk Orchestra ... 12

1. Wind Instruments ... 16
   Dizi ... 16
   Xiao ... 18
   Suona ... 20
   Sheng ... 23
   Guan ... 28

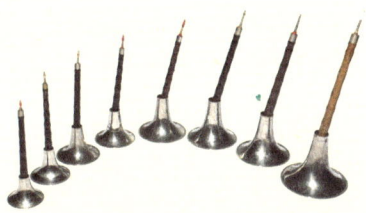

2. Plucked Stringed Instruments ... 31
   Pipa ... 31
   Liuqin ... 34
   Zhongruan ... 36
   Daruan ... 36
   Yangqin ... 37
   Guzheng ... 41
   Konghou ... 43
   Sanxian ... 44

3. Percussion Instruments ... 46

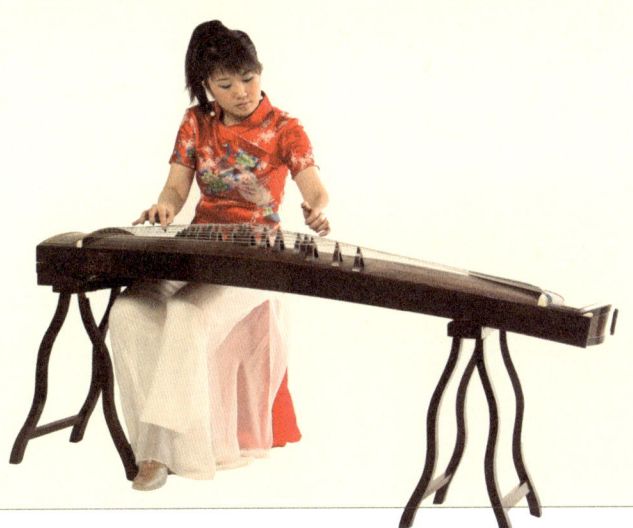

   Bianzhong ... 47
   Dagu ... 48
   Xiaobo (xiaocha) ... 48
   Xiaoluo ... 50
   Jingluo ... 50
   Daluo ... 51
   Yunluo ... 53
   Paigu ... 54
   Muyu ... 55
   Bangu ... 56
   Nanbangzi ... 57
   Bangzi ... 57

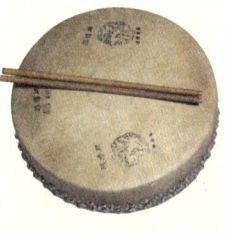

4. Bowed Stringed Instruments ... 58
   Erhu ... 59
   Gaohu ... 64
   Zhonghu ... 65
   Laruan ... 66

Chapter Two The History of Chinese Music ... 68

1. **The Rudimentary Stage**
   (From the 2100 BC to 221 BC) ... 69
2. **The Thriving Stage**
   (From 221 BC to 960 AD) ... 83
3. **The Mature Stage**
   (From 960 AD to 1840) ... 105
4. **The Modern and Contemporary Stage**
   (From 1840 to present) ... 108

Dynasties in Chinese History ... 114

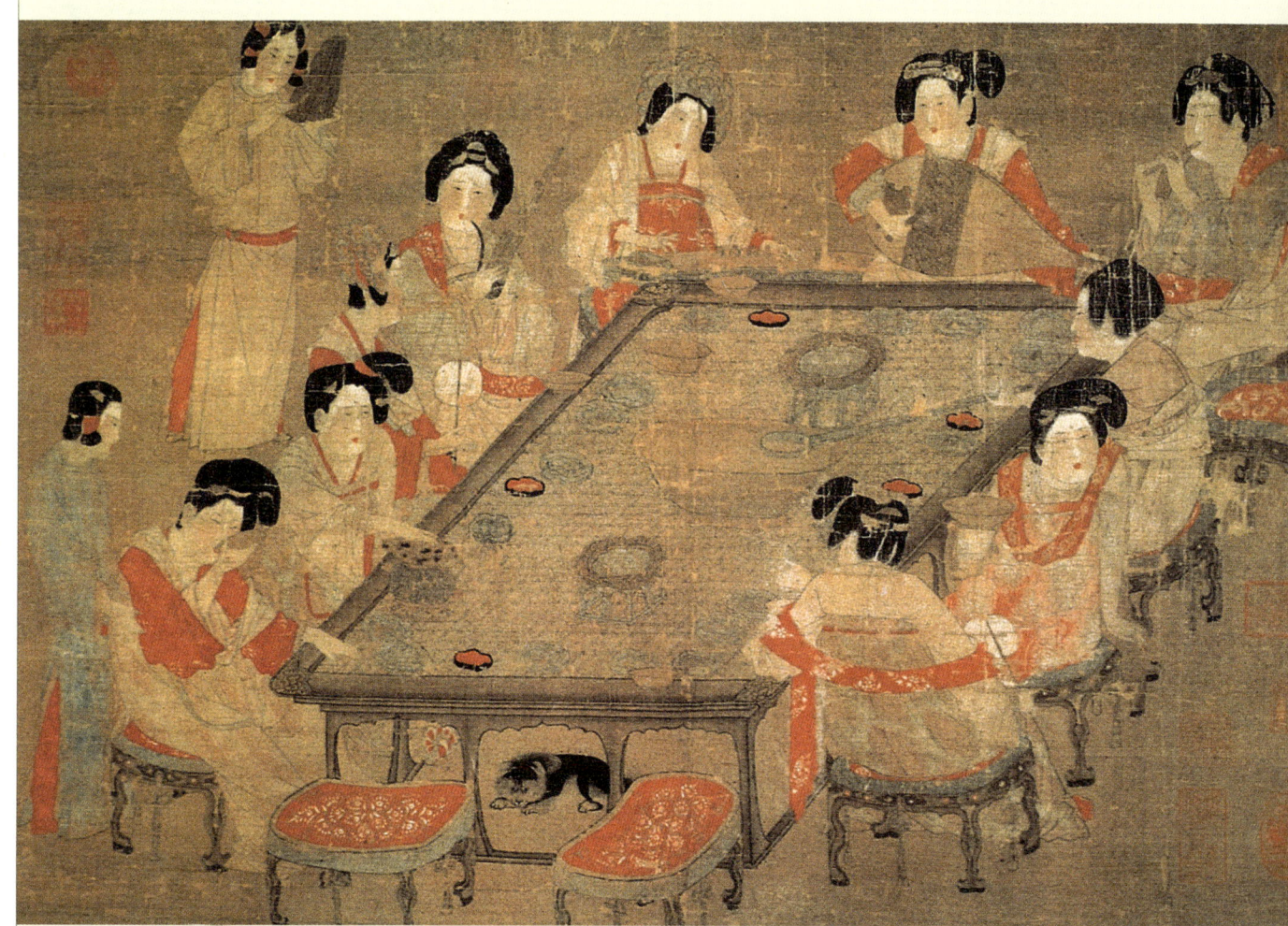

Revelry in Tang Court
Unknown painter, Tang Dynasty
Ink and color on silk
48.7×69.6cm
Palace Museum, Taipei
Revelry in Tang Court depicts life in the harem in a Tang court. Ten aristocratic ladies waited on by two maids sit around a dinner table sipping tea or playing music. The musical instruments include *sheng* (reed pipe), *ban* (clappers), zither, *pipa* and the short flute.

Preface

The Chinese music illustrated in this book categorizes traditional Chinese music and various types of music developed from it.

Traditional Chinese music possesses a special charm. Chinese music is distinguished by its musical compositions, musical instruments and famous musicians. When appreciating Chinese music, priority should be given to the following three elements: the "inherit richness" of tunes, the "resemblance in form and in spirit" and the quality and style of the music.

The "inherit richness" of tunes means a musician processes and upgrades melody in respect of timbre, intensity and pitch so that his music has its distinctive personal and local color.

Resemblance in spirit is as important as form. This concept does not apply to music only, to be more exact, it is the general principles and high ideals pursued in Chinese culture. The balance between yin and yang is emphasized in traditional Chinese medicine, Taoist teachings of essence, energy and this mentality is followed in Chinese calligraphy. All are closely related to the performing art of Chinese music. When playing the same musical piece, different performers may produce different effects, such as quick or slow rhythm, and bright or dark timbre, due to their different interpretations of music. As a result music can display happiness, anger, grief and joy in its spiritual character.

Stress is laid on the character and style of Chinese music, especially of the imperial ceremonial music created by scholars. Here "character" means the mental outlook of a person and "style" means the artistic style of the music. The well-known literary theorist Liu Xie (465 – 532 AD) pointed out in his classic work of literary criticism *The Literary Mind and the Carving of the Dragon* that an artist's mental outlook plays an important role in his artistic creation and determines the character and style of his work.

Music is an emotional art. Chinese music is entirely different from Western music in style. While importance is attached to harmony, polyphony and orchestration in Western music, in Chinese music the ethnic feature is displayed by its melodious tune and implicit richness as well as the tone colors of different instruments. In a word, style is the overall manifestation of musical instruments, works, performance and aesthetic taste. So far as the composition of musical instruments is concerned, ancient Chinese musical instruments are divided into eight categories according to the material they are made of. The eight different kinds of "sound" recorded in history are metal (*zhong* and *ling*), stone (*qing*), pottery (*xun*), wood (*paiban*),

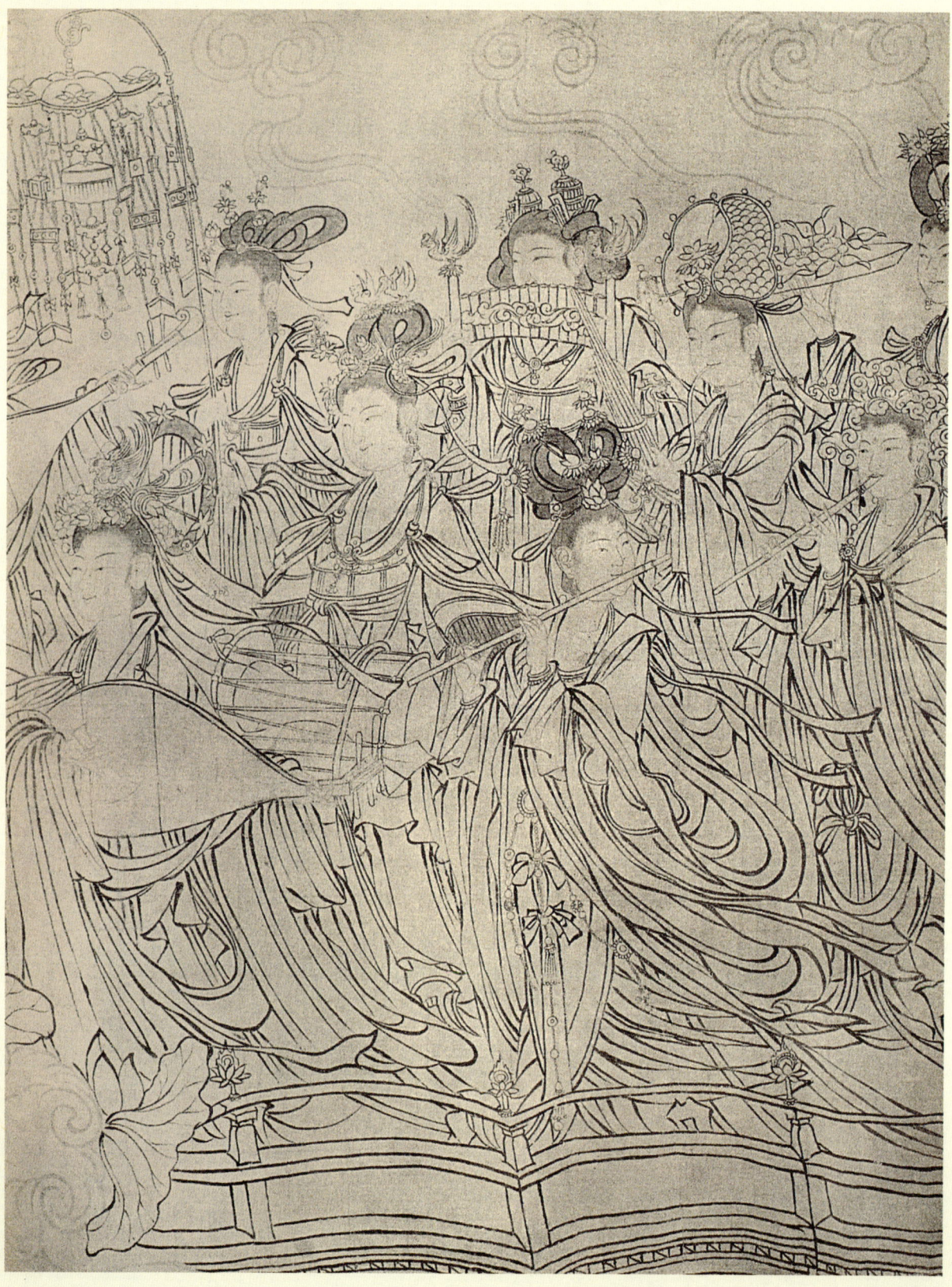

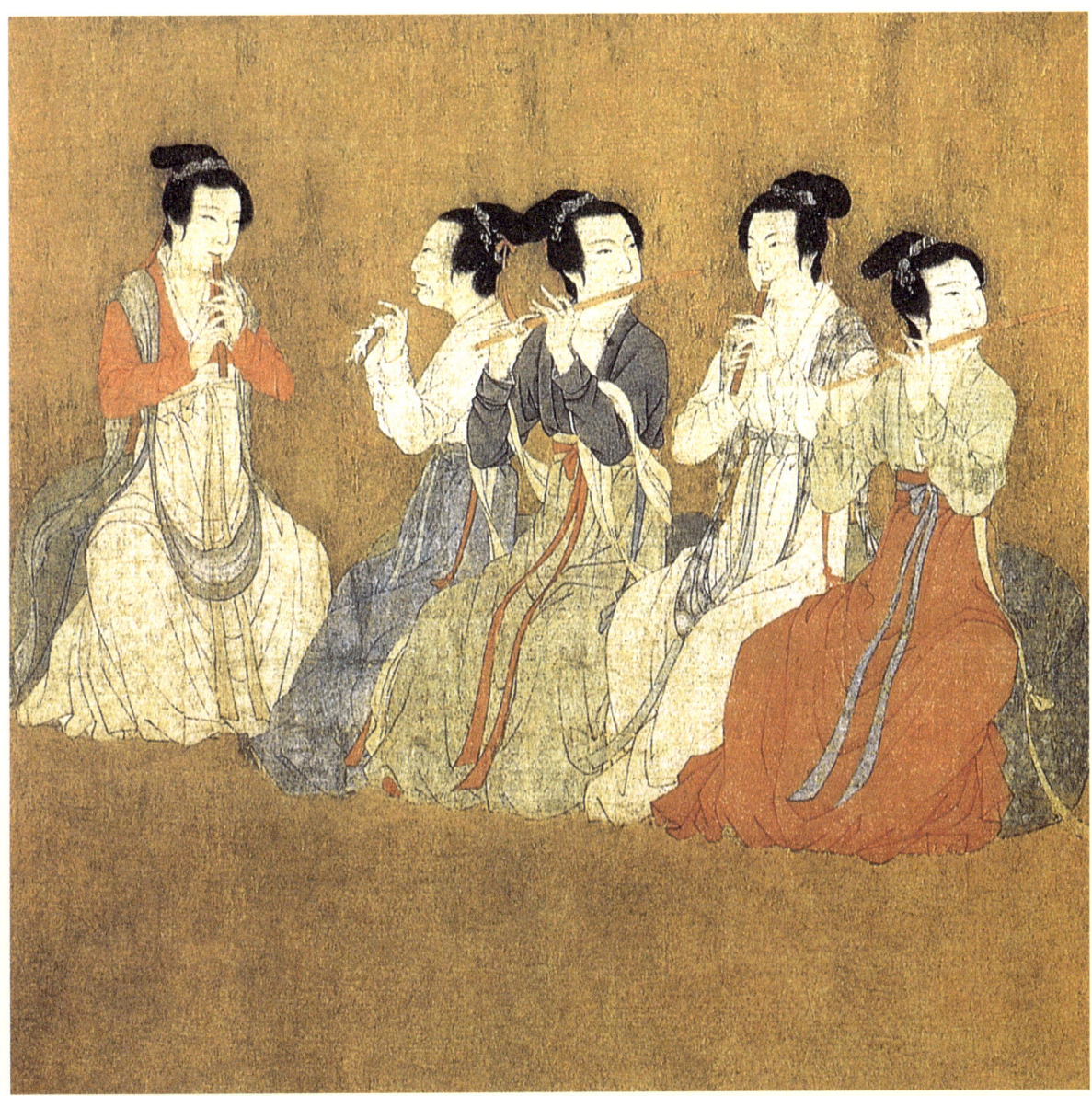

Left: *Procession of Gods* (detail)
Wu Zongyuan 武宗元 (? – 1050)
Ink on silk
58×777.55cm
Collection of C. C. Wang (US)
Wu Zongyuan was a folk painter in the Northern Song Dynasty. He specialized in Buddhist and demon painting. He was once appointed by Emperor Zhenzong of the Song Dynasty as director of the imperial task force for temple murals. This painting is a draft for a mural, depicting a procession of 87 Taoist gods. The stately figures are executed with flowing, rhythmical, long lines, exhibiting movement and cadence in a long but orderly procession. The dozen or so musical instruments are all played while the musicians are on the move.

Above: *The Night Revels of Han Xizai* (detail)
Gu Hongzhong 顾闳中 (Painter of the Five Dynasties, years of birth and death unknown)
Ink and color on silk
28.7×335.5cm
Palace Museum, Beijing
This painting is one of the major works in China's art history. The painting is in five sections that depict people wining and dining, watching the performance of a dance, lounging, music playing or flirting, with Han Xizai appearing in various sections. Of particular artistic merit is the section featuring five flute-playing courtesans, in which music seems to flow from their facial expressions and the rhythmic colors of their clothing. Some art critics consider it to be a forerunner of picture story books.

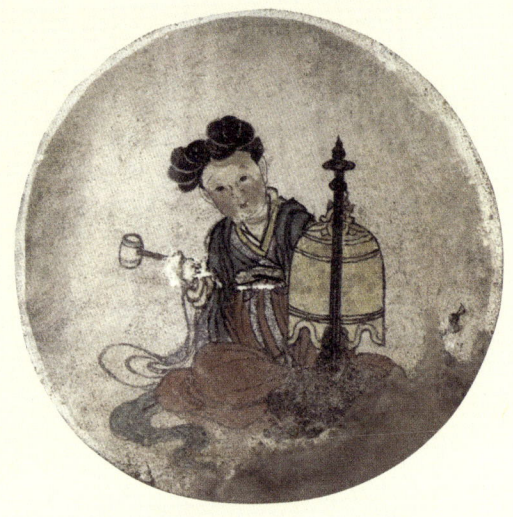
Metal

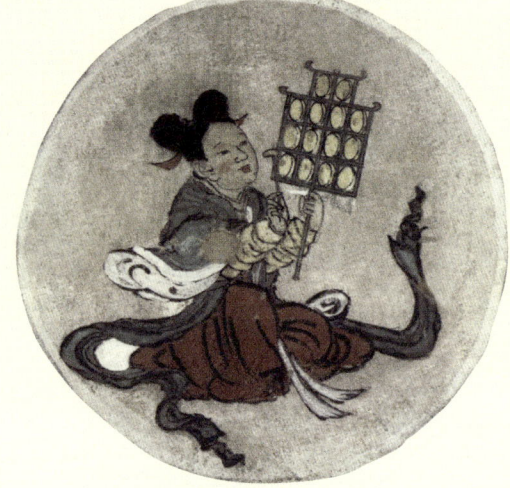
Stone

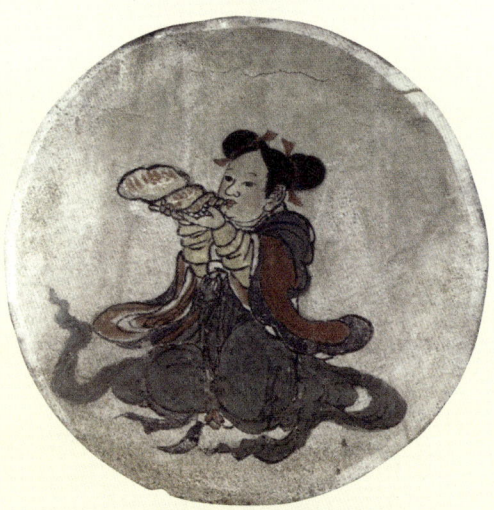
Pottery

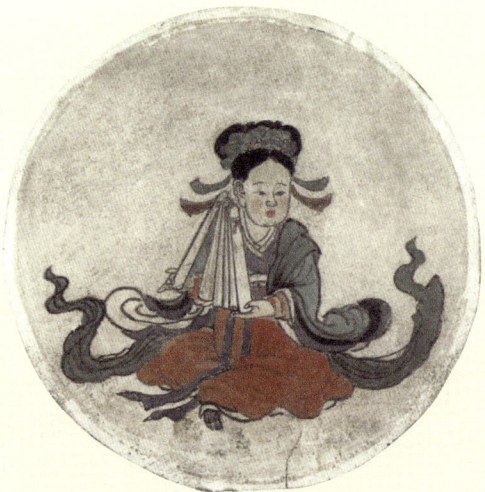
Wood

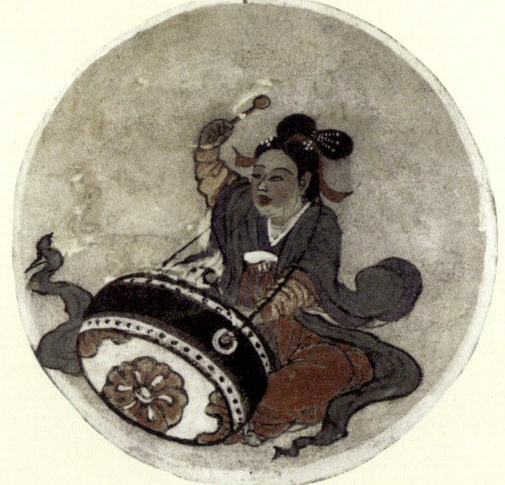
Leather

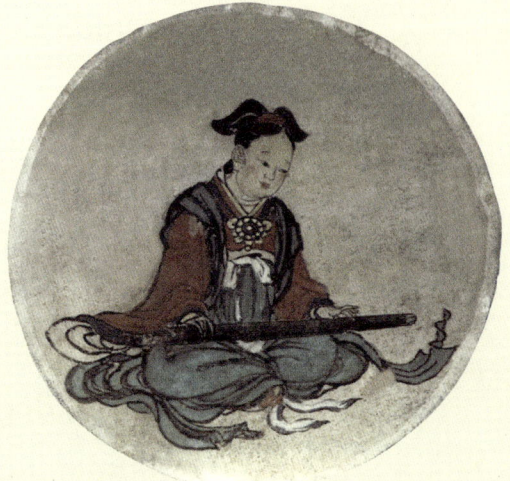
Silk

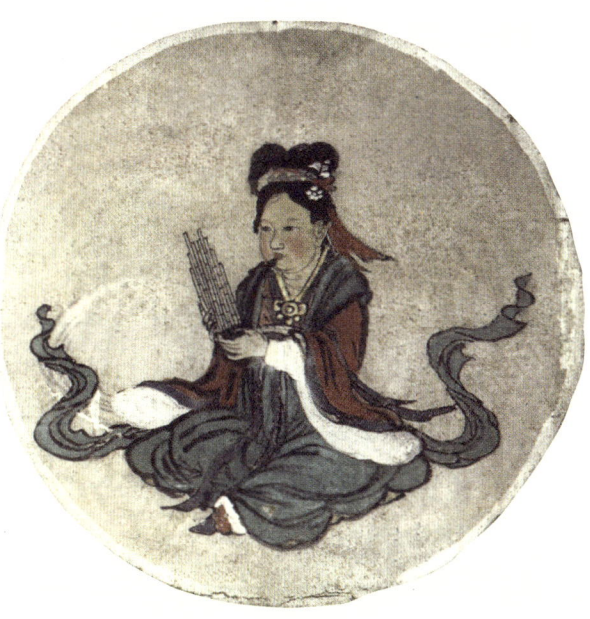

Gourd

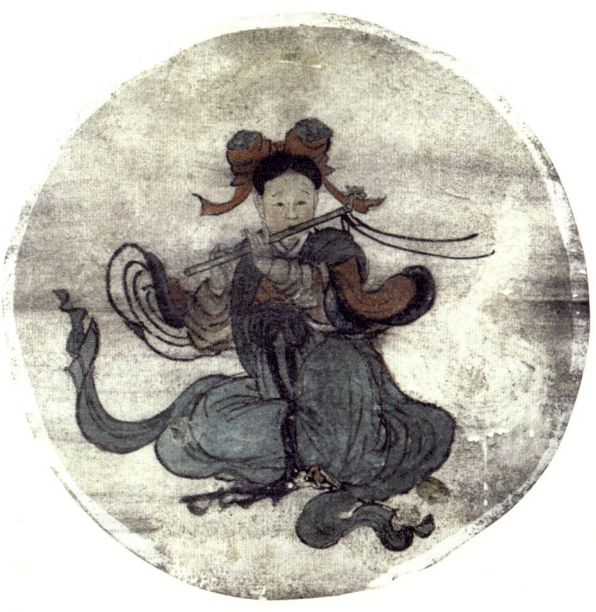

Bamboo

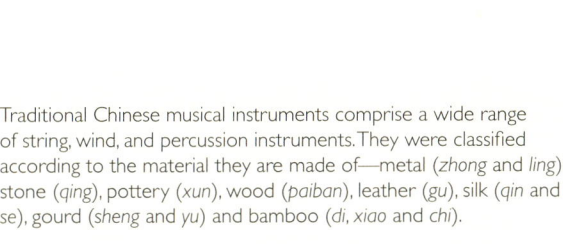

Traditional Chinese musical instruments comprise a wide range of string, wind, and percussion instruments. They were classified according to the material they are made of—metal (*zhong* and *ling*), stone (*qing*), pottery (*xun*), wood (*paiban*), leather (*gu*), silk (*qin* and *se*), gourd (*sheng* and *yu*) and bamboo (*di*, *xiao* and *chi*).

leather (*gu*), silk (*qin* and *se*), gourd (*sheng* and *yu*) and bamboo (*di*, *xiao* and *chi*). Ancient Chinese musical instruments have undergone great changes and development. The present-day Chinese music is composed of four types according to the playing method of blowing, bowing, plucking and striking. Therefore musical instruments are divided into four sections: wind instruments (*dizi*, *suona*, *sheng*, etc.), plucked stringed instruments (*pipa*, *yangqin*, *guzheng*, *qin*, *ruan*, *sanxian*, etc.), percussion instruments (*yunluo*, *paigu*, *dagu*, *bianzhong*, etc.) and bowed stringed instruments (*erhu*, *jinghu*, *banhu*, *gaohu*, *zhonghu*, etc.). The three sections of wind instruments, bowed and plucked stringed instruments, complete with high-pitched, alto and bass instruments, are able to play concerted musical pieces. As a result, a Chinese folk orchestra is distinctive for its great variety of unique instruments as well as for its superb acoustic effects.

As an important part of Chinese culture, Chinese music embodies rich and colorful traditions and anticipates a prosperous future.

This book describes in detail the musical instruments with which a Chinese folk orchestra is equipped and their working and sounding principles. This book is also devoted to the description of the development of Chinese music and the introduction of some music-related tales of profound significance.

CHAPTER ONE
Present-day Chinese Folk Orchestras

A present-day Chinese folk orchestra is usually comprised of about 90 musicians who perform mostly professional compositions. Such orchestras have only a short history and it wasn't until the 1920s that Liu Yaozhang, Liu Tianhua and some other musicians established the Datong Music Society in Shanghai; this is considered the beginning of the Chinese folk orchestra. In the fall of 1935 the Nanjing Central Broadcasting Station Chinese Folk Orchestra was set up. After 1949 the concerted efforts of many middle-aged and elderly composers of Chinese music brought a new phase in the development of the Chinese folk orchestra. Ever since the 1980s a large number of young composers have produced innovative works different from those of their predecessors both in style and technique.

Composition

In the 1950s a group of aspiring musicians of Chinese music such as Peng Xiuwen, Li Huanzhi, Liu Wenjin, Qin Pengzhang and Piao Dongsheng

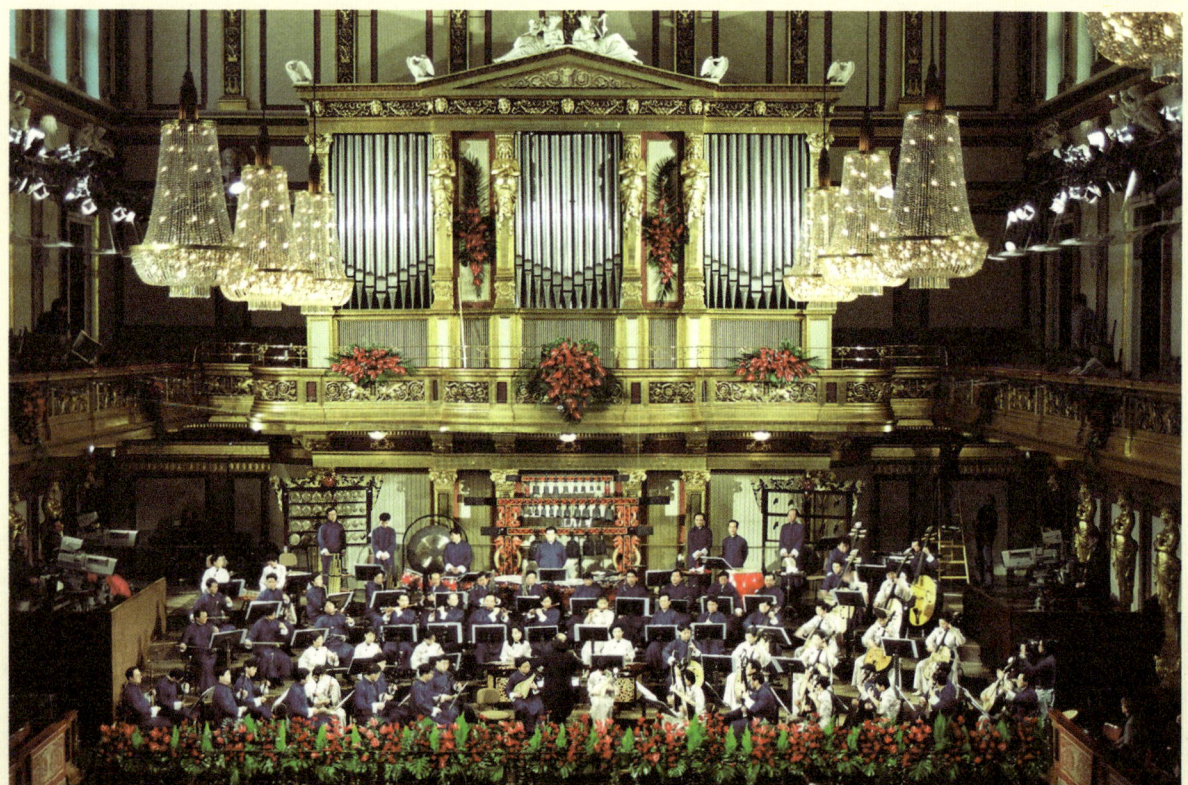

The China National Orchestra's performance at Vienna's Golden Hall in 1999

started to compose for the orchestra. Some of their compositions are modifications of traditional folk tunes, e.g., *Chunjianghuayueye* and *Erquanyingyue*, however they also wrote new compositions with modern themes. Their representative works are *Qin Dynasty Terra Cotta Warriors and Horses* (by Peng Xiuwen), *Caprice of the Long Wall* (by Liu Wenjin), *Local Ballads of Western Yunnan Province* (by Guo Wenjing) and *Suite of Northwestern China* (by Tan Dun). These works brought into full play the striking contrast of colorful Chinese instruments.

General Musical Score

A general musical score is a written representation of a musical composition showing all the instrumental sections arranged one after

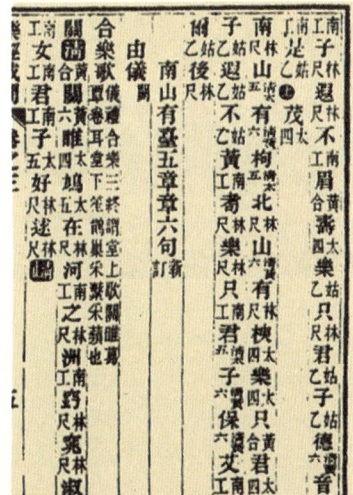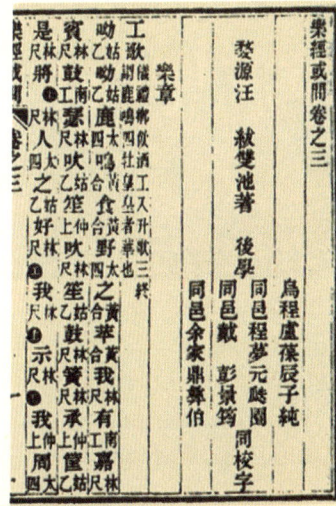

A copy of *Yuejinghuowen*, which is a worded score written by Wang Fu in the middle of the Qing Dynasty

Ancient Musical Scores

The history of Chinese music witnessed a great variety of musical scores. Scores were classified in various ways, either according to the time a kind of instrument and a genre of music were prevalent, different master performers or different schools of tunes. Musical scores were also divided into different forms of musical notation, e.g., worded notation, instrument-oriented notation and curve-diagrammed notation.

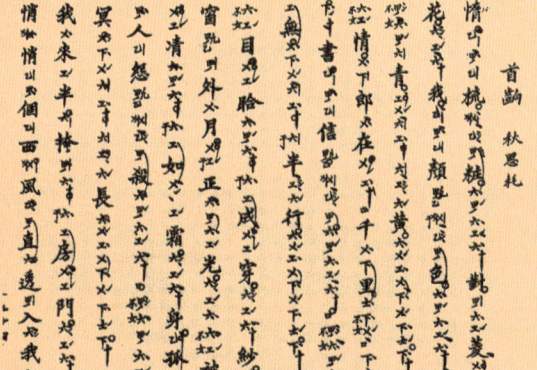

The lithographic copy of a score of southern music written in 1912 when the Republic of China was founded

The full score of the instrumental ensemble in *Stringed Music for Reference* from the Qing Dynasty. In ancient China music was passed on from a master to his pupil. In order to save ancient scores from being lost, Rong Zhai, a musician of China's Mongolian ethnic group, collected and sorted out 13 tunes of Chinese ancient stringed music in 1814. He compiled a hand-written copy of these 13 tunes and entitled it *Stringed Music for Reference*, which was also known as *Thirteen Tunes of Stringed Music*. This book is considered one of the most ancient scores ever recorded.

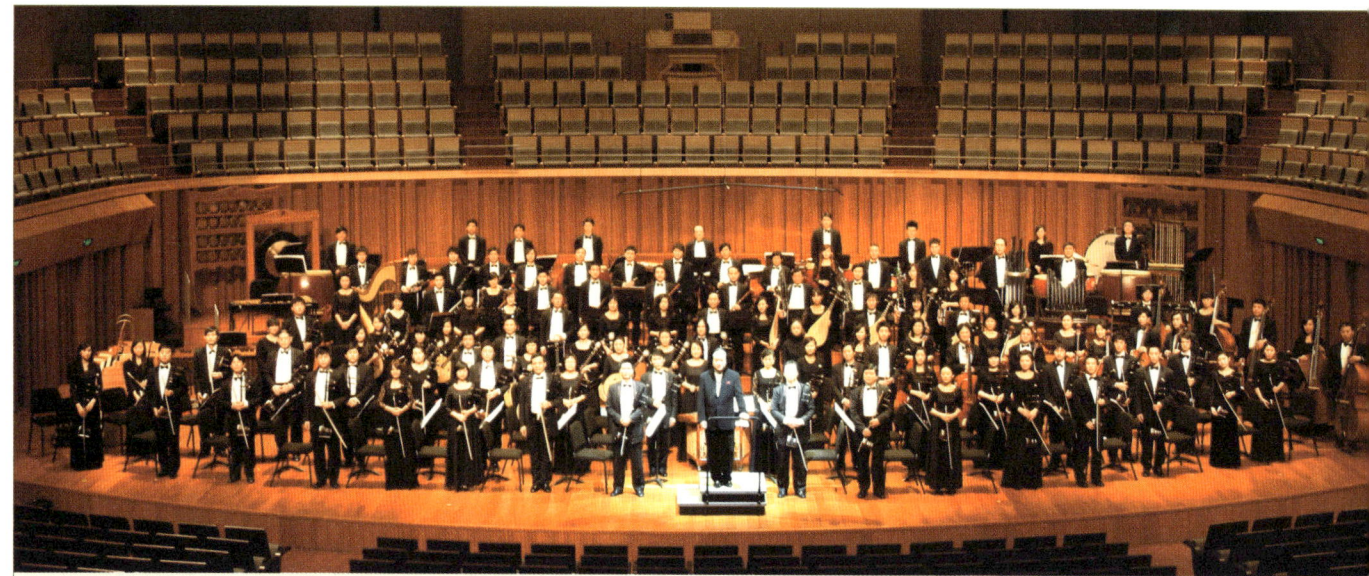

China National Orchestra

another. The score used for a specific instrument is called sectional score. A general score is mainly used for rehearsal, recording and performance.

The earliest general scores were written for stringed and woodwind instruments and wind and percussion instruments. The tunes were recorded in the form of traditional worded, sub-worded or *gongchi* (naming after two of the Chinese characters) musical notation. The present-day general scores of an orchestra are arranged in different sections according to the timbre, volume and harmonization of specific instruments.

Conductor

The role of a conductor is to direct the orchestral musicians to play their respective instruments according to the general score and in the mood required by it. The conductor, who stands in front of the orchestra, plays a key role in an orchestra.

During the initial stage of its development, the instrumental ensemble was performed without a conductor. With the emergence of Chinese folk orchestras and chamber-music-like performance, a dramatic change took place in the technique, structure, performance and style of Chinese music. Many experimental works were entirely different from traditional Chinese folk music. As a result, the position of a conductor was added to an orchestra.

Structure of an Orchestra

A Chinese folk orchestra is composed of four sections: wind, plucked, percussion and bowed.

There are as many as a thousand different kinds of musical instruments in China. Only a tiny portion of them are used in an orchestra. The selection of musical instruments for an orchestra depends on how well they compliment one another.

As wind and percussion instruments give much more volume than bowed and plucked instruments, priority is given to bowed and plucked sections in the overall layout of acoustics. In this way, the audience in the theatre will be able to enjoy comprehensive and balanced sound effects.

Conductor in Ancient Times

Among the relics of the Spring and Autumn Period and the Warring States Period unearthed in Sui county, Hubei Province, the *jiangu*—a percussion instrument—is found in a bell and drum band. A *jiangu* player holds sticks in both hands and beats the *jiangu*. At that time the *jiangu* performer acted like the conductor of a modern-day orchestra.

Like the *jiangu* performer, the players of *jiegu*, *zhonggu*, *zhongqing*, *paiban* and *bangu* also used conductors. At that time a conductor was also a performer who was proficient in all kinds of melodies and instruments. He used his percussion instrument to set the rhythm of music and played the role of conductor.

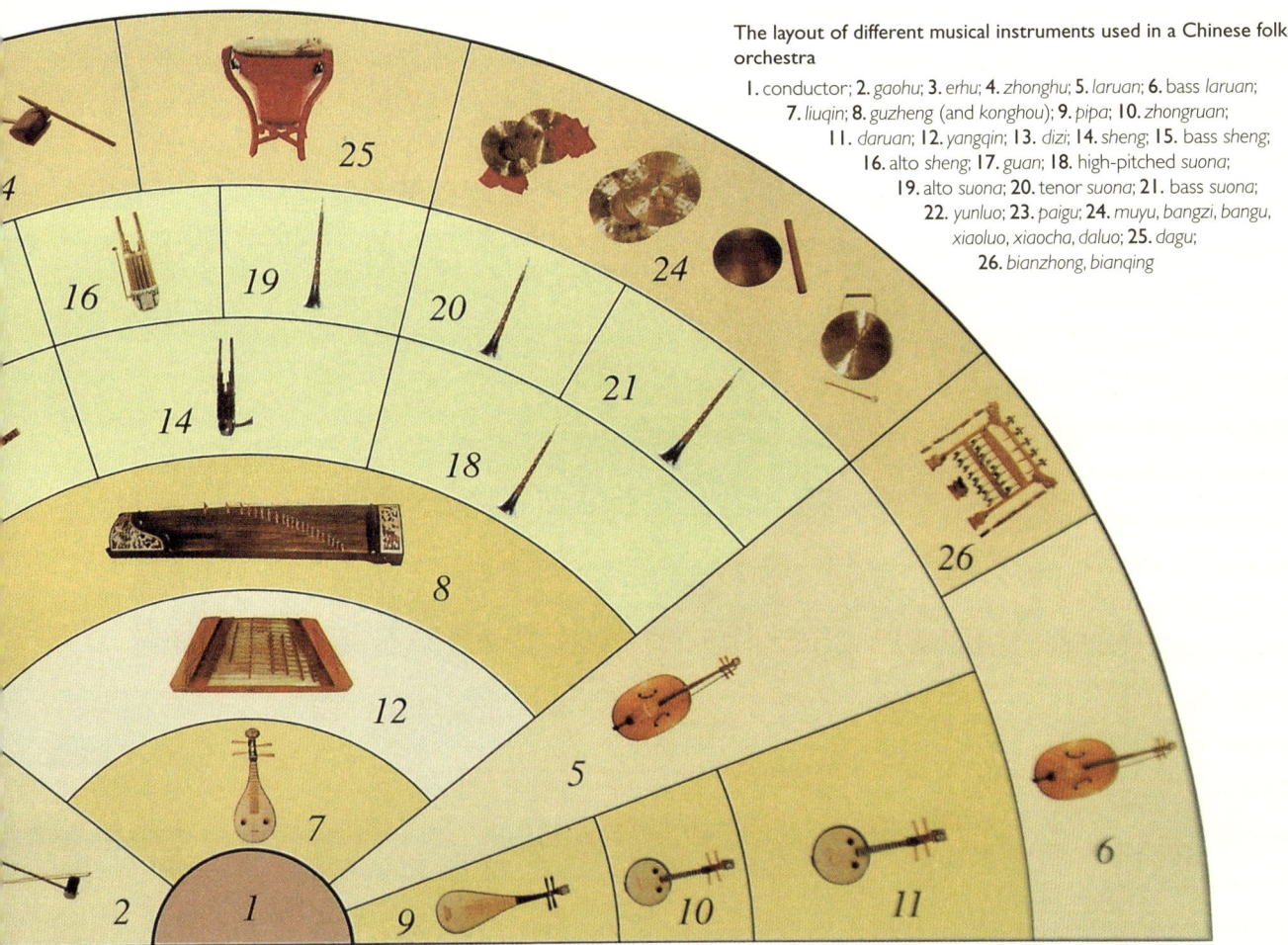

The layout of different musical instruments used in a Chinese folk orchestra

1. conductor; 2. *gaohu*; 3. *erhu*; 4. *zhonghu*; 5. *laruan*; 6. bass *laruan*; 7. *liuqin*; 8. *guzheng* (and *konghou*); 9. *pipa*; 10. *zhongruan*; 11. *daruan*; 12. *yangqin*; 13. *dizi*; 14. *sheng*; 15. bass *sheng*; 16. alto *sheng*; 17. *guan*; 18. high-pitched *suona*; 19. alto *suona*; 20. tenor *suona*; 21. bass *suona*; 22. *yunluo*; 23. *paigu*; 24. *muyu, bangzi, bangu, xiaoluo, xiaocha, daluo*; 25. *dagu*; 26. *bianzhong, bianqing*

1 Wind Instruments

A bamboo flute

The wind instruments used by present-day Chinese folk orchestras are composed of three parts: *dizi*, *suona* and *sheng*. The *dizi* is a perfect combination of fortitude and softness. The high pitch of the *suona* is as shrill and clear as the singing of a magpie. The *sheng* is distinguished by its steady, melodious and sentimental sound. As the only harmonic instrument of all the traditional Chinese instruments, it plays the role of harmonizing the wind ensemble in the orchestra.

Dizi

The *dizi* (also known as "Chinese flute" or "bamboo flute") is one of the transverse wood instruments commonly used in traditional Chinese music. Most *dizi* are made of bamboo. The traditional *dizi* with a vibrating cover are classified by their length and range in four groups: *xiaodi*, *bangdi*, *qudi* and *dadi*. The modern *dizi* without a vibrating cover is called the *xindi* (which literally means "new flute"). The *dizi* players are positioned in the middle row of the orchestra. Every kind of *dizi* is played by two musicians.

The *bangdi*, which is prevalent in the north of China, is mainly used to accompany local operas

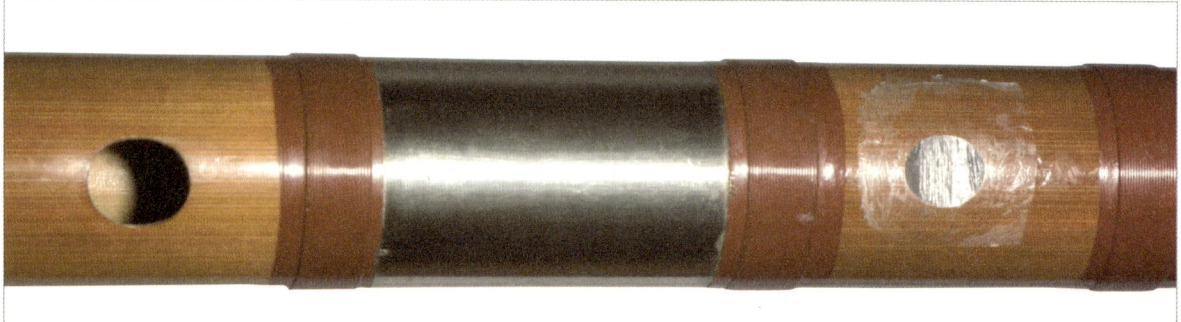

A bamboo membrane

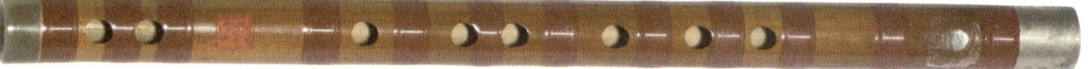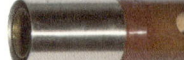

A *dizi* with a plug-in mouthpiece. The attached telescopic brass hoop can be extended to adjust the accuracy in pitch.

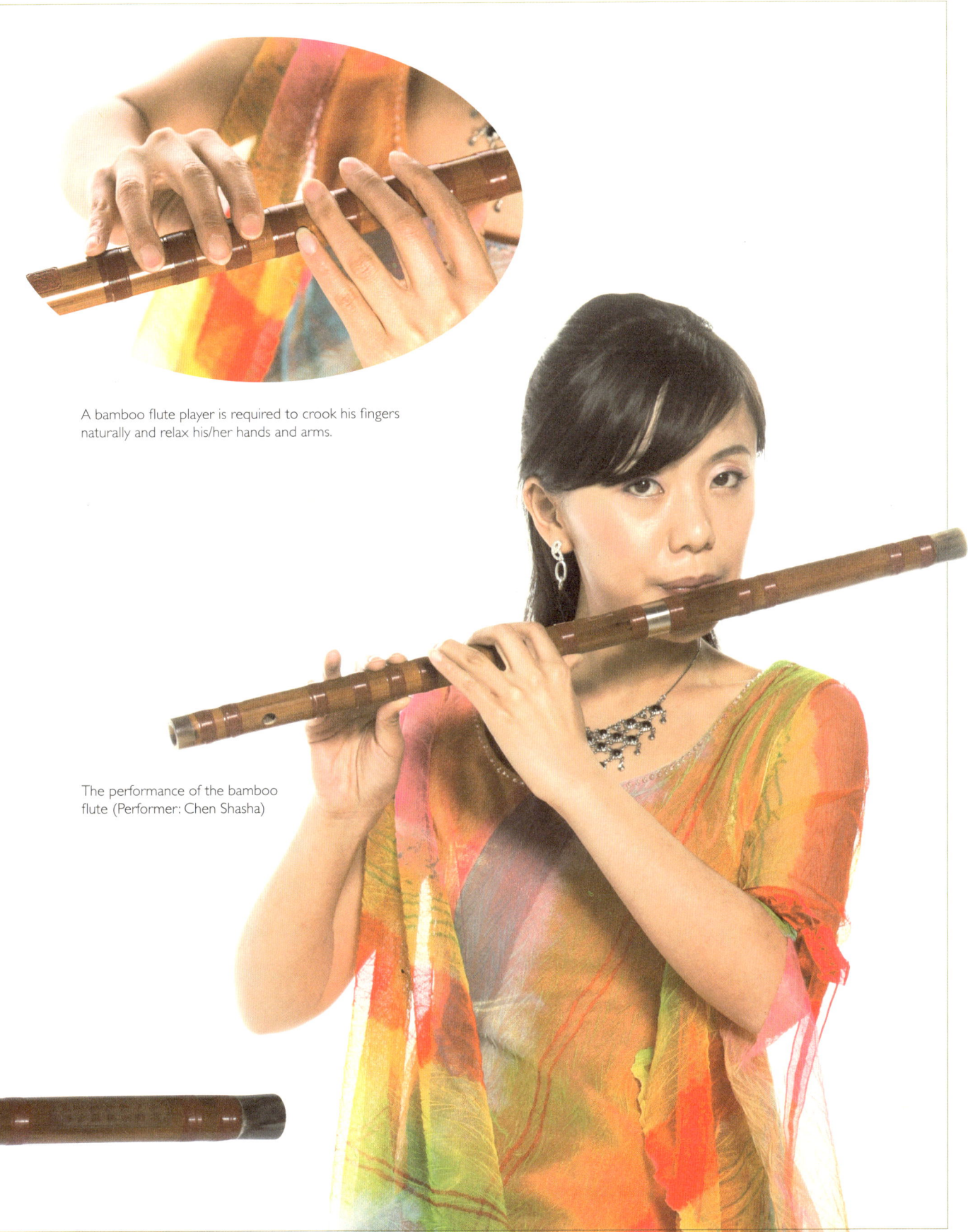

A bamboo flute player is required to crook his fingers naturally and relax his/her hands and arms.

The performance of the bamboo flute (Performer: Chen Shasha)

The Source of the *Dizi*

Tradition has it that a man called Linglun made the *dizi* 4,600 years ago by order of the Yellow Emperor. However, the archaeological finding proved that the *dizi* appeared eight or nine thousand years ago. Xun Xun, an expert in temperament in the Western Jin Dynasty, invented in 274 AD the 12 temperament set of *dizi* for the purpose of tuning instruments to fit the scale of music. Each *dizi* is used to produce a different tone. This set of *dizi* serves as a tone adjuster.

In the Western Han Dynasty the *dizi* was called the "*hengchui*" (which literally means "horizontal blowing"). After the missions of Zhang Qian (? – 114 BC) to the Western Regions (139 – 126 BC for the first time, 119 – 115 BC for the second time) the *dizi* and the related tunes of the ethnic groups were introduced into the hinterland. The spread and use of the *dizi* reached a thriving stage in the Tang Dynasty. Many poets described the melodious sound of the *dizi*. In the Song and Yuan dynasties the *dizi* were adopted to accompany local operas and singing. In later years the *dizi* was divided into two main categories: *bangdi* and *qudi*, which were adopted according to their different tones as an instrument to accompany respectively the Northern local operas and Southern local operas.

Section of *Departure Herald*, painted in Ming Dynasty. The horserider in the picture is blowing the *dizi* transversely.

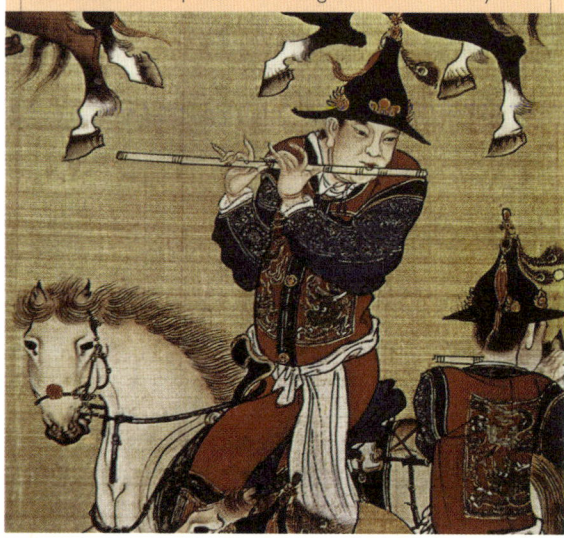

and perform folk tunes. It is known for its bright, loud and rustic sound. The *qudi*, which is popular south of the Yangtze River, especially in Jiangsu, Zhejiang, Guangdong and Fujian provinces, is often used to accompany the *kunqu* opera and in local music. In sharp contrast with the musical style of the *bangdi*, the tone of the *qudi* is a representative example of the typical features of Chinese *sizhu* music: soft, melodious and exquisite. The *xindi* was specially designed and produced to meet the needs of the present-day Chinese folk orchestra. It plays the function of harmonizing the tones of the *bangdi* and *qudi*.

Xiao

As an age-old traditional bamboo-made wind instrument, the *xiao* is similar to the *dizi*. The only difference is that the *xiao* is played by blowing from the top. In the Qin and Han dynasties *paixiao* (also known as "panpipes") came into being with a row of short pipes of varying length fixed together. The *xiao* can be seen in cave paintings since the Tang and Song dynasties and is often mentioned in historical accounts. Different from the loud, bright and vigorous sound of the *dizi*, the tone color of the *xiao* is soft, gentle and melodious, possibly why many poets had a special liking for this instrument.

A *xiao*

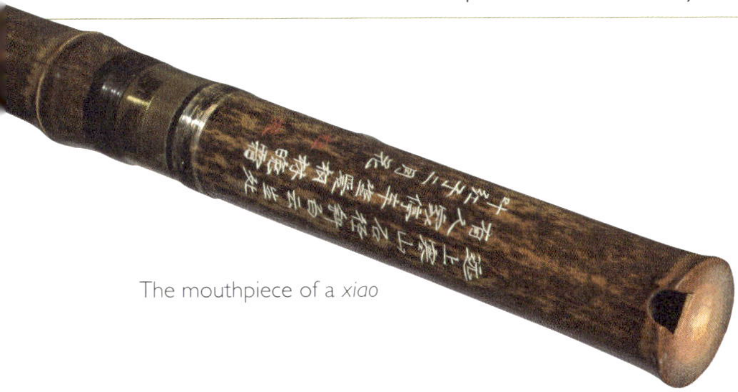

The mouthpiece of a *xiao*

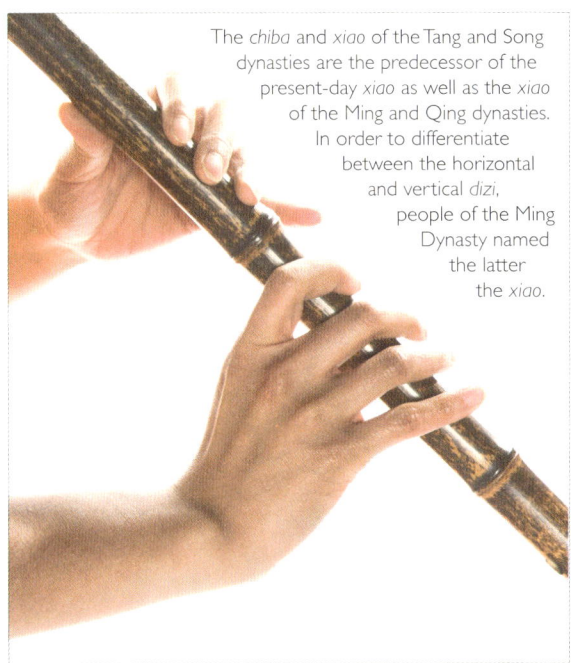

The *chiba* and *xiao* of the Tang and Song dynasties are the predecessor of the present-day *xiao* as well as the *xiao* of the Ming and Qing dynasties. In order to differentiate between the horizontal and vertical *dizi*, people of the Ming Dynasty named the latter the *xiao*.

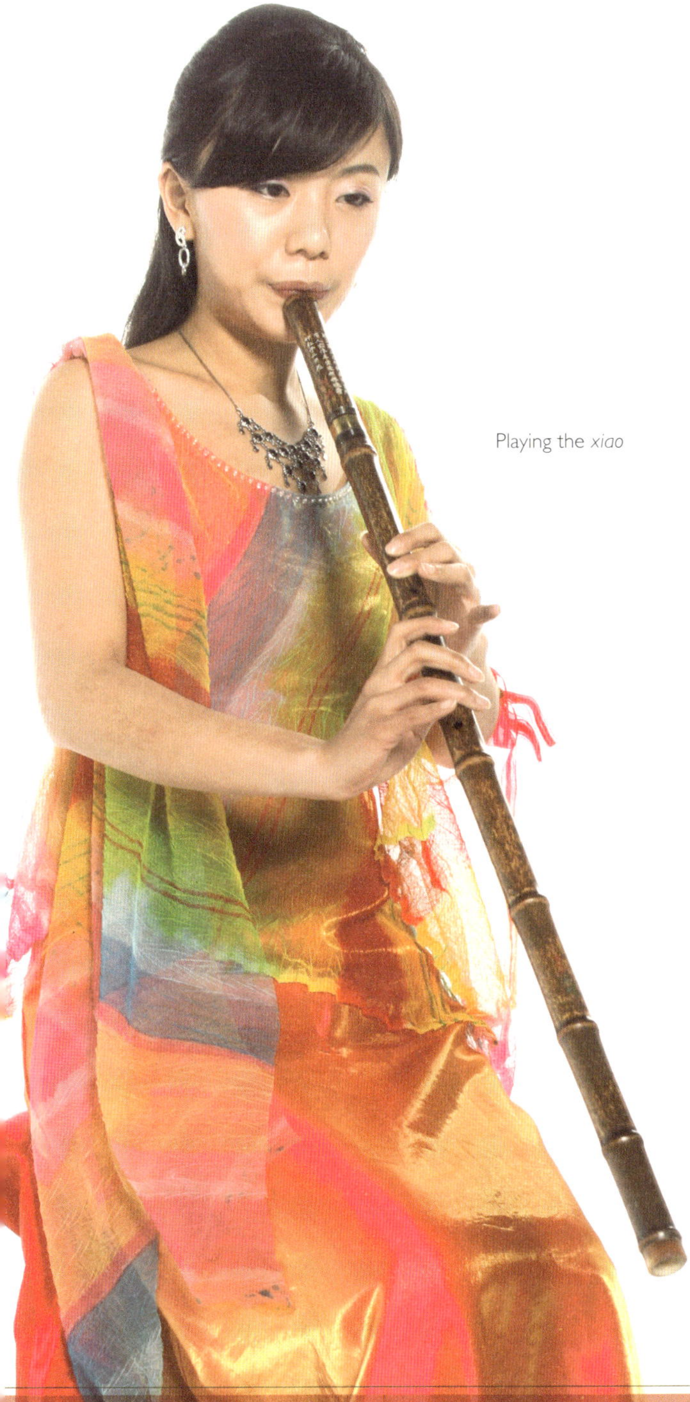

Playing the *xiao*

Attract the Phoenix by Playing the *Xiao*

During the Spring and Autumn Period and the Warring States Period, Duke Mugong of the Qin State had a beautiful and talented daughter called Longyu. She was fond of playing the *sheng*. One day the sound of the *xiao* floated into her chamber complimenting her performance of the *sheng*. When the *xiao* player Xiao Shi was brought to the throne, the Duke, impressed by this handsome player's free and easy manner, told him to play the *xiao*. Xiao Shi played three pieces in a composed way and his melodies attracted a fragrant breeze, rosy clouds and golden phoenixes. The delighted Duke gave Xiao Shi his daughter's hand in marriage.

One night as the couple were playing the *xiao* and the *sheng* together. They saw a phoenix fly over and land on their left and a dragon fly land on their right. Xiao Shi declared, "I am an immortal. With the blessing of Heaven, I married you. But the mandate of Heaven forbids me to stay in this world for long. Now that the dragon and the phoenix have come to fetch us, it's time for us to leave." With these words Xiao Shi mounted the dragon and Longyu mounted the phoenix and together they flew off to Heaven.

Suona

In a Chinese folk orchestra the *suona* family is composed of high-pitched, alto and bass parts. The high-pitched *suona* is the traditional *suona* nicknamed the *xiaohaidi*. The sharp and penetrating sound of the high-pitched *suona* drowns out the sound of other instruments. Another fairly important traditional *suona* is called the *dasuona* (or "big *suona*"). Different from the high-pitched

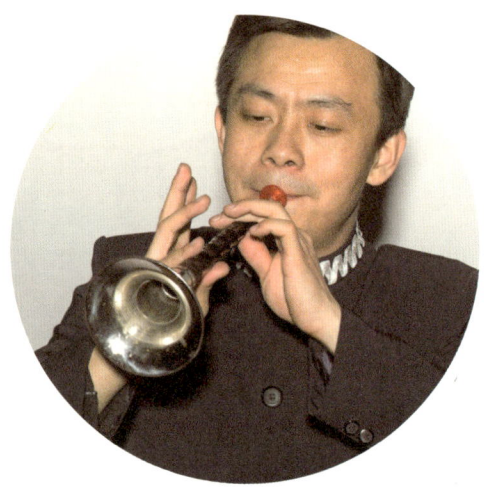

A performance of the traditional *suona* (Performer: Niu Jiandang)

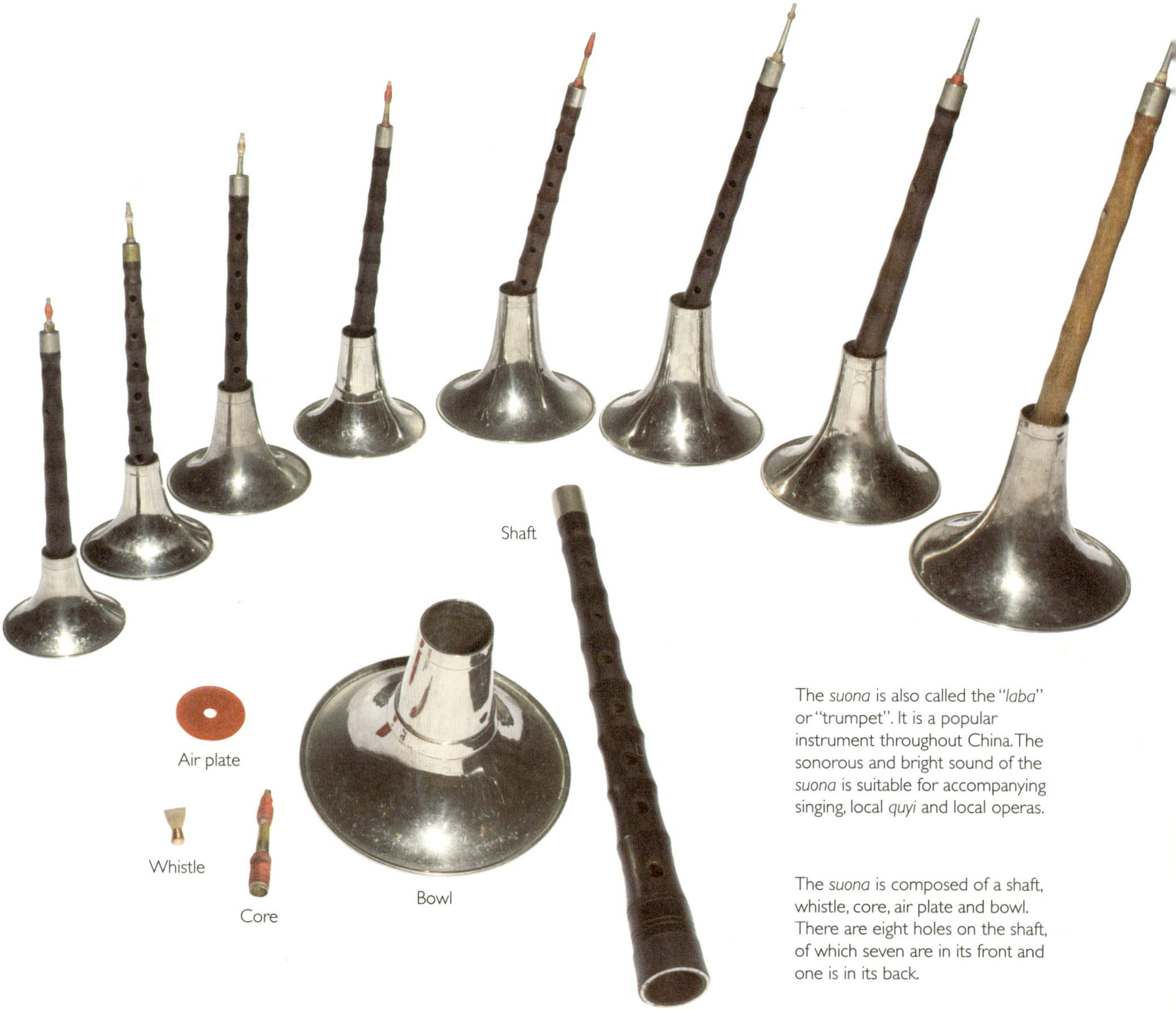

Air plate

Whistle

Core

Bowl

Shaft

The *suona* is also called the "*laba*" or "trumpet". It is a popular instrument throughout China. The sonorous and bright sound of the *suona* is suitable for accompanying singing, local *quyi* and local operas.

The *suona* is composed of a shaft, whistle, core, air plate and bowl. There are eight holes on the shaft, of which seven are in its front and one is in its back.

suona, the big *suona* is known for its rustic and stirring tone which is well suited to certain local folk tunes, e.g., *xintianyou* (which literally means "Ramble in the sky" popular in the loess plateau in northern China) and *hetaoshanqu* (which literally means the mountainous tunes popular in the Hetao Area). The key-added *suona* used by a Chinese folk orchestra is divided into the alto *suona* and the bass *suona*.

The Working Principle of the Key-added *Suona*

The key-added *suona*, is composed of three inserted tubes. Inserting the tubes at different lengths can adjust its tune. Most varieties of the *suona* are keyed. The timbre of the key-added *suona* is low and deep while the sound of its upper register is bright and resonant.

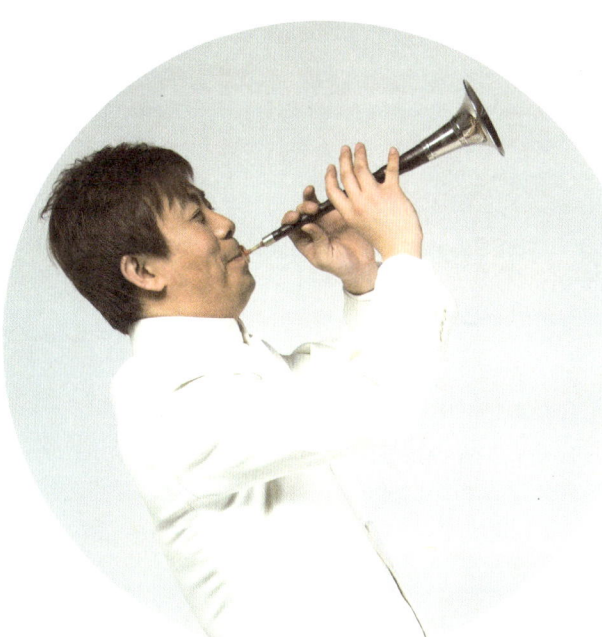

A performance of the traditional *suona* (Performer: Niu Jiandang)

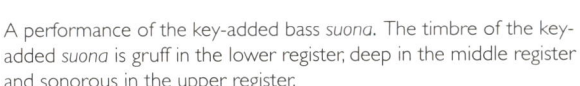

A performance of the key-added bass *suona*. The timbre of the key-added *suona* is gruff in the lower register, deep in the middle register and sonorous in the upper register.

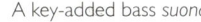

A key-added bass *suona*

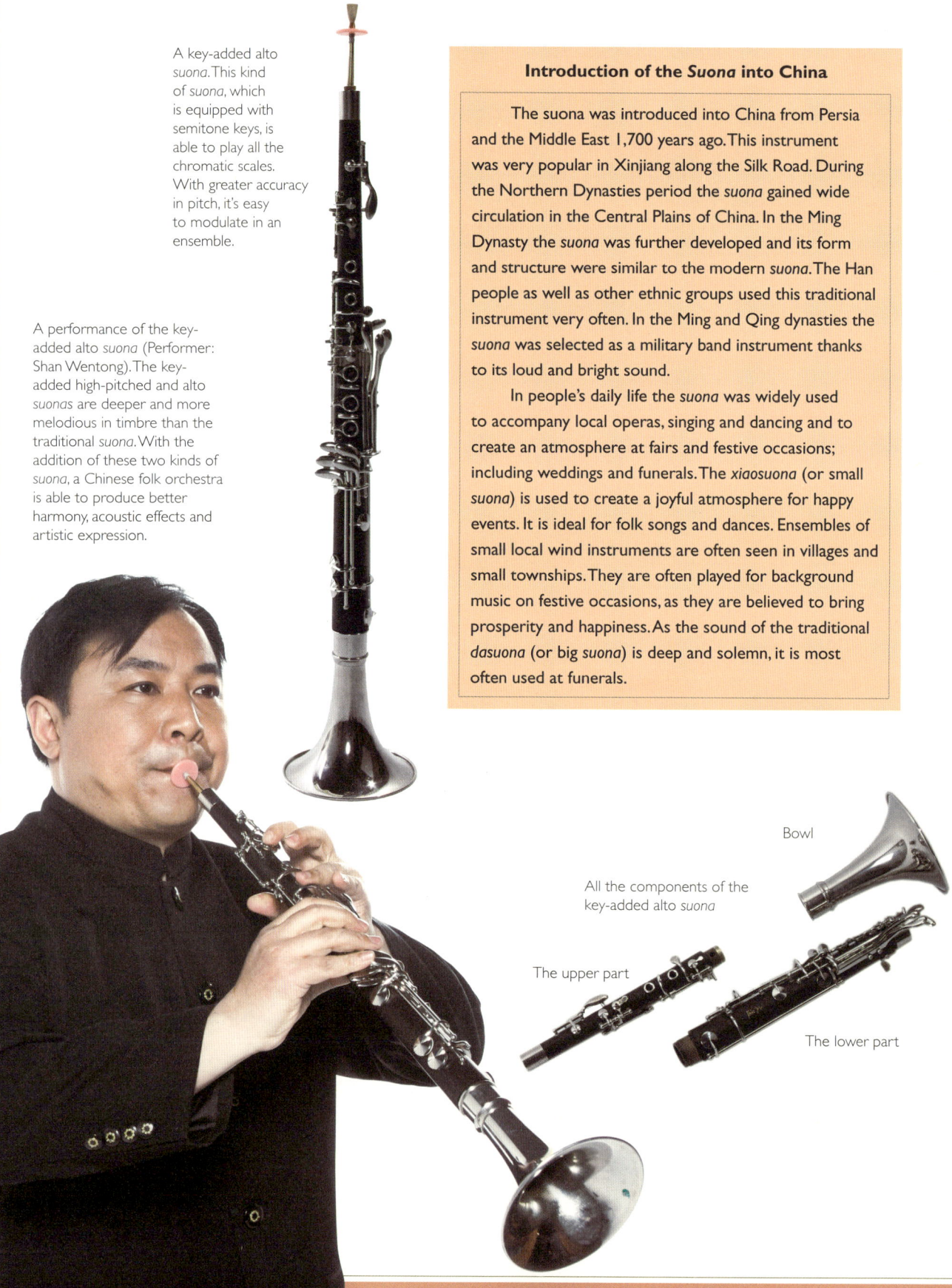

A key-added alto *suona*. This kind of *suona*, which is equipped with semitone keys, is able to play all the chromatic scales. With greater accuracy in pitch, it's easy to modulate in an ensemble.

A performance of the key-added alto *suona* (Performer: Shan Wentong). The key-added high-pitched and alto *suonas* are deeper and more melodious in timbre than the traditional *suona*. With the addition of these two kinds of *suona*, a Chinese folk orchestra is able to produce better harmony, acoustic effects and artistic expression.

Introduction of the *Suona* into China

The suona was introduced into China from Persia and the Middle East 1,700 years ago. This instrument was very popular in Xinjiang along the Silk Road. During the Northern Dynasties period the *suona* gained wide circulation in the Central Plains of China. In the Ming Dynasty the *suona* was further developed and its form and structure were similar to the modern *suona*. The Han people as well as other ethnic groups used this traditional instrument very often. In the Ming and Qing dynasties the *suona* was selected as a military band instrument thanks to its loud and bright sound.

In people's daily life the *suona* was widely used to accompany local operas, singing and dancing and to create an atmosphere at fairs and festive occasions; including weddings and funerals. The *xiaosuona* (or small *suona*) is used to create a joyful atmosphere for happy events. It is ideal for folk songs and dances. Ensembles of small local wind instruments are often seen in villages and small townships. They are often played for background music on festive occasions, as they are believed to bring prosperity and happiness. As the sound of the traditional *dasuona* (or big *suona*) is deep and solemn, it is most often used at funerals.

All the components of the key-added alto *suona*

Bowl

The upper part

The lower part

Sheng

In a Chinese folk orchestra the *sheng* family is composed of high-pitched, alto and bass parts. While the *sheng* can be played solo, its varied and harmonic effects can be utilized to bind all the other wind instruments. Its keyboards come in various forms and can

The *sheng* pipe

The finger holes of the *sheng*

look like either a piano keyboard or an organ keyboard. Every musical hole is equipped with an amplifying metal tube. *Sheng* players are usually in a seated position.

High-pitched *Sheng*

The high-pitched *sheng* generally refers to the *jiansheng* (which literally means "the *sheng* with a keyboard"), e.g., the 32-reed-pipe *sheng*. The high-pitched *sheng* has a soft and melodious timbre. By pressing the keys with both hands, the player can adjust the volume during a performance.

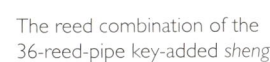

The reed combination of the 36-reed-pipe key-added *sheng*

Chinese Music and Musical Instruments

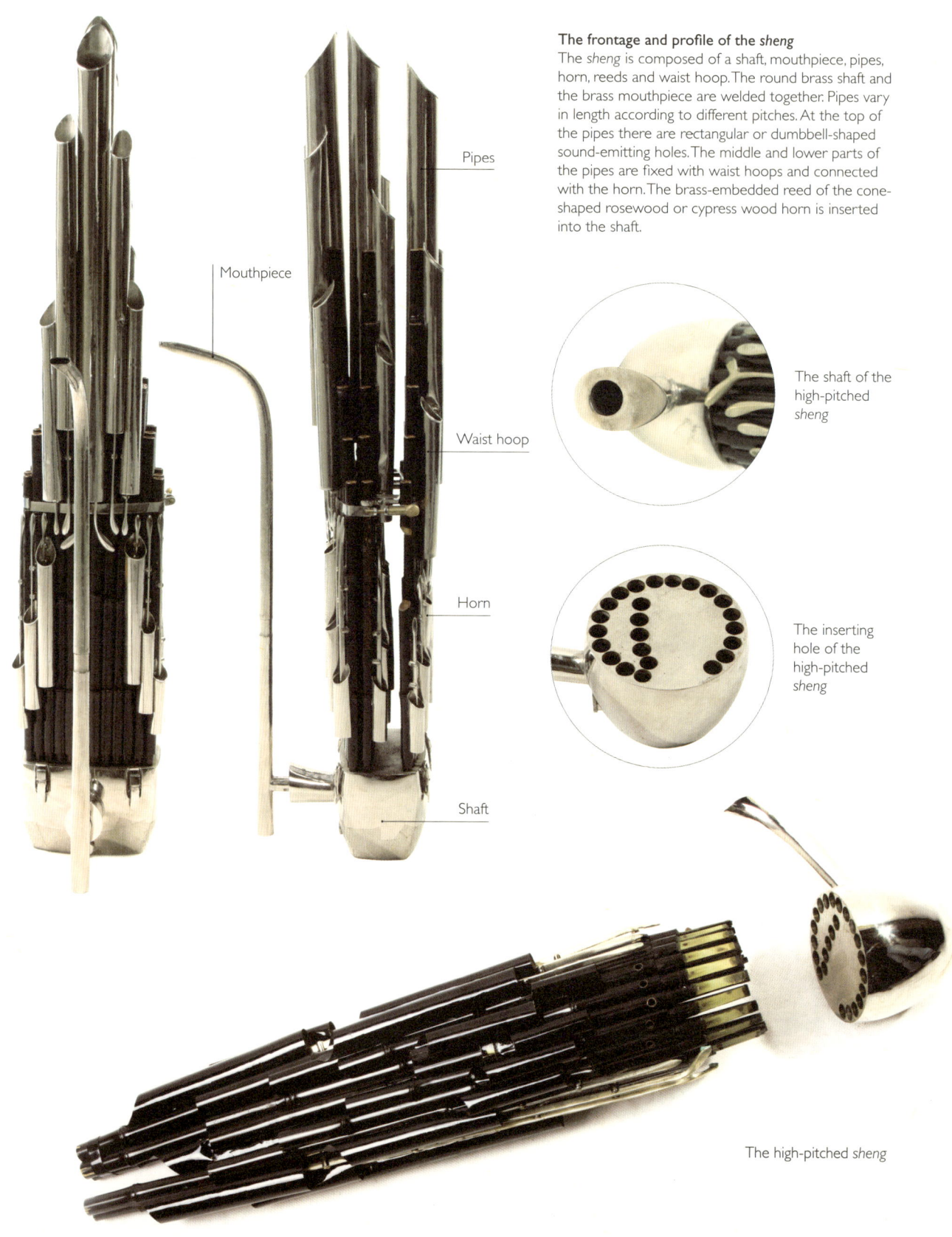

The frontage and profile of the *sheng*
The *sheng* is composed of a shaft, mouthpiece, pipes, horn, reeds and waist hoop. The round brass shaft and the brass mouthpiece are welded together. Pipes vary in length according to different pitches. At the top of the pipes there are rectangular or dumbbell-shaped sound-emitting holes. The middle and lower parts of the pipes are fixed with waist hoops and connected with the horn. The brass-embedded reed of the cone-shaped rosewood or cypress wood horn is inserted into the shaft.

Pipes

Mouthpiece

Waist hoop

Horn

Shaft

The shaft of the high-pitched *sheng*

The inserting hole of the high-pitched *sheng*

The high-pitched *sheng*

Chapter One Present-day Chinese Folk Orchestras Wind Instruments

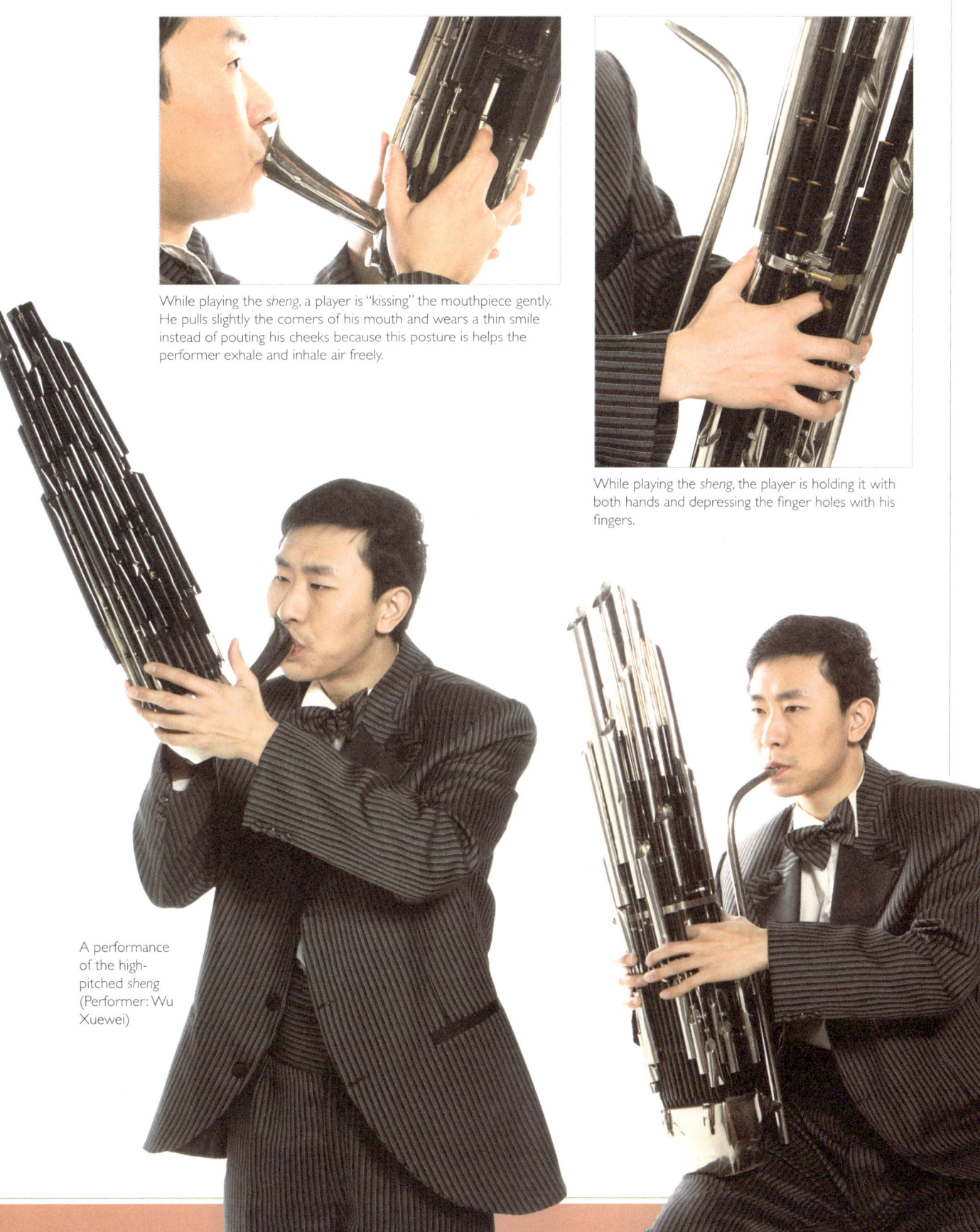

While playing the *sheng*, a player is "kissing" the mouthpiece gently. He pulls slightly the corners of his mouth and wears a thin smile instead of pouting his cheeks because this posture is helps the performer exhale and inhale air freely.

While playing the *sheng*, the player is holding it with both hands and depressing the finger holes with his fingers.

A performance of the high-pitched *sheng* (Performer: Wu Xuewei)

Alto *Sheng*

The alto *sheng* is also called the *baosheng*. With a bigger size than the *jiansheng*, the *baosheng* is usually sat vertically on the player's lap. The player holds the *sheng* with both hands while blowing. The pleasant harmony of the alto *sheng* sounds like a soft and melodious song. Bigger in size, the *baosheng* has a loud sound. By bridging the high-pitched *sheng* and the bass *sheng*, the alto *sheng* harmonizes the sound of the wind instruments.

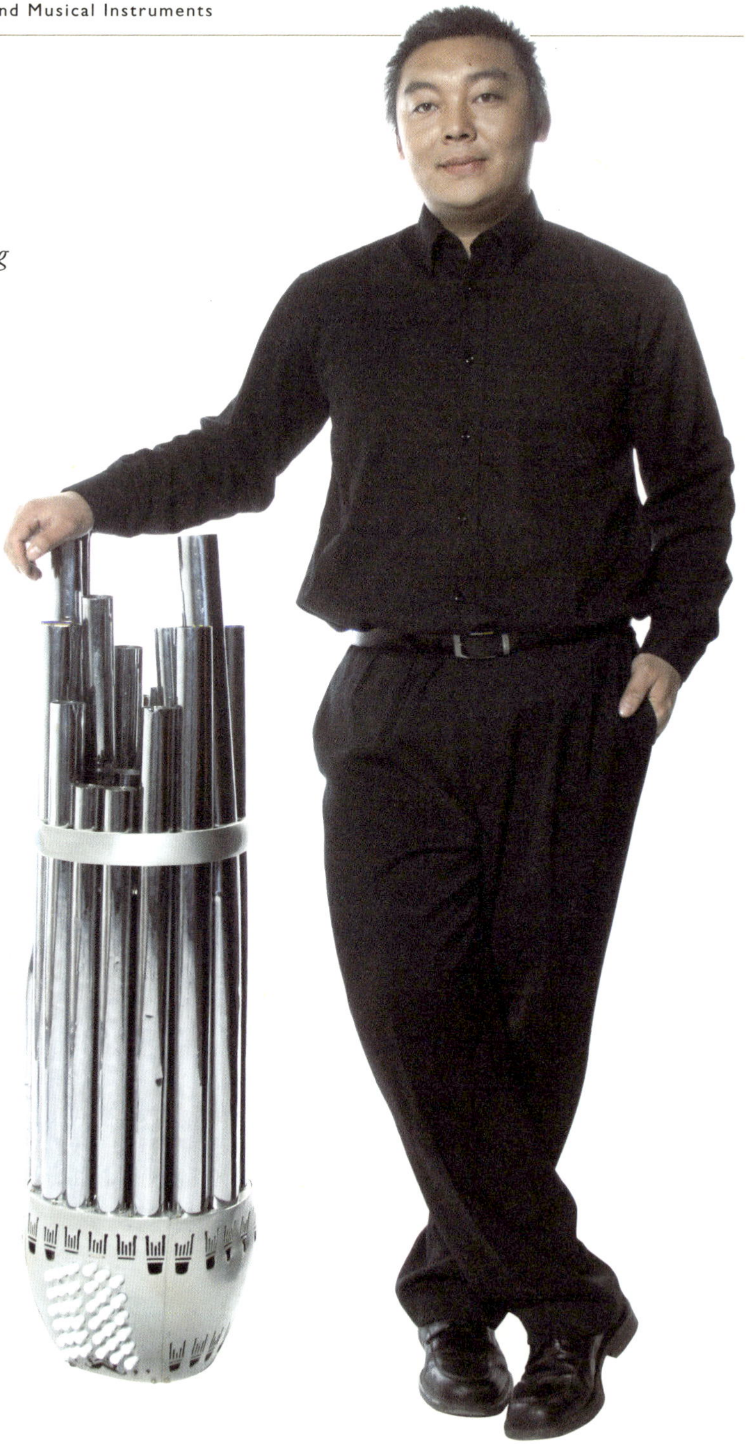

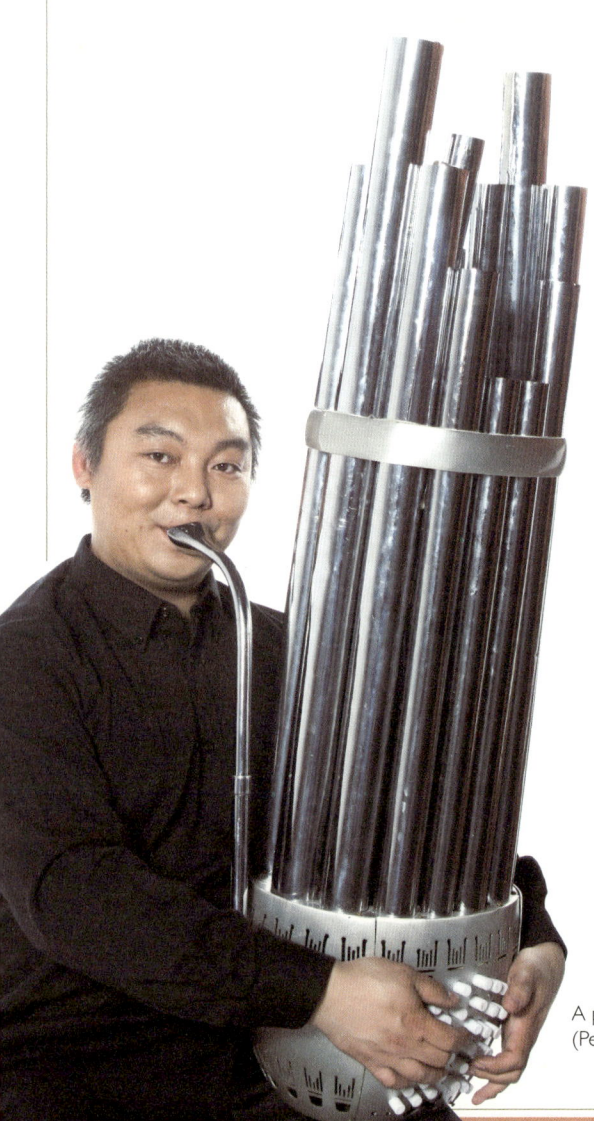

The alto *sheng* is almost half the height of the performer.

A performance of the alto *sheng* (Performer: Wang Wei)

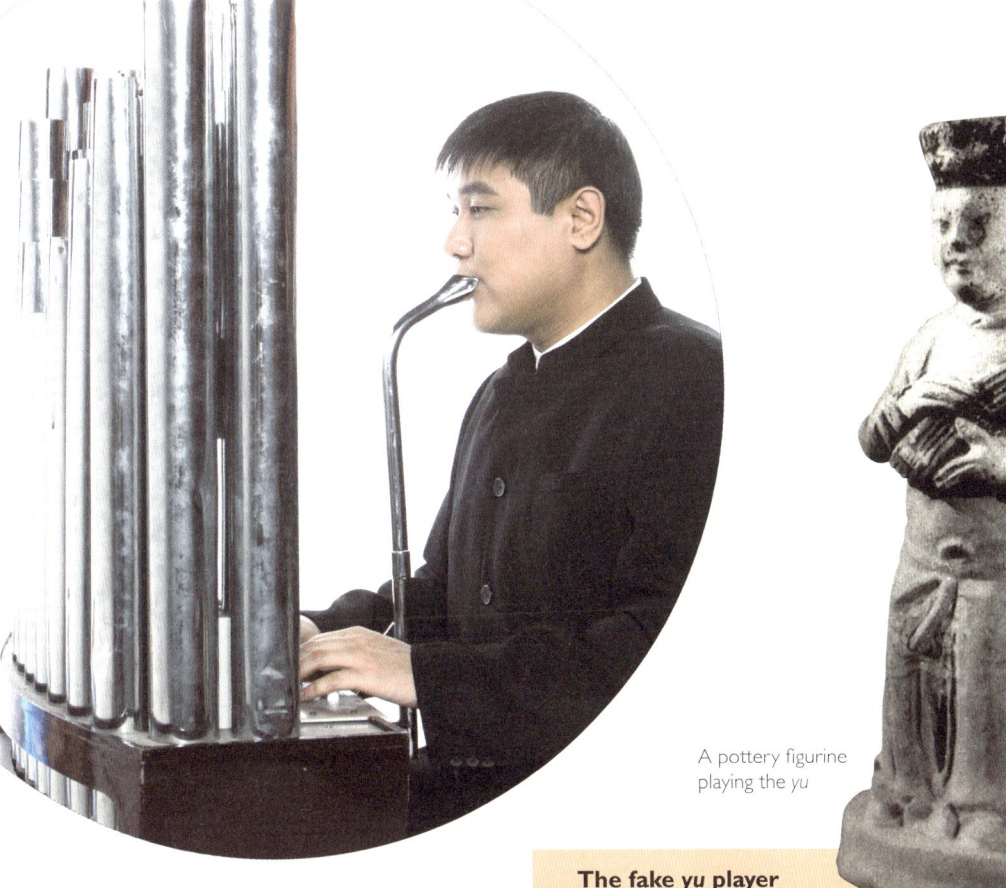

A performance of the bass *sheng* (Performer: Tang Dazhi)

A pottery figurine playing the *yu*

Bass *Sheng*

The bass *sheng* is as big as a small organ and is fixed in a special box. The bass *sheng* player is required to have superior lung capacity. As the bass *sheng* is big in size, it can produce the deepest notes in an orchestra, which are usually known as basic notes. With its deep and rich sound the bass *sheng* plays the role of a stabilizer in the bass section.

The fake *yu* player

Before the Song Dynasty the *yu* and the *sheng* were two similar musical instruments. Duke Xuanwang of the Qi State had a special liking for this instrument. When he listened to the *yu* ensemble, he demanded at least 300 musicians play the *yu* in unison. He thought only music played by a large number of musicians was pleasant. One musician, Nanguo, did not know how to play the *yu*, but he was able to hide among the band undetected. For a long time he enjoyed the same benefits as the other musicians. After Duke Xuanwang died, his son Min succeeded the throne. The new Duke, unlike his father, preferred a *yu* solo to a *yu* ensemble. Nanguo could no longer conceal his deception and soon disappeared.

Guan

As a component of this musical part, the *guan* used in present-day Chinese folk orchestras has been modified from its earlier designs. Developed from the ancient *guan*, the serial *guan* is only used in ensembles. The *suona* and *dizi* distinguished by their unique timbre, are complemented well by the the soft and rich sound of the *guan*. The birth of the alto and bass key-added *guan* makes up for the deficiencies in the sound range.

Though similar to the traditional *guan* in timbre, the reformed key-added *guan* has a lower range and is able to play all the chromatic scales and modulate with ease. As a result it can produce ideal effects in both solo and ensemble performances.

A performance of the alto *guan*. With a penetrating sound, the alto *guan* is played solo or used to lead the ensemble of a folk orchestra. It is sometimes used to strengthen the alto-range section. (Performer:Shan Wentong)

A performance of the bass *guan*. The bass *guan* is suited for playing sentimental pieces. Its gloomy and melancholy timbre is especially fit for playing sad and sorrowful tunes.

Chapter One Present-day Chinese Folk Orchestras Wind Instruments

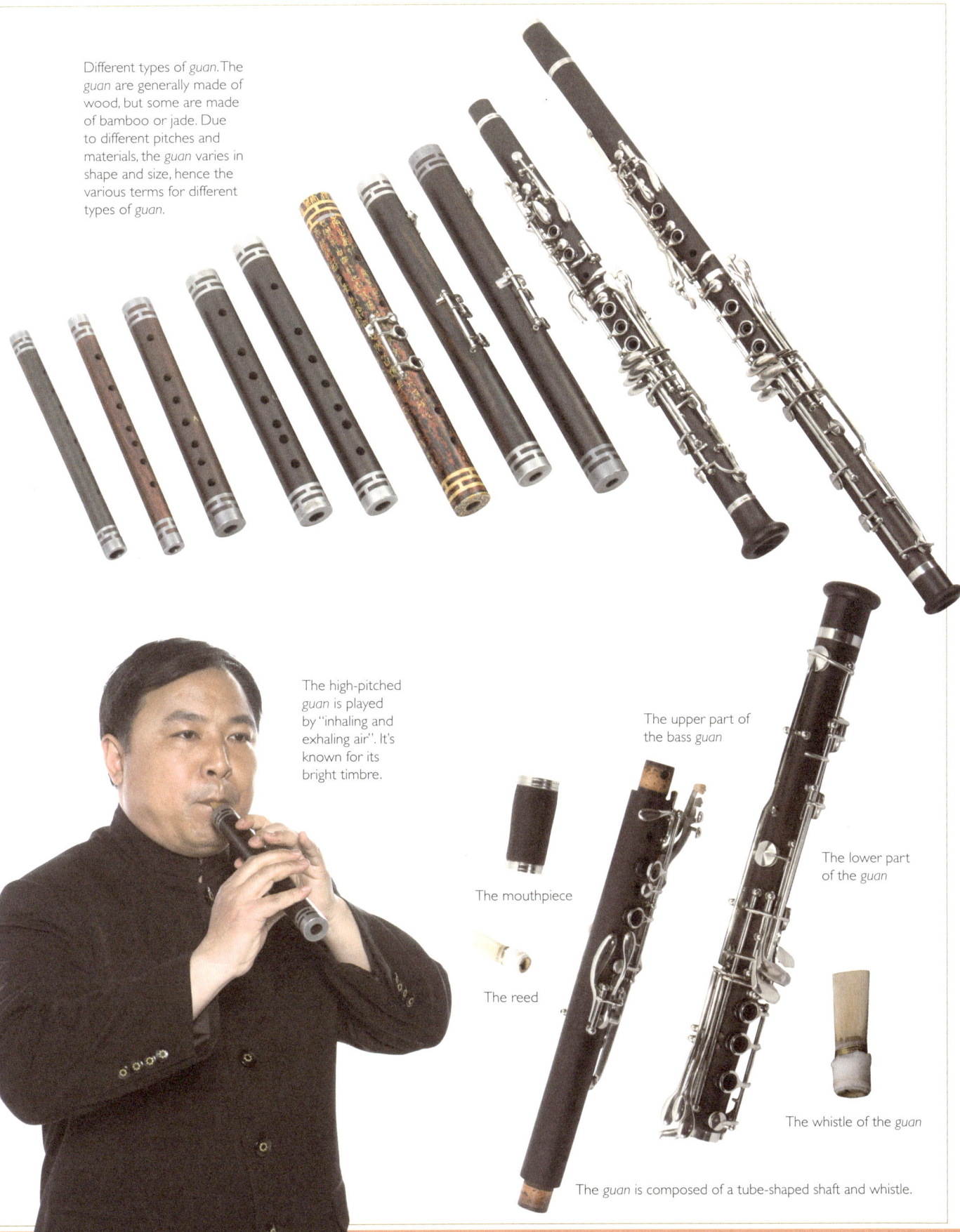

Different types of *guan*. The *guan* are generally made of wood, but some are made of bamboo or jade. Due to different pitches and materials, the *guan* varies in shape and size, hence the various terms for different types of *guan*.

The high-pitched *guan* is played by "inhaling and exhaling air". It's known for its bright timbre.

The upper part of the bass *guan*

The mouthpiece

The reed

The lower part of the *guan*

The whistle of the *guan*

The *guan* is composed of a tube-shaped shaft and whistle.

29

Bili—the ancient *guan*

The *bili*, the predecessor of the modern *guan*, is a reed pipe instrument made of wood. The range of 11 musical notes is produced through a double-reed whistle. There are 8 or 9 finger holes. This kind of wind instrument is known for its solemn and bright timbre. According to research, the word "*bili*" is the transliteration of a word from the ancient Qiuci language. Scenes of *bili* performances can be seen in many ancient scriptures and murals.

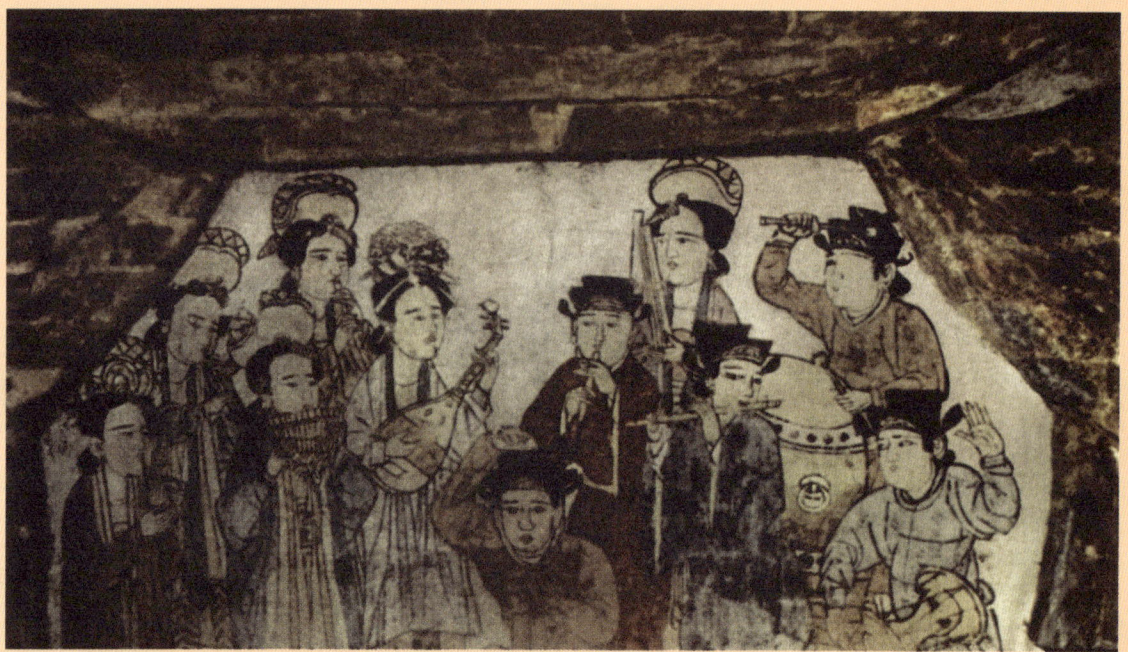

This mural of group entertainment was unearthed in 1951 in a Song Dynasty grave at Baisha reservoir of Yuzhou, Henan Province. The mural is praised for its bright color and lifelike painting. The mural is made of bricks. There are 10 entertainers in the mural.

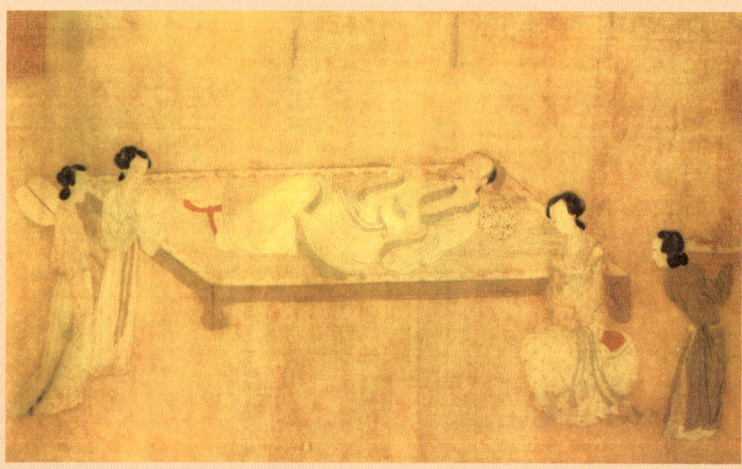

There were quite a number of outstanding *bili* players in the palace and among the common people. Even Emperor Xuanzong himself was adept at composing and playing *bili* tunes. One of the most popular tunes was *Yulinlingqu*, which he composed in commemoration of his deceased concubine Yang.

Painting of Minghuang of Tang Enjoying Himself with Musical Performance from the Tang Dynasty (Painter: Zhang Xuan)

2 Plucked Stringed Instruments

Plucked stringed instruments are played by pulling and plucking strings with one's finger or a plectrum. The plucked stringed instruments in a Chinese folk orchestra were carefully chosen from among a large number of traditional stringed instruments in China. These instruments are often some of the most recognizable in traditional Chinese music and illustrate the main differences between Chinese and Western music.

The conventional plucked stringed instruments include the *pipa*, *liuqin*, *yangqin*, *zhongruan*, *daruan*, *guzheng*, *konghou* and *sanxian*. Those instruments combine to display their unique and colorful style with a contrast in register and timbre.

Pipa

With a long history, the *pipa* is played by pulling and plucking its strings with the fingers of one's right hand and pushing, pulling and pressing the strings with the fingers of one's left hand. The overtone is sounded by pressing the fingers of one's left hand on the overtone points to produce clear musical notes. It can also be used to make harmonious notes in combination with other plucked stringed instruments. The melody produced by the *pipa*'s long succession of notes is extremely melodious.

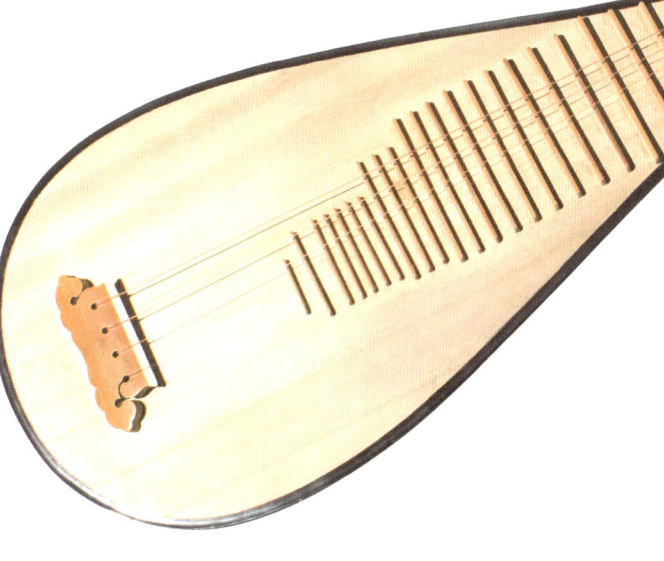

The *pipa* is referred to as the "king of Chinese folk music", "king of plucked stringed instruments" and "leading plucked stringed instrument". This wood-made *pipa* has a half-pear-shaped sound box and four strings.

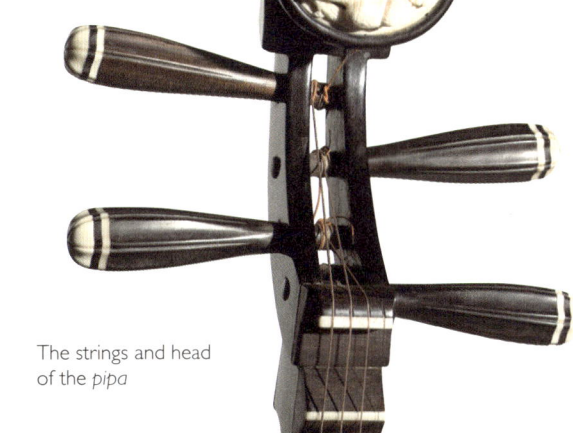

The strings and head of the *pipa*

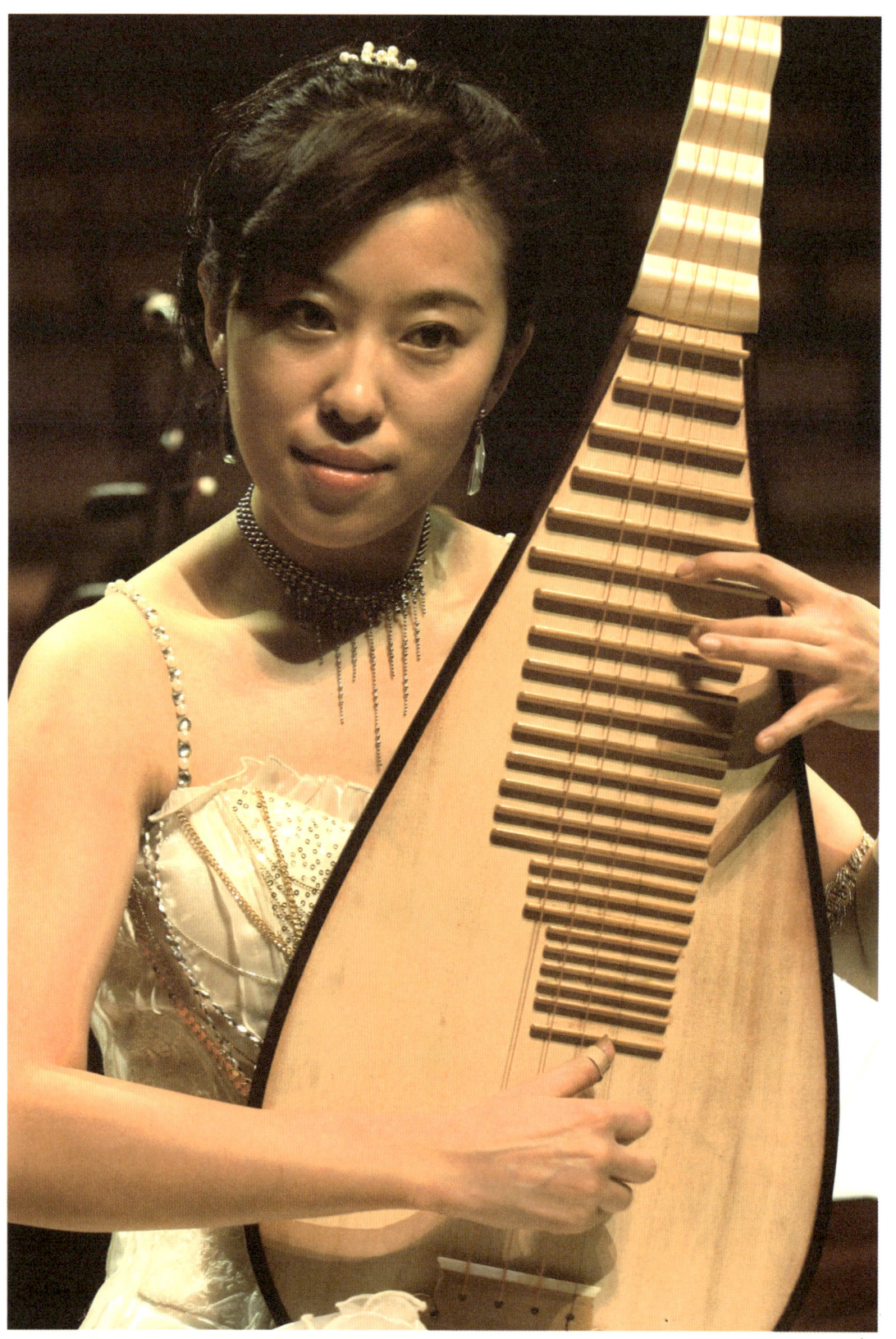

While playing the *pipa*, the player, who is holding it vertically, is plucking the strings with her right hand and pressing the strings with her left hand. (Performer: Zhao Cong)

Bai Juyi and his famous poem—*Pipaxing*

In the fall of 816 Bai Juyi, a famous poet of the Tang Dynasty, went to see a friend off by the side of the Xunyang River. They heard the melodious tune of a *pipa* which floated above the serene water. Bai Juyi and his friend followed the pleasant music and found a small boat where a girl was playing the *pipa*. She came from Chang'an and was a professional *pipa* player at the office in charge of court music. A highly skilled *pipa* player, she married a merchant afterward. However, her husband put business above his affection for her so she ended up spending her days and nights weeping in an empty boat.

Bai Juyi wrote a poem entitled *Pipaxing* to honor this girl. In this popular poem Bai Juyi described in detail the different techniques of playing the *pipa*. What's more, the poet gave a profound analysis of the musical styles of the *pipa* and the inner feelings of the *pipa* player. From the angle of a listener, the poet

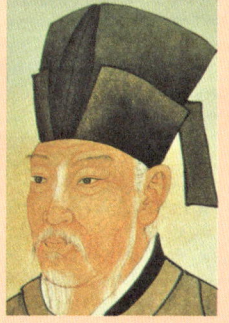

Bai Juyi's poem *Pipaxing* is considered a representative work of poetry from the Tang Dynasty. Later generations commended it as one of the "three best poems about music".

depicted the mentality of the player as well as the sound of the performance. The lines are some of the greatest in Chinese poetry about music.

The thick strings loudly thrummed like the pattering rain
The fine strings softly tinkled in murmuring strain
When mingling loud and soft notes were together played
'Twas like large and small pearls dropping on a plate of jade.

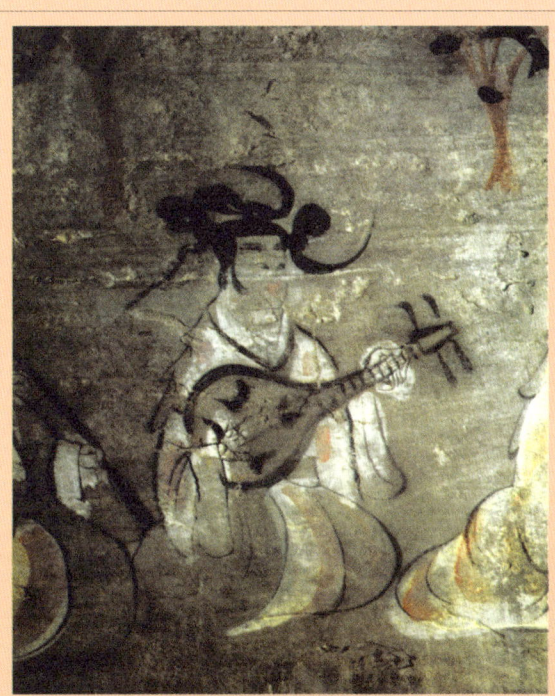

Pipa performers shown in ancient murals

Wenqu and *Wuqu*

The music of the *pipa* can be divided into two categories—*wenqu* (which literally means gentle tunes) and *wuqu* (which literally means vigorous tunes). The representative piece of *wuqu* is *Shimianmaifu* (which literally means "fall into an ambush from all sides"). This vigorous piece of music is impressive for its powerful range. In the war between Liu Bang and Xiang Yu during the last years of the Qin Dynasty, Xiang Yu's 100,000-strong army were surrounded by Liu Bang's 300,000-strong army at Gaixia. In the still of the night the troops of the Han sang the Chu songs in unison to sap the fighting will of the enemy troops. Ultimately, leading 800 cavalrymen, Xiang Yu attempted to break through the encirclement. When hopelessly outnumbered, Xiang Yu was compelled to kill himself with a sword by the Wujiang River. Two *pipa* compositions were written about this battle. Those in favor of Liu Bang liked to play *Shimianmaifu* in praise of the gallant valor of the Han troops. Those in favor of Xiang Yu often played *Bawangxiejia* (which literally means "the Conqueror Xiang Yu removes his armor") to express sorrow over Xiang Yu's tragic defeat.

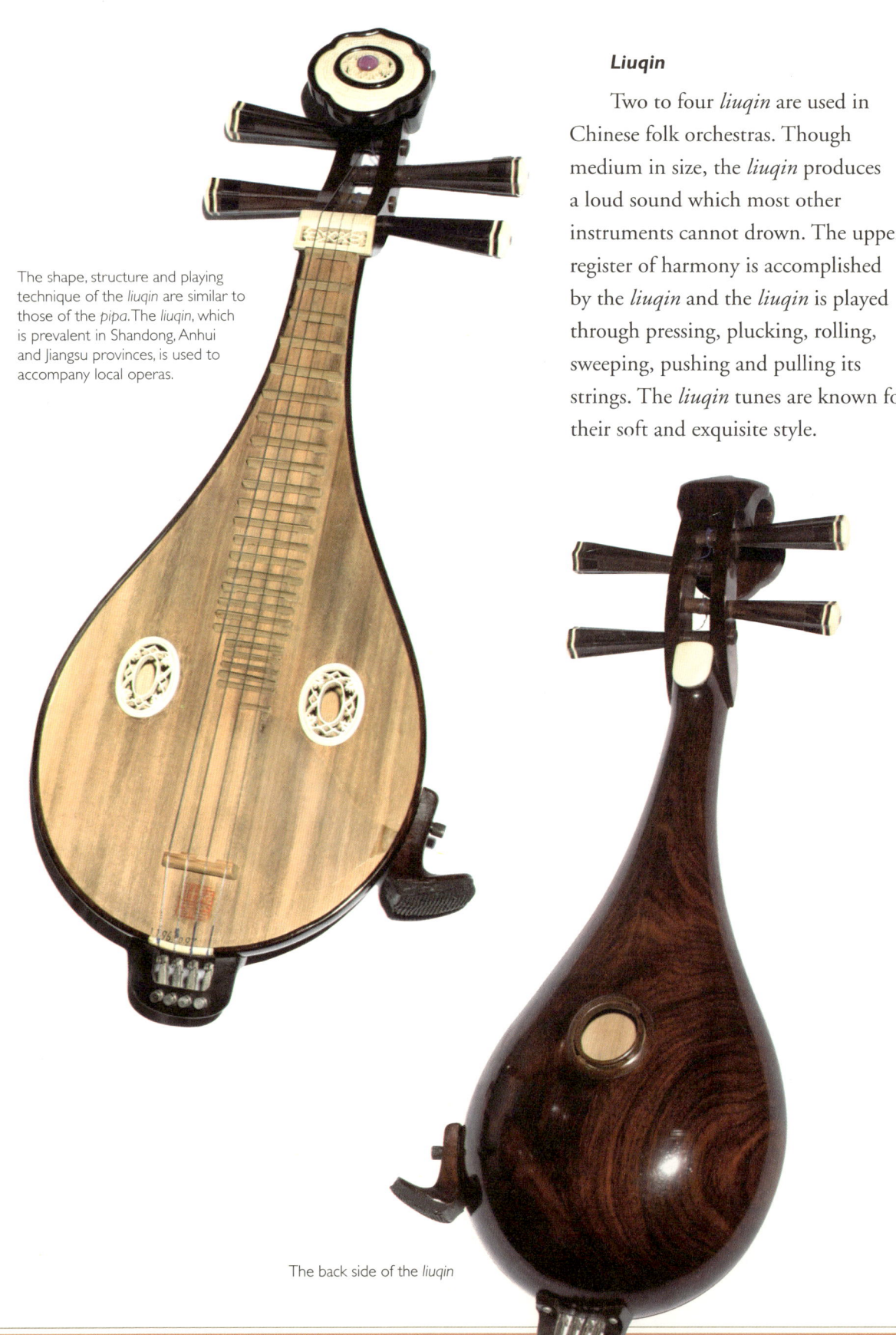

The shape, structure and playing technique of the *liuqin* are similar to those of the *pipa*. The *liuqin*, which is prevalent in Shandong, Anhui and Jiangsu provinces, is used to accompany local operas.

Liuqin

Two to four *liuqin* are used in Chinese folk orchestras. Though medium in size, the *liuqin* produces a loud sound which most other instruments cannot drown. The upper register of harmony is accomplished by the *liuqin* and the *liuqin* is played through pressing, plucking, rolling, sweeping, pushing and pulling its strings. The *liuqin* tunes are known for their soft and exquisite style.

The back side of the *liuqin*

Chapter One Present-day Chinese Folk Orchestras Plucked Stringed Instruments

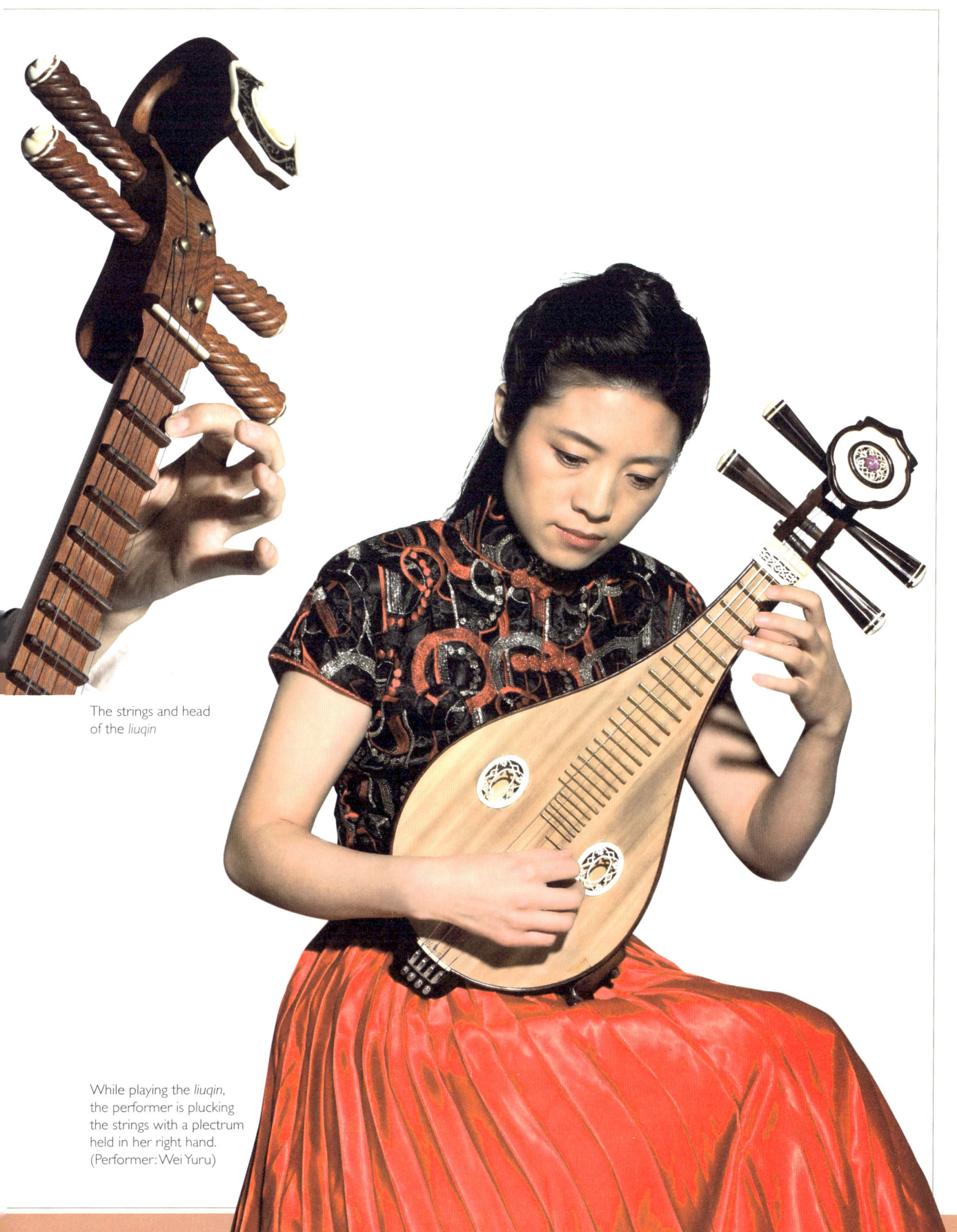

The strings and head of the *liuqin*

While playing the *liuqin*, the performer is plucking the strings with a plectrum held in her right hand. (Performer: Wei Yuru)

Zhongruan

The 4-stringed instrument is divided into alto and bass *zhongruan* (or medium *ruan*). A Chinese folk orchestra is usually equipped with 6 to 8 alto *zhongruan* and 4 to 6 bass *zhongruan*. The soft and sweet timbre of the *zhongruan* is well suited for producing a bright and melodious sound in the middle and upper registers. The *zhongruan* is usually used in an orchestra to play harmonious double-notes and chords. Its soft and sweet timbre is similar to that of a guitar. Different from the traditional single-note performance, the present-day *ruan* is used to play tunes with rich harmony and complex rhythm.

Daruan

The *daruan* (or big *ruan*), which is bigger in size and lower in pitch than the *zhongruan*, is played in the same way as the *zhongruan*. An extra effort is required on the part of the *daruan* player to produce its resonant and rich sound. It is used in an orchestra as part of the lower register of plucked stringed instruments. There are now several varieties of *ruan*. In all cases the main body is made of hardwood and the surface and back boards are made of tung wood.

The playing technique and symbols of the *ruan* are similar to those of the *liuqin*. The *ruan* is played with a plectrum. The player uses her right hand to pluck the strings and her left hand to press the strings.

The *daruan* is the main instrument of the *ruan* family used in a present-day Chinese folk orchestra.

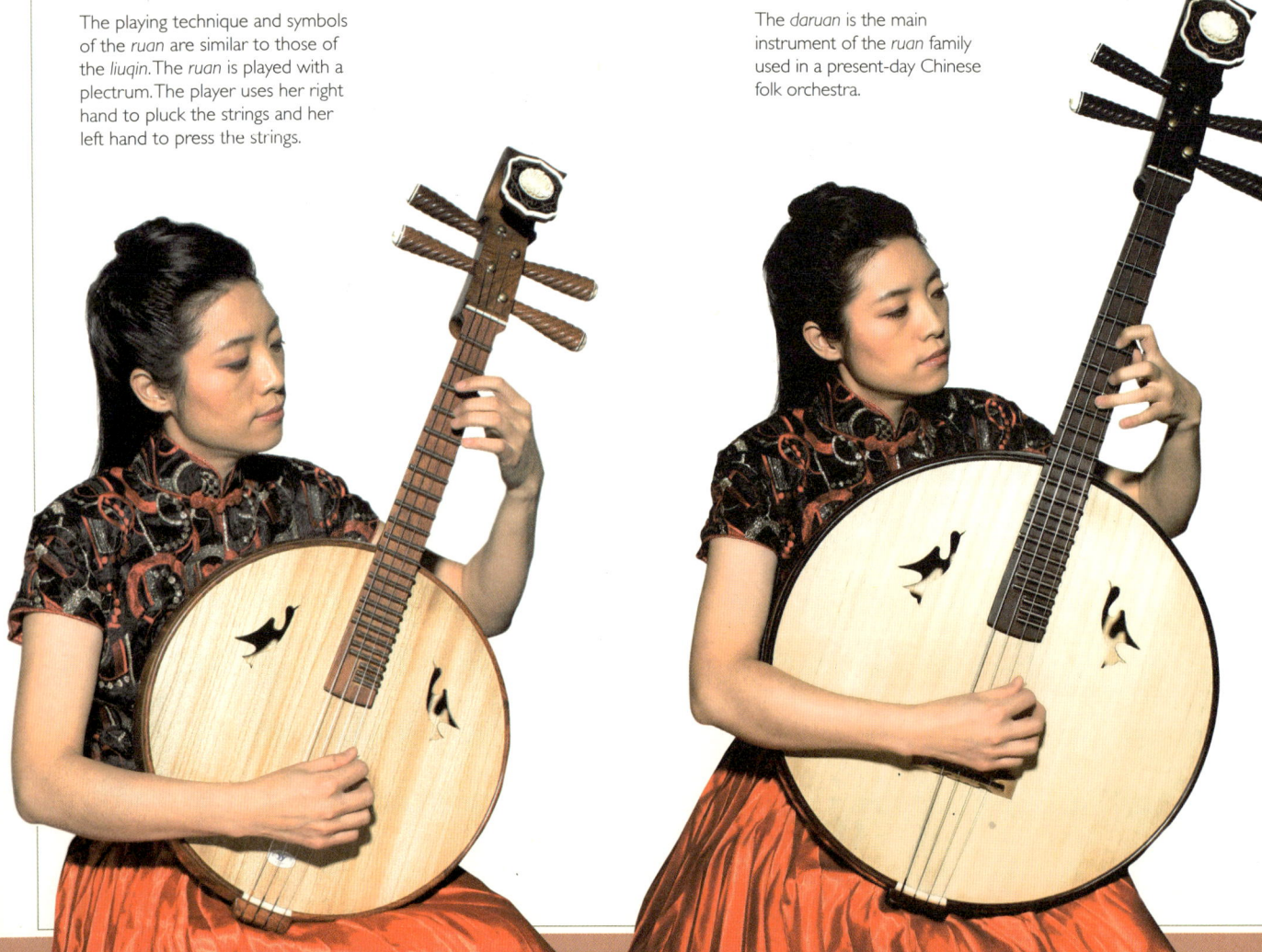

Ruan Xian, a skillful *ruan* player

Ruan Xian, one of the well-known "seven wise scholars in the bamboo grove" in the literary world of the Eastern Jin Dynasty, was especially good at playing the *ruan*. In the brick-carved mural titled *A Painting of Seven Wise Scholars in the Bamboo Grove*, unearthed from an Eastern Jin Dynasty grave at Nanjing's Xishanqiao in Jiangsu Province, the graceful charm of Ruan Xian playing the *ruan* is vividly depicted. Ruan Xian modified the *ruan* by enlarging its sound box and increasing the number of frets. As a result, the modified *ruan* improved in timbre and in range.

The *ruan*, which used to be regarded as a refined instrument, was only used at the official conservatory or at the office in charge of court music for solo or ensemble performances. The *ruan* can be seen in many landscape and figure paintings as well as in many murals in Chinese history. Among the Dunhuang frescoes the *zhongruan* appears in dozens of murals. Differing in shape and performing posture, all the performers of the *zhongruan* are vividly portrayed.

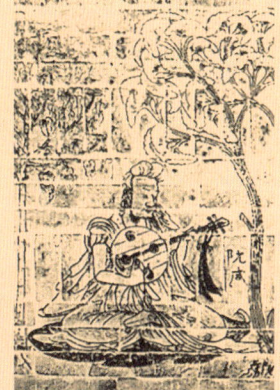

The brick-carved mural entitled *A Painting of Seven Wise Scholars in the Bamboo Grove* was unearthed in 1960 in a grave at Xishanqiao in Nanjing, Jiangsu Province. In the painting the bare-foot Ruan Xian sits on a fur blanket with his legs crossed and holds a straight-necked four-stringed pipa. As Ruan Xian was good at playing this instrument, people of later generations called it "the ruanxian".

Yangqin

The *yangqin* is played by striking its strings with two hammers. With a loud resonance in the lower range and a bright, clear and soft sound in the middle and upper ranges, the *yangqin* is usually used in an orchestra to play a double-ranged harmony. In the plucked section the *yangqin* plays the role of coordinating and harmonizing different ranges and balancing sound effects. Without the coordinating power of the *yangqin*, other parts of the sound range would be dull and insipid and the overall sound effects would be unbalanced.

In 1600 or so the *yangqin* was introduced into China from Persia during the Ming Dynasty. After repeated modifications the *yangqin*, known for its wide range and easy modulation, is used in an orchestra to play complex notes. Some professional *yangqin* are equipped with the foot-operated damper to mute the sound, thus solving the problem of echoing sound produced during a performance.

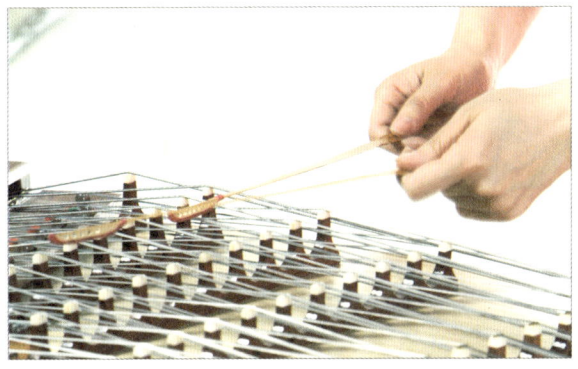

The basic technique of using bamboo hammers is to alternate hands while striking the strings. The *yangqin* is suited for playing quick-rhythm tunes and expressing a lively and joyous mood.

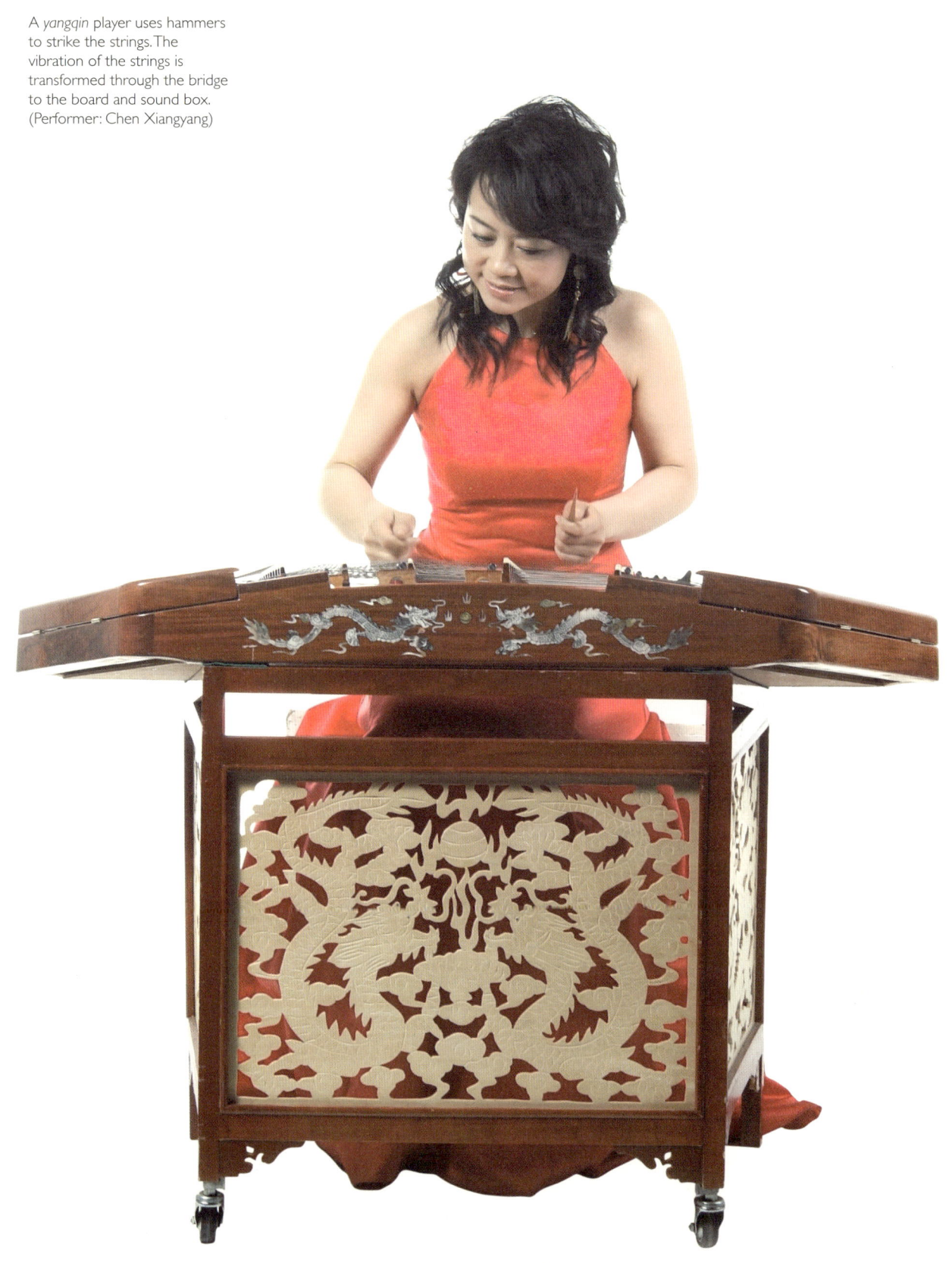

A *yangqin* player uses hammers to strike the strings. The vibration of the strings is transformed through the bridge to the board and sound box. (Performer: Chen Xiangyang)

Chapter One　Present-day Chinese Folk Orchestras　Plucked Stringed Instruments

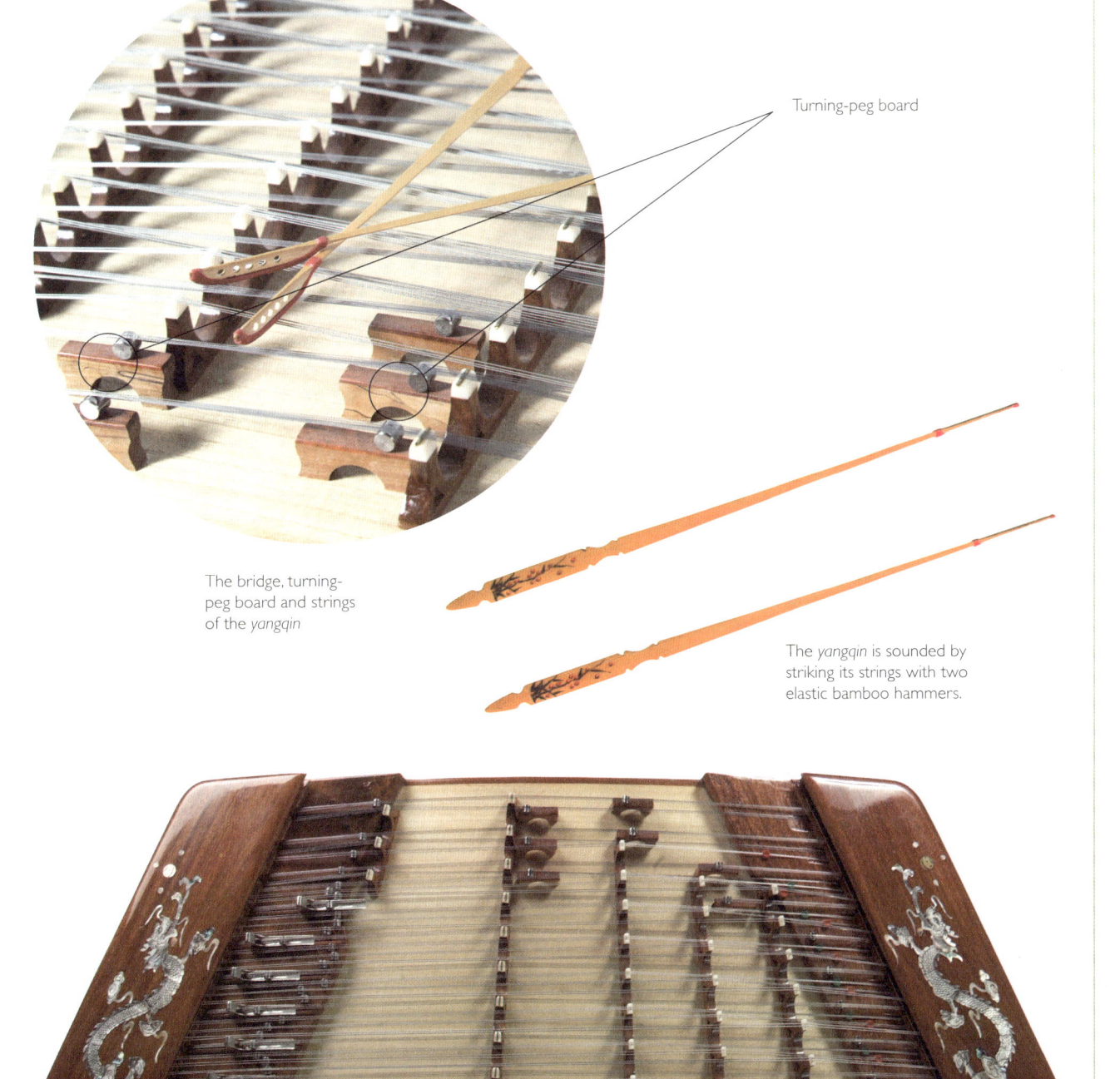

The bridge, turning-peg board and strings of the *yangqin*

The *yangqin* is sounded by striking its strings with two elastic bamboo hammers.

The bridge, turning-peg board and strings of the *yangqin*

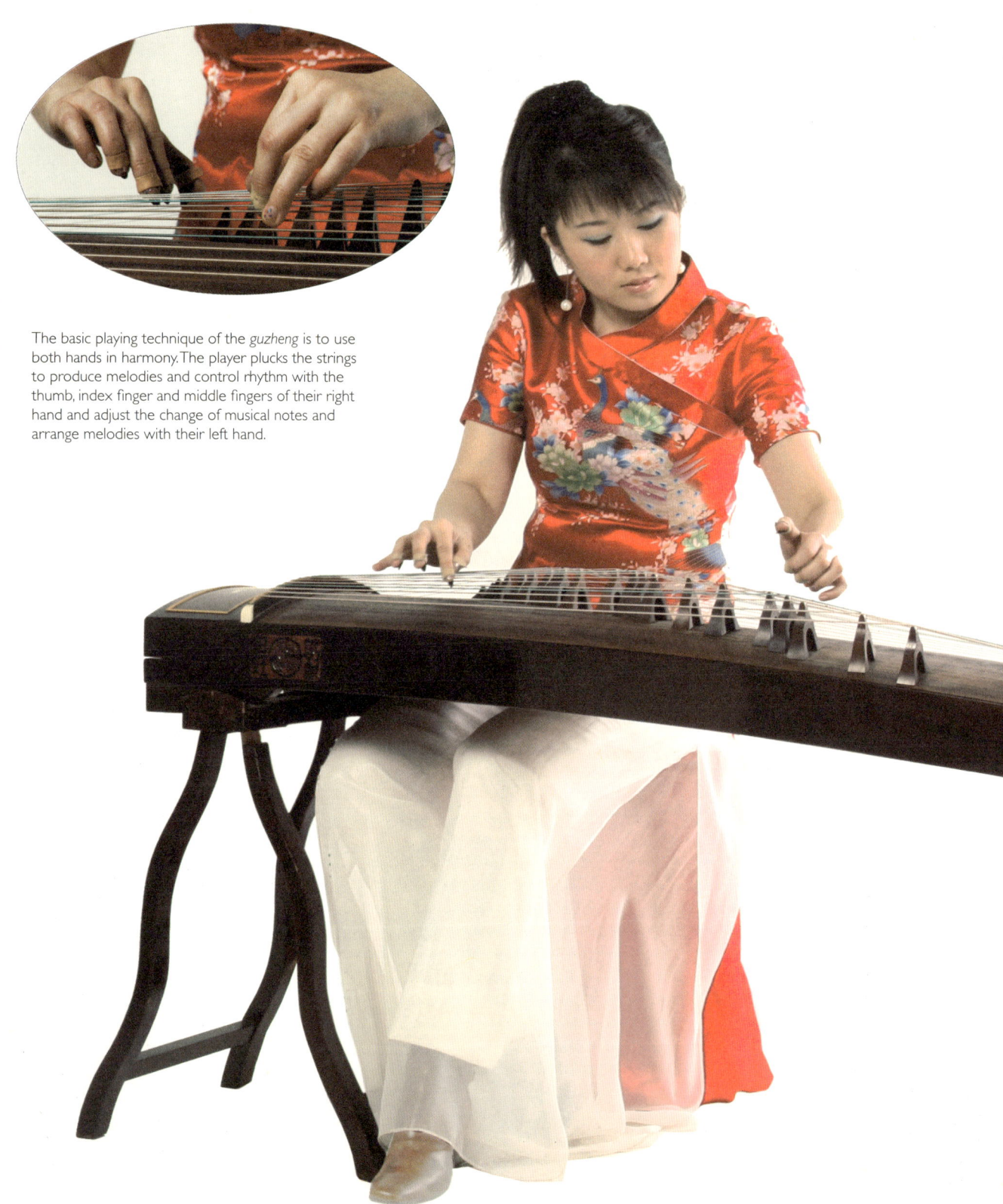

The basic playing technique of the *guzheng* is to use both hands in harmony. The player plucks the strings to produce melodies and control rhythm with the thumb, index finger and middle fingers of their right hand and adjust the change of musical notes and arrange melodies with their left hand.

The performance of the *guzheng* (Performer: Zhang Lu)

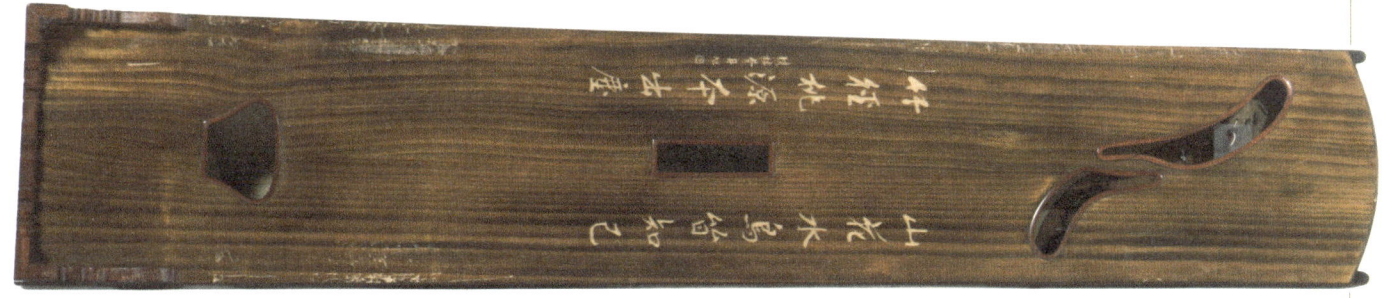

The *guzheng* is an ancient plucked stringed instrument, which originated in Shaanxi and Gansu provinces and was prevalent during the Sui and Tang dynasties. Throughout history, the *yangqin* has been introduced through China and other places in Asia.

Guzheng

The *zheng* used in a Chinese folk orchestra is a modified 21-stringed instrument. It is used to play some lovely and colorful melodies. The player uses their fingernails or a plectrum to play the *guzheng* (or ancient *zheng*). The thumb, middle finger and index finger of one's right hand are used to pluck strings while the fingers of one's left hand are used to press the strings to modulate sound. As a suspended instrument without a fingerboard, the *guzheng* is known for its variation in pitch. It can produce notes of various types.

The modern *guzheng* is an innovation in Chinese folk music. The modified *zheng* family is composed of 21-, 23- and 25-stringed *zheng* with different sound ranges and functions. The present-day leading players are Cao Zheng, Zhao Yuzhai, Cao Dongfu, Luo Jiuxiang and Wang Changyuan. The concerto *Canghaifu*, which Mr Liu Wenjin composed by adapting Cao Cao's famous work *Guancanghai*, has become a representative work of the time. The Japanese composer Miki Minoru's *Pine Trees* is also an excellent example of a modern *guzheng* concerto.

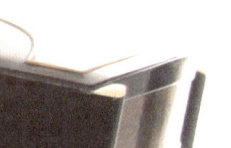

> #### Popular *Zheng*
>
> As one of the eight musical sounds made by ancient instruments, the *zheng* was widely used in musical activities in the Qi, Lu, Zheng, Wei and Zhao States during the Spring and Autumn Period and the Warring States Period. Most people were fond of playing the *zheng* and the *guzheng* became more popular after the First Emperor of the Qin Dynasty unified China.
>
> The *zheng* is not only a traditional instrument of long standing in China. As early as the Northern and Southern Dynasties people in ancient Korea used the Chinese *guzheng* as a model and invented a *jiayeqin* characteristic of Korean tastes. The *zheng* was also introduced into Japan in the first half of the 7th century AD and became a leading instrument in the performance of traditional Japanese music.

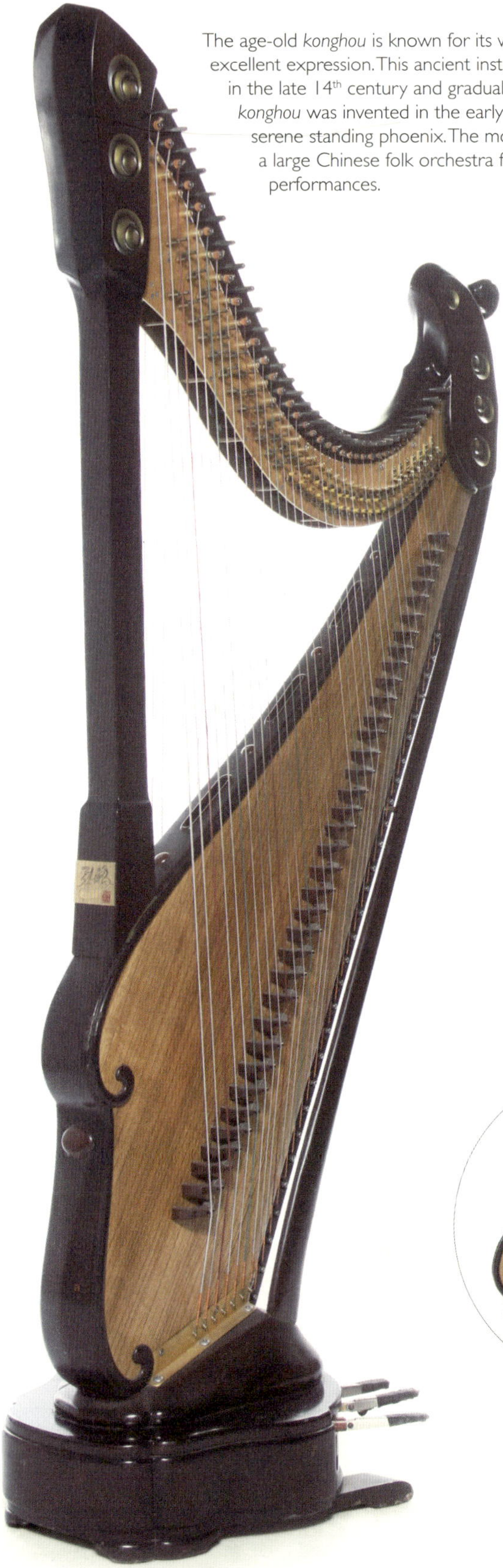

Chinese Music and Musical Instruments

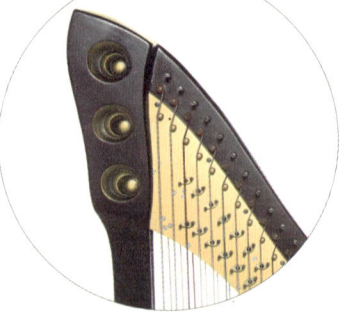

The two sides of the curved wood in the upper part of the *konghou* are inlaid with brass plates where metal turning pegs are installed.

The age-old *konghou* is known for its wide range, melodious timbre and excellent expression. This ancient instrument was no longer prevalent in the late 14th century and gradually disappeared. The modern *konghou* was invented in the early 1980s. The shaft looks like a serene standing phoenix. The modern *konghou* is often used by a large Chinese folk orchestra for solo, ensemble or backup performances.

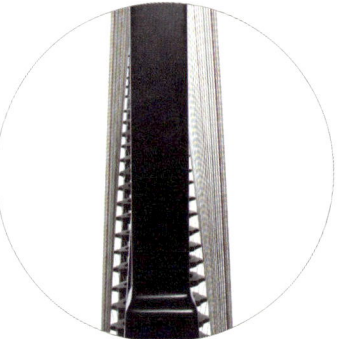

There are 44 strings each side.

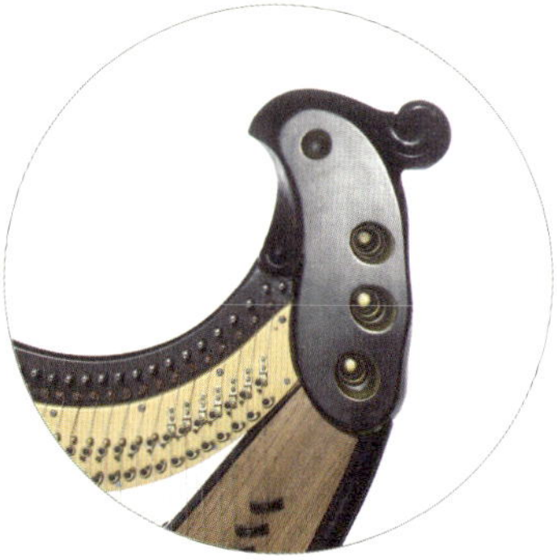

The head of the *konghou* is carved with the decoration of "the phoenix turning its head".

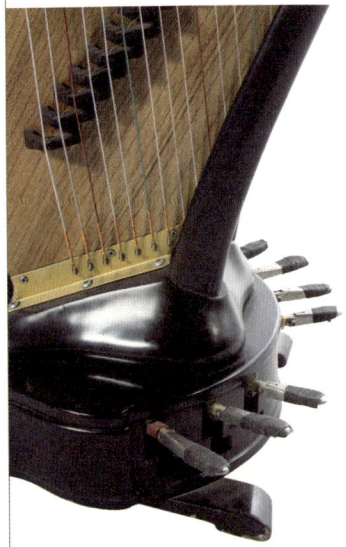

The pedal is used to modulate from one key to another.

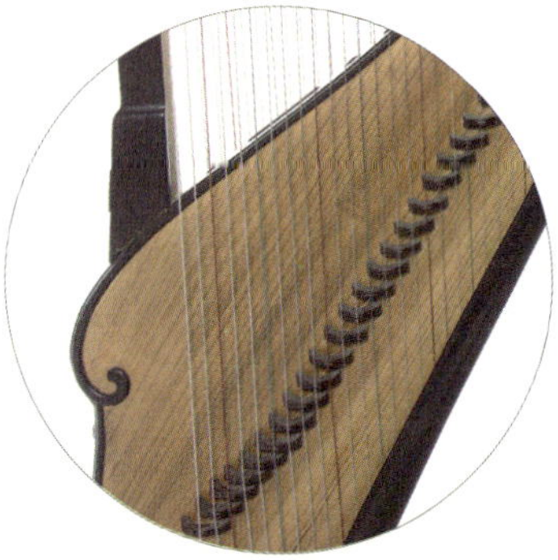

The resonance box in the lower part of the *konghou* assumes the shape of a vertical double-faced *pipa* covered with surface boards on both flanks.

Konghou

The *konghou* used in present-day Chinese folk orchestras mainly plays a supporting role in the family of plucked stringed instruments. Sometimes it is also played solo in order to showcase the great variety of colorful Chinese instruments. While similar to a harp, it is different from the single row of strings of a harp; the tonic train of the Chinese *konghou* is distinguished by two rows of symmetrical chord strings. The player can use both hands to stroke and press strings or play the *konghou* in a portamento style. The musical sound thus produced is very melodious. The leading performer of the modern *konghou* is Cui Junzhi. With its soft and exquisite sound, the *konghou* can also play the harmonic scale. In a seated position, the player holds the *konghou* with both arms and touches the strings on both sides with both hands. The sound produced in a portamento style is as impressive as the flowing water.

The player is in a seated position while playing the *konghou*. The player clutches the resonance box to her chest and plays the strings on both sides with both her hands. Thanks to the excellent structure and high performance of the instrument, the *konghou* player can produce melodies and harmony at the same time with both hands. (Performer: Wu Lin)

The Horizontal *Konghou* and Vertical *Konghou*

The *konghou*, similar to a harp, was introduced to China via the Silk Road during the Eastern Han Dynasty. It is divided into the horizontal and vertical varieties. It was at its most prevalent during the Sui and Tang dynasties and was later introduced to Japan. As the *konghou* is a popular instrument, many descriptions of this instrument can be read in ancient Chinese poetry.

The vertical *konghou* was commonly played by the ethnic groups in northern China. The *konghou* is mainly shaped like the head of a phoenix or a dragon. The horizontal *konghou* looks like the ancient *qin* and *se* of the Spring and Autumn Period. The ancient horizontal *konghou* appears in the brick paintings of ancient graves of the Wei and Jin States unearthed at Jiayuguan, Gansu Province.

The modern *konghou* used today are remodeled after the style of the ancient *konghou* as a result of meticulous textual research.

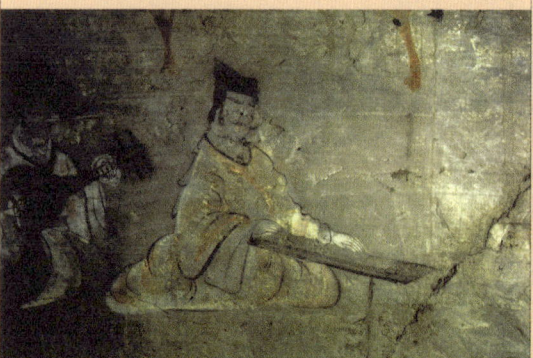

The horizontal *konghou*

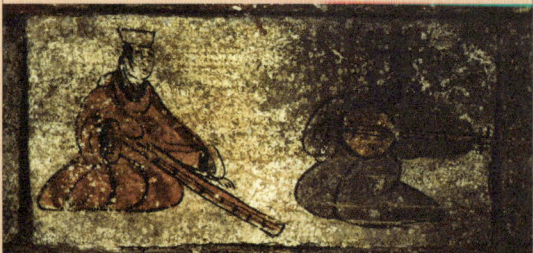

The horizontal *konghou*

Sanxian

The *sanxian* (which literally means "three-stringed"), a type of lute, comprises of three parts: the head, shaft and drum (resonance box).

Its head looks like a shovel. Its shaft is the longest of all the plucked stringed instruments. Its drum is its resonance box. The oval drum frame is made of rosewood and its two sides are covered with snake skin. It is played with a plectrum. Its crisp and clear sound and full and melodious timbre are complemented with a gradual slide from one note to the other.

The *sanxian* is often played solo and the sound produced when a player uses his or her left hand in a portamento style is unique and impressive. As the modern *sanxian* is equipped with nylon-wrapped wire strings, its penetrating sound is swiftly produced.

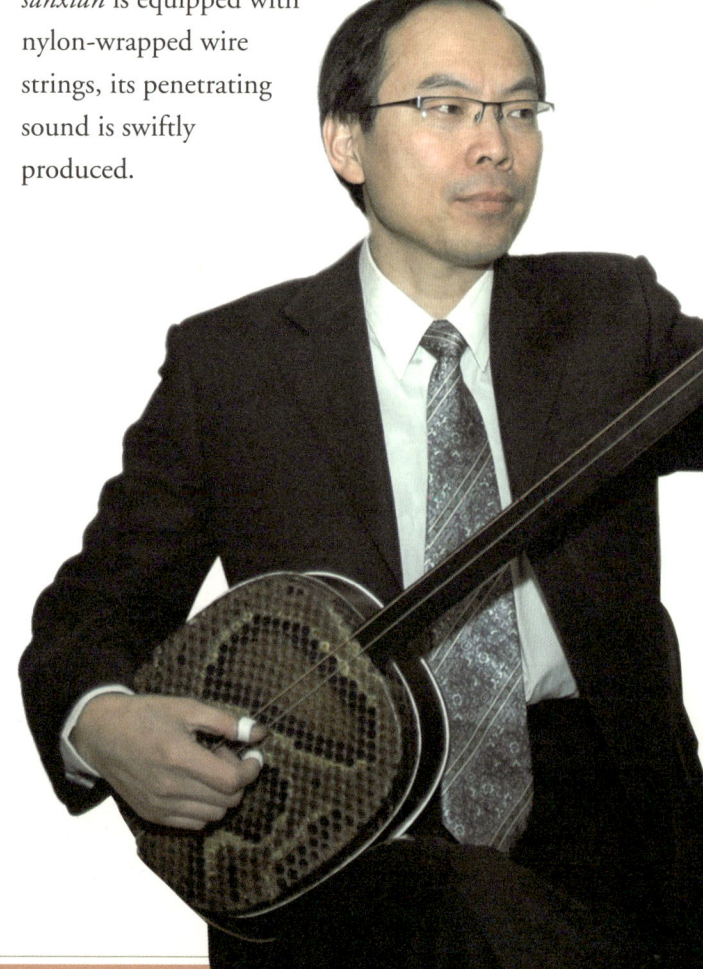

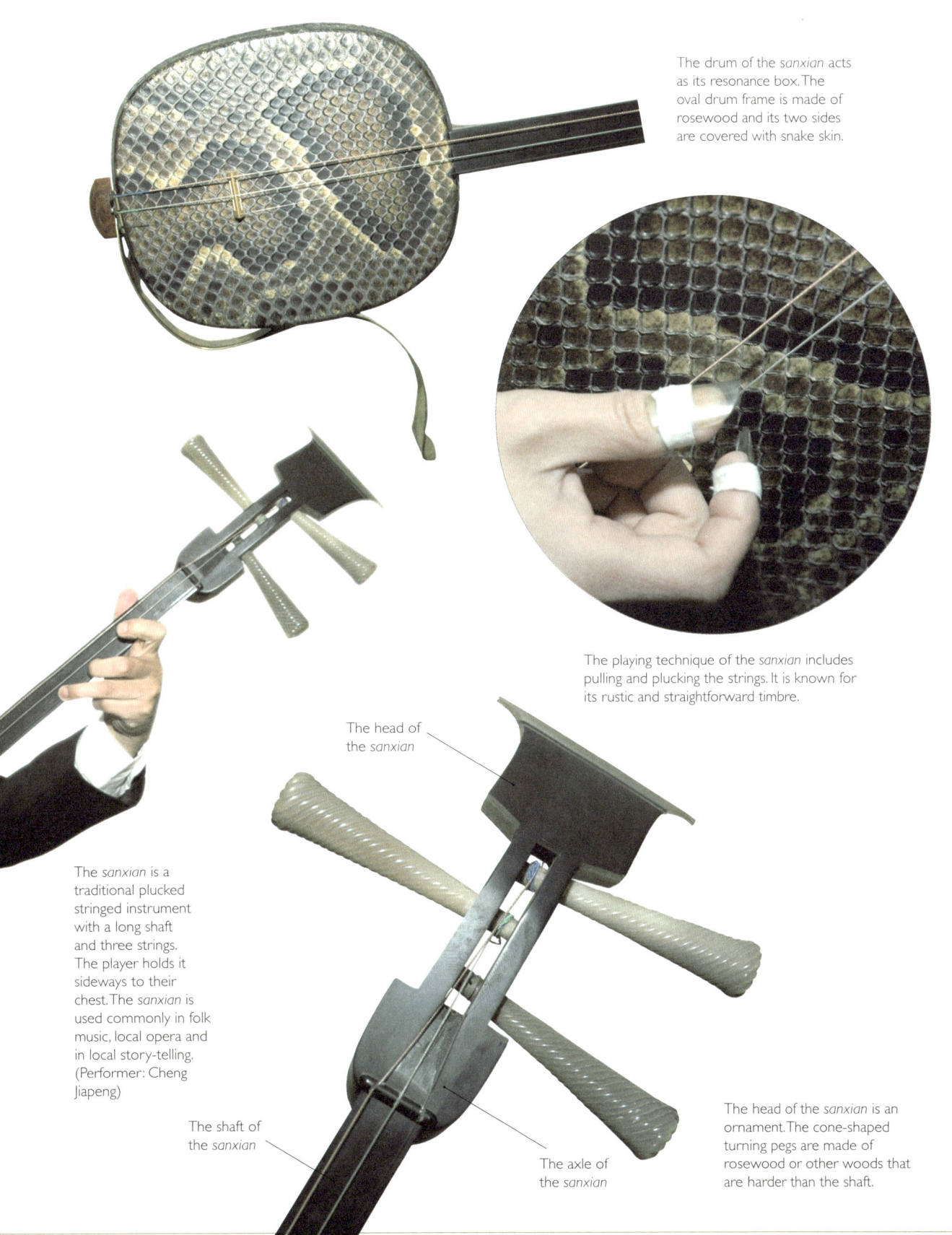

The drum of the sanxian acts as its resonance box. The oval drum frame is made of rosewood and its two sides are covered with snake skin.

The playing technique of the sanxian includes pulling and plucking the strings. It is known for its rustic and straightforward timbre.

The head of the sanxian

The sanxian is a traditional plucked stringed instrument with a long shaft and three strings. The player holds it sideways to their chest. The sanxian is used commonly in folk music, local opera and in local story-telling. (Performer: Cheng Jiapeng)

The shaft of the sanxian

The axle of the sanxian

The head of the sanxian is an ornament. The cone-shaped turning pegs are made of rosewood or other woods that are harder than the shaft.

3 Percussion Instruments

A Chinese folk orchestra is equipped with a great variety of percussion instruments. In ancient China musical sounds were divided into eight types according to the eight different materials the musical instruments were made of. When the performance of a Chinese folk orchestra reaches its climax, the brass-made *bianzhong*, *daluo* and *yunluo*, the stone-made *bianqing*, the leather-made *dagu* and *paigu* combine to produce a roaring sound, thus creating a strong artistic atmosphere. In the performance of a light and joyful tune, the sounding of the *pengling*, *linggu* and *guban* can add harmonious rhythm to the tune and make the music clear and exquisite.

Being without pitch or tone percussion instruments must be directed by a conductor in order to create a melody. In a Chinese folk orchestra percussionists are required to play a variety of percussion instruments. It is common practice for a player to move from one percussion instrument to another during a performance.

The characteristics of percussion instruments:

Most percussion instruments are played by striking a stick. The sticks are made of wood, rubber or metal. Some instruments are played by striking their leather surface with one's hands, for example, the *shougu* (which literally means "hand drum"). The metal-made percussion instruments, such as the *luo*, *bo*, *ling* and *zhong*, create sound through their vibrations after being struck. The leather-covered *gu* (or drum) is sounded by the vibration of its taut skin after it is beaten.

The pitch of many percussion instruments used in present-day Chinese folk orchestras can be

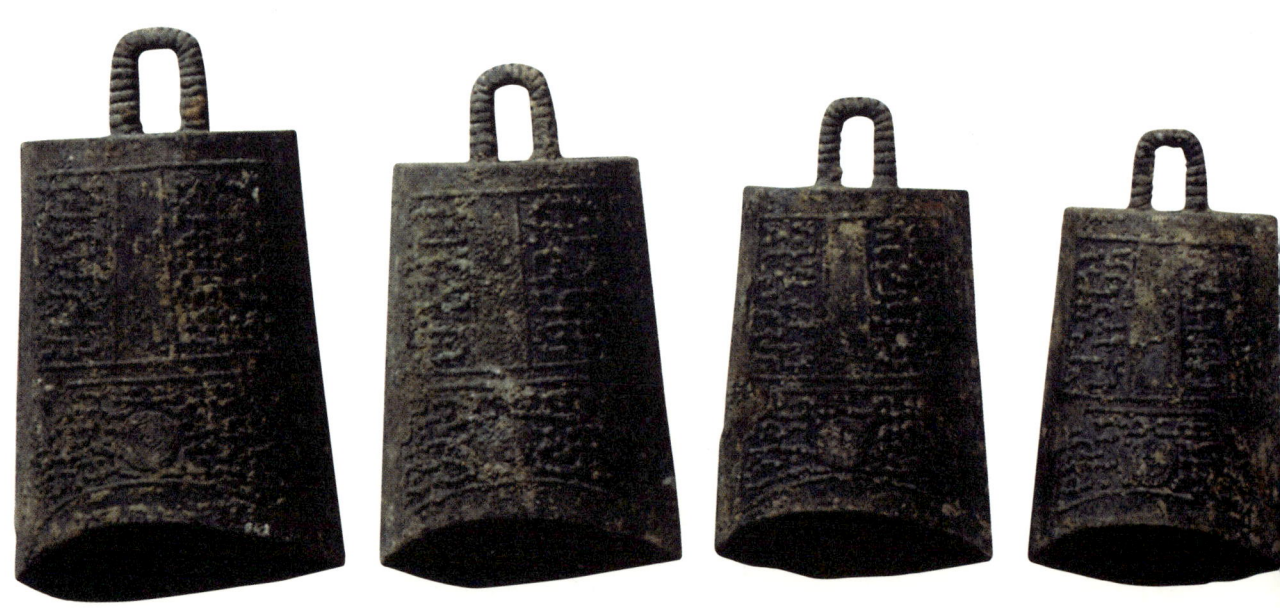

adjusted. For example, each of the five-piece *paigu* has a unique pitch. Even the brass-made percussion instruments are adjusted before a performance. An experienced player will tune their instruments with a hammer to modify the range and pitch to meet the needs of the orchestra. The pitch of the *daluo* and *yunluo* is adjusted in this way.

Bianzhong

The *bianzhong* (also known as "chime bells" or "serial bells") are played by striking the rim of each bell. The force of striking is of fundamental importance. If struck too hard, the sound will be broken. If struck too lightly, the sound will not be loud and resonant enough due to the insufficient vibration of the bell.

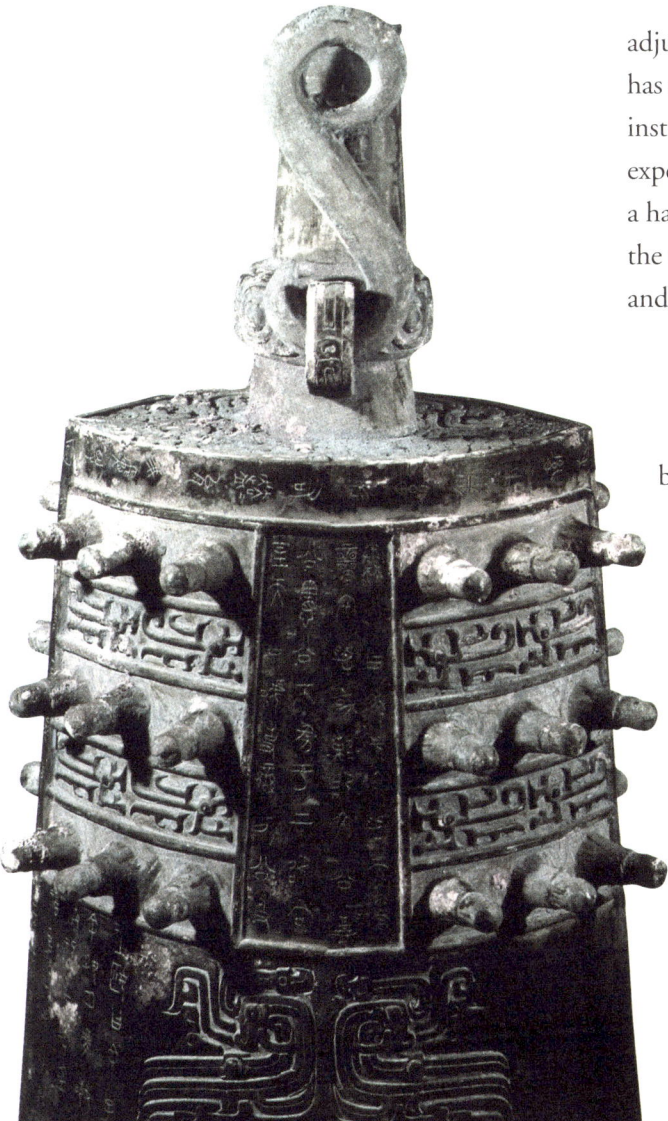

Lord Qin's Chimes
The so-called "Lord Qin's Chimes" are a set of bronze bells from the Spring and Autumn Period and the Warring States Period unearthed in 1978 at Taigongmiao Village in Baoji, Shaanxi Province. As a relic of the Feng Palace of Pingyang or an ancestral temple, they are kept at the Baoji Bronze Museum. The inscription on Lord Qin's Chimes is the oldest bronze inscription preserved in China.

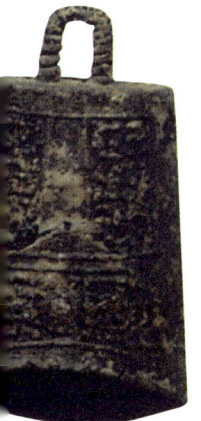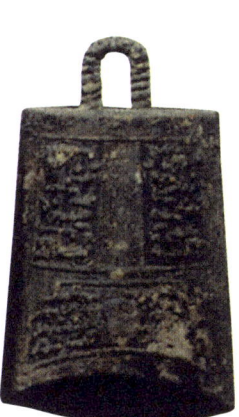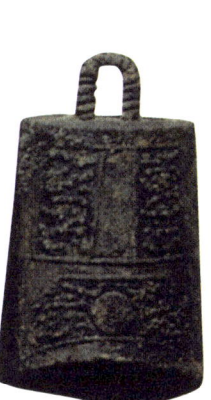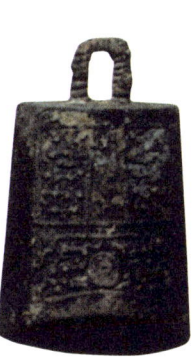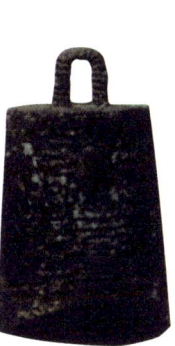

A set of *bianzhong*

Dagu

The *dagu* (also known as "big drum") is sounded by beating its skin with a pair of wood sticks. The vibration will sound best when a player beats the 2/3 section of the skin. The player sometimes beats the frame of the drum to achieve specific sound effects. The skins of the *dagu* are made or calf skin of other animal hide.

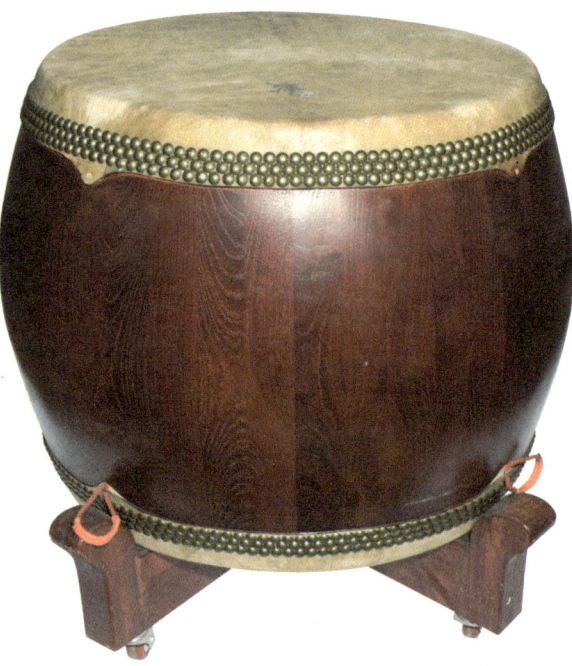

With a diameter of about one meter, the *dagu* (also known as "big drum") is actually a wood frame covered with animal hide.

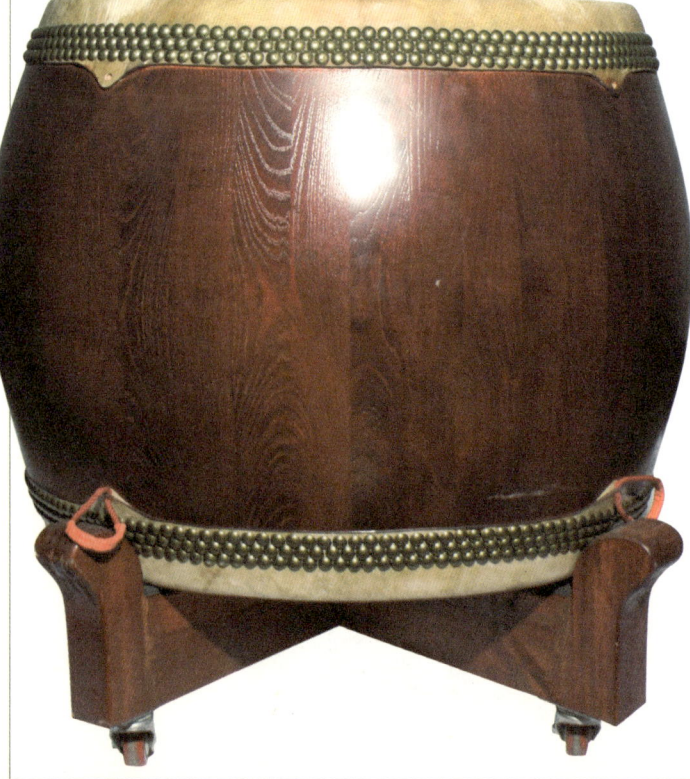

Xiaobo (xiaocha)

The *xiaobo* (or small *bo*) consists of a pair of very thin round brass plates. In the center of the plate a hole used to tie a string handle. The player puts his hands into the string handles and strikes the two plates against each other. When playing the *xiaobo*, the player, guided by the mood of the tune, will strike the *xiaobo* in the postures of open arms or arms close to each other to produce different sound effects.

The *dagu* is placed vertically in front of the player. Although it is covered with a skin on each side, only one side is used. The player beats the *dagu* with a single drumstick, which is called the *dagu* stick. Either head of the drumstick can be used to beat the *dagu*. Both heads are wrapped up with wool or felt. (Performer: Yu Xin)

Chapter One Present-day Chinese Folk Orchestras Percussion Instruments

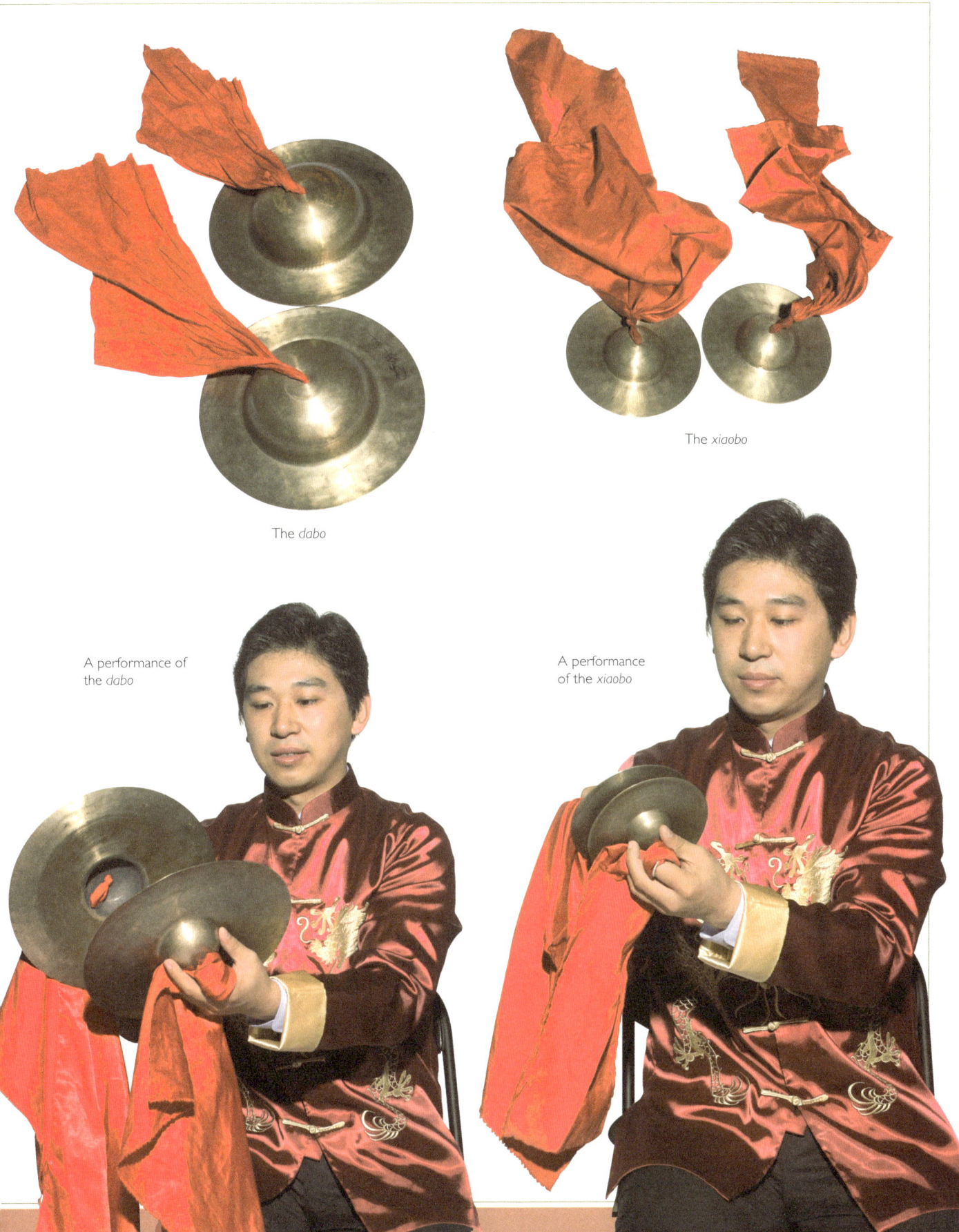

The *dabo*

The *xiaobo*

A performance of the *dabo*

A performance of the *xiaobo*

Xiaoluo

The *xiaoluo* (also known as "small gong") is known for its thrilling and bright sound. A player holds the rim of the *luo* in their left hand and strikes its center with a thin wooden plate. Its ringing sound is difficult to control. While known for its clear and pleasant sound, when struck in the wrong position, the sound produced can be unpleasant.

Jingluo

The *jingluo* first appeared in Suzhou, Jiangsu Province and Zhoucun, Shandong Province, also called *suluo* or *huyinluo* (literally meaning "gong of a tiger's voice"). As it was later used to accompany Beijing opera, people started to call it the *jingluo* (literally meaning "Beijing gong"). It is known for its loud and sonorous sound. The player uses a small hammer to strike the center of *jingluo* to control timbre and volumn.

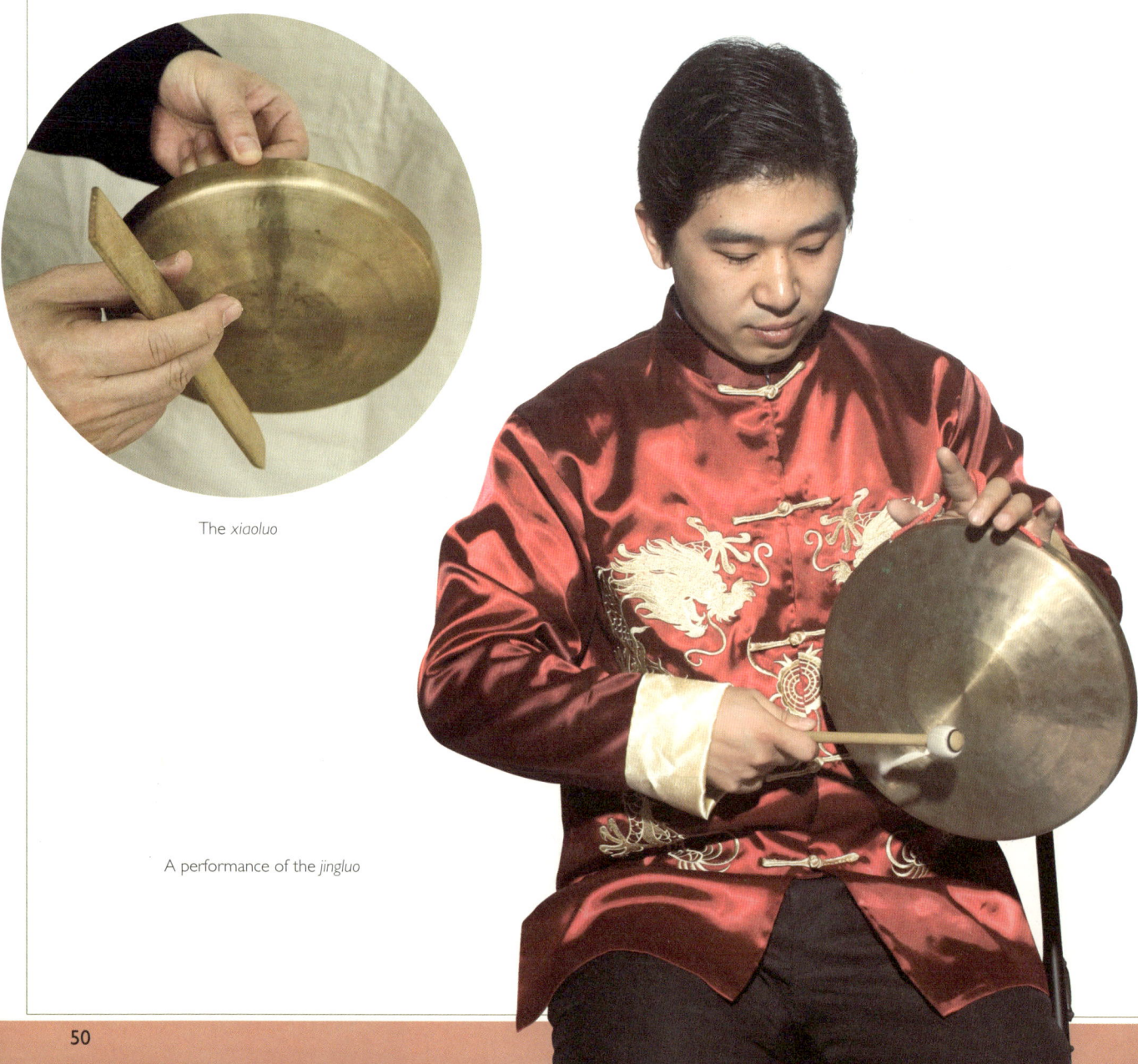

The *xiaoluo*

A performance of the *jingluo*

Daluo

The *daluo* (also known as "big gong") is the biggest brass-made *luo* in an orchestra. A player puts his right hand against the back side of the *luo* to control its timbre and volume and to help stabilize the *luo* and its frame, otherwise the *luo* will sway unsteadily. A player uses a mallet in his left hand to strike the central part of the *luo*. Sometimes the player deliberately strikes the other section of the *luo* to meet the requirements of a particular tune.

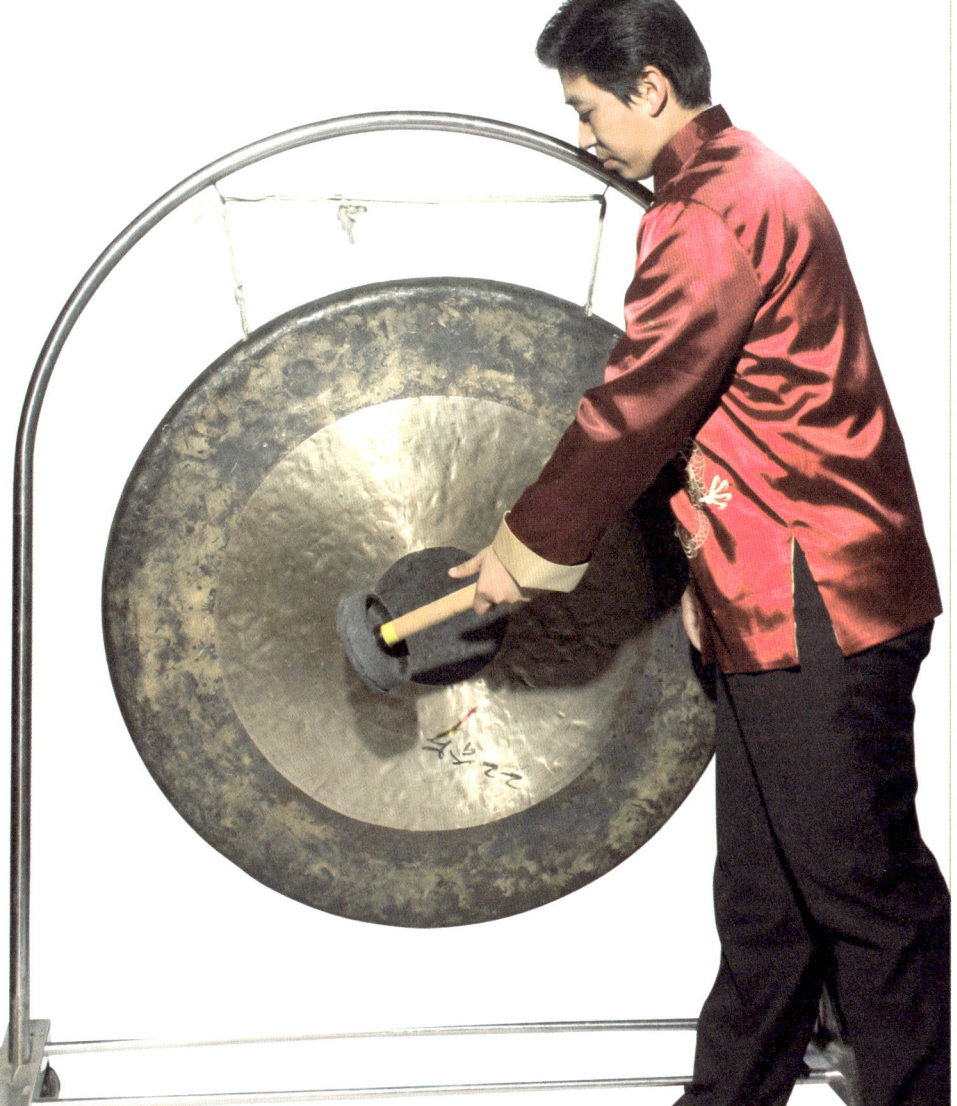

The *jingluo* was first made in Suzhou, hence also known as *suluo*. As it is commonly used to accompany the local operas, the choices of its range vary according to the need of each play. That's why high-pitched, alto, bass *jingluo* are made to their own specifications.

A performance of the *daluo*

Chinese Music and Musical Instruments

The *yunluo* first appeared during the Yuan Dynasty. Of the *luo* family, the *yunluo* is the only instrument which can be used to play melodies. It is often used in folk music, local operas and temple music. At one time, the *yunluo* was prevalent in Taoist ceremonies and later gained popularity among the people.

A performance of the *yunluo*

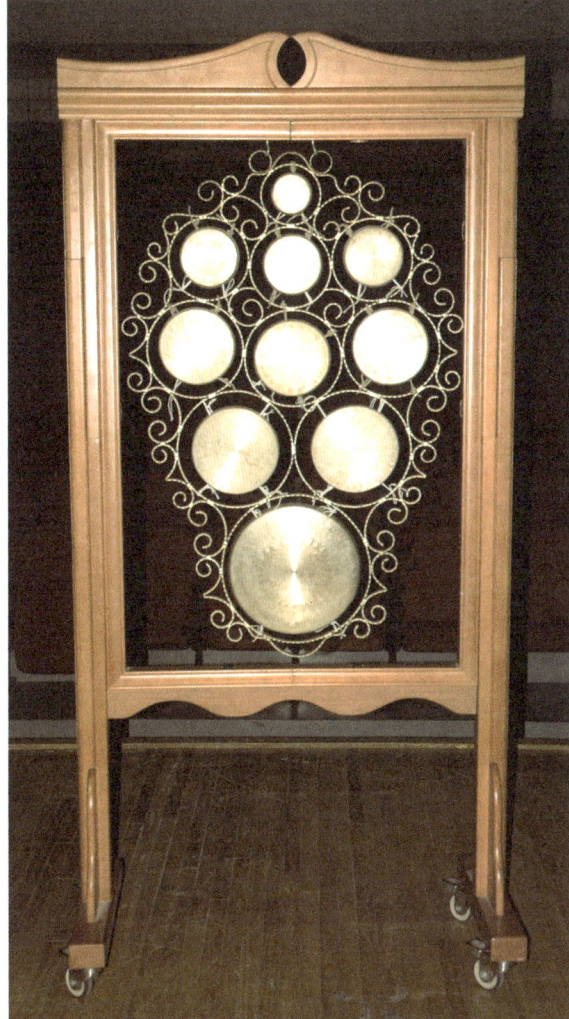

The *shimianluo* (which literally means "ten gongs") is popular in the coastal areas of southeast China. They are played by one player only. The *shimianluo* can produce rich and lively acoustic effects. Regarded as a colorful instrument, the *shimianluo* is often used in ensembles.

Yunluo

The *yunluo* consists of a dozen of small *luo* which differ in size and pitch. The player strikes the *luo* with two hand-held mallets. Some players even hold two mallets in each hand and can produce four harmonic notes at the same time. In the famous piece *Yuzhoukaige* a passage of the *yunluo* solo is commended for its penetrating and melodious sound and vivid and natural performance.

"Brass-resonant" Percussion Instruments

The joyous scenes of singing and dancing to the accompaniment of the *luo* (or gong) and *gu* (or drum) are enjoyed by Chinese people. The "brass-resonant" percussion instruments are often used on the following occasions: official ceremonies, folk fairs, festive activities and religious rites. The playing of percussion instruments reached the professional level due to need of the selection, combination and regulation of instruments.

The introduction of Buddhism into China from India during about the Eastern Han Dynasty brought some "brass-resonant" percussion instruments into China's Central Plains, including the brass *bo* (or cymbals). Instruments of this kind could produce loud, sonorous and stirring sounds and were used in ancient times as verbal commands to issue battle orders. The Chinese idiom *Mingjinshoubing* means "to sound a brass gong for retreat in battle".

In Chinese history, emperors, princes and other dignitaries liked to beat brass gongs to clear the way when they left their residence and passed through the streets. On the one hand, the sounding of brass gongs in this way could disperse a crowd and clear a passage. On the other hand, the deep and sonorous sound of brass gongs could create a solemn atmosphere to display their awe-inspiring power. Hence another Chinese idiom, *Mingluokaidao* (which literally means "to sound a brass gong to clear the way").

"Sound a *luo* to clear the way"

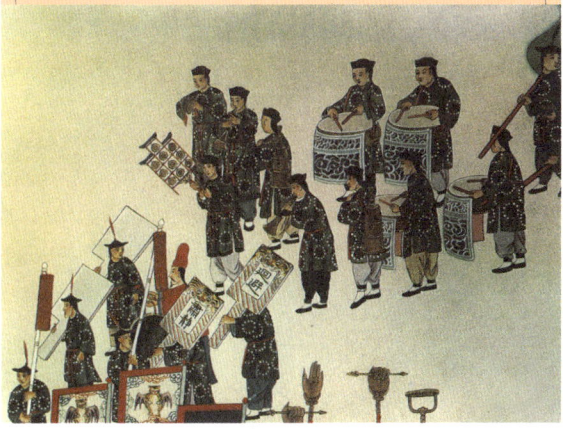

Yiguzuoqi—a Chinese idiom, meaning (rousing the spirits with the first drum roll)

During the Spring and Autumn Period the Qi State launched an attack on the Lu State. Nevertheless, the weak Lu State defeated the strong Qi State. The reason for their victory was that they adopted Cao Gui's tactics of command, i.e., to beat drums to boost the morale of the soldiers. With the first round of drumbeating their own soldiers mustered their courage. With the second round of drumbeating the enemy soldiers were discouraged. With the third round of drumbeating the enemy troops lost their nerve completely. The courageous troops of the Lu State ultimately won the battle.

Jigumingyuan—a Chinese idiom, meaning (beat the drum and appeal for justice)

Yao, Shun and Yu—legendary rulers in ancient China—installed big drums in front of the government offices to show their concern for the common people. People were encouraged to beat the drums to ask the magistrate for restitution. This practice worked for several thousand years. It was a set pattern for the magistrate to hold court when he heard someone beat the drum.

Paigu

The *paigu* is a set of 5 small drums used as kettledrums to set pitch. The drum is covered with animal hide on both sides. The drummer uses a pair of wooden mallets with both hands to beat the skins on both sides. The five drums are arranged in a spectacular way according

A performance of the *paigu*

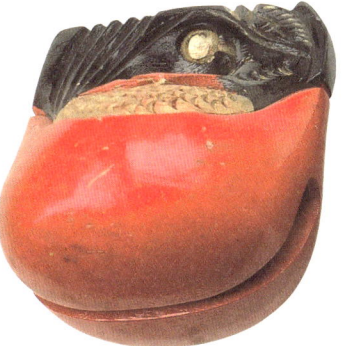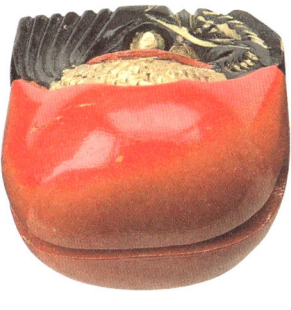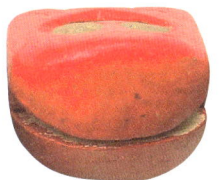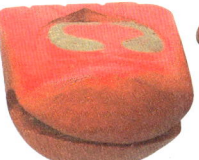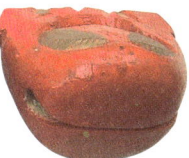

The *muyu* is mainly used in the Buddhist and Taoist temples as well as in folk music. This is a set of *muyu* in different sizes. They can make sounds in different pitches. The fish-shaped hollow *muyu* has a mouth at the top and a slope on the back. The player strikes the *muyu* to produce a crisp and soft sound.

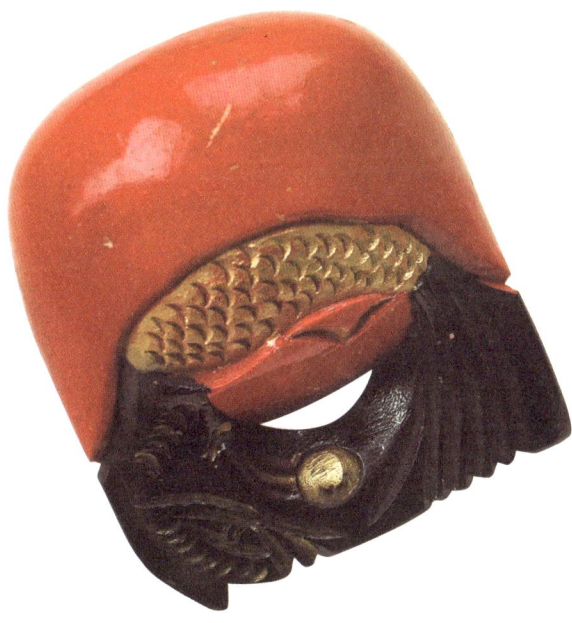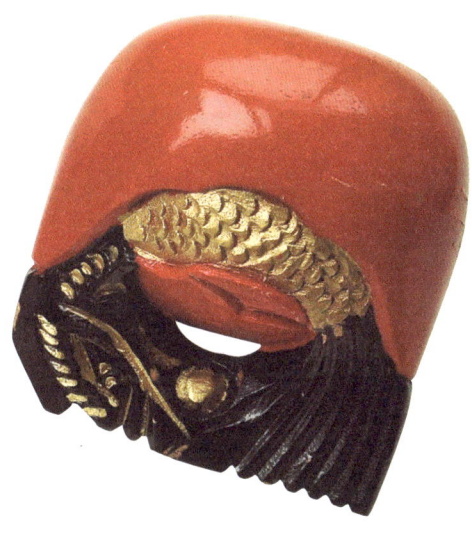

to their pitch. Some solo passages of the *paigu* are full of vigor and excitement. Sometimes the drummer will keep his hands crossed to play complex tunes. This kind of performance is a good showcase of a *paigu* player's talents.

Muyu

The *muyu* (literally meaning "the wooden fish") can be seen in many temples. Differing in shape, the *muyu* is a hollow wooden block used as a percussion instrument. Usually five or six *muyu* of different sizes are used in Chinese folk orchestras. When it is beaten, the *muyu* will make a sound similar to the clatter of hoofs.

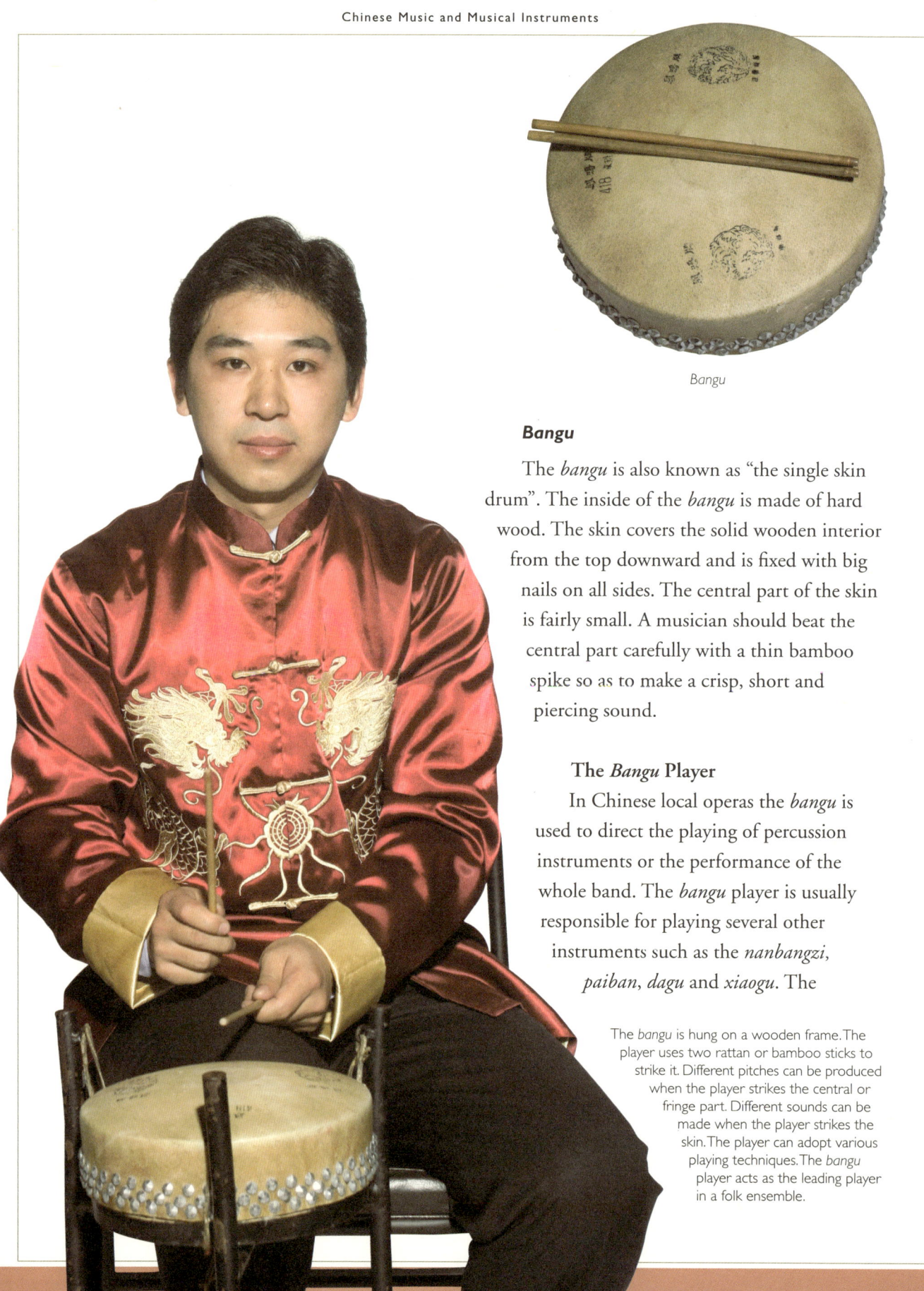

Bangu

Bangu

The *bangu* is also known as "the single skin drum". The inside of the *bangu* is made of hard wood. The skin covers the solid wooden interior from the top downward and is fixed with big nails on all sides. The central part of the skin is fairly small. A musician should beat the central part carefully with a thin bamboo spike so as to make a crisp, short and piercing sound.

The *Bangu* Player

In Chinese local operas the *bangu* is used to direct the playing of percussion instruments or the performance of the whole band. The *bangu* player is usually responsible for playing several other instruments such as the *nanbangzi*, *paiban*, *dagu* and *xiaogu*. The

The *bangu* is hung on a wooden frame. The player uses two rattan or bamboo sticks to strike it. Different pitches can be produced when the player strikes the central or fringe part. Different sounds can be made when the player strikes the skin. The player can adopt various playing techniques. The *bangu* player acts as the leading player in a folk ensemble.

player uses his left hand to beat the *bangu* with a bamboo spike and his right hand to play the *paiban* to control the rhythm.

Nanbangzi

The *nanbangzi*, which is made of rosewood, makes a rattling sound when struck. On both sides of its top there is a sounding and vibrating groove.

Bangzi

The *bangzi*, which is also made of rosewood, is composed of two clappers of different thickness. The player holds a clapper in each hand and strikes them against each other. The *bangzi* can produce a crisp sound and is used to make strong beats in an instrumental ensemble.

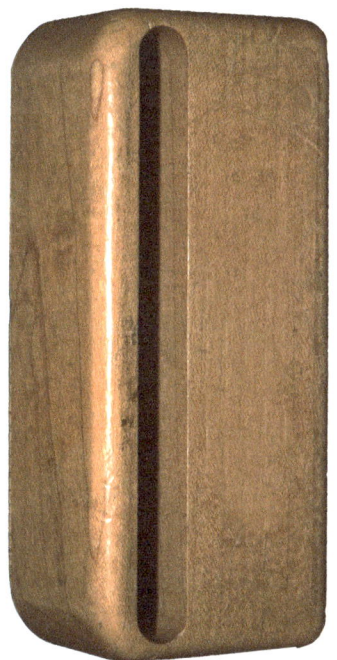

The *nanbangzi* (literally meaning "south *bangzi*") is so named because this kind of *bangzi* is often used in local operas and *quyi* performance in southern China.

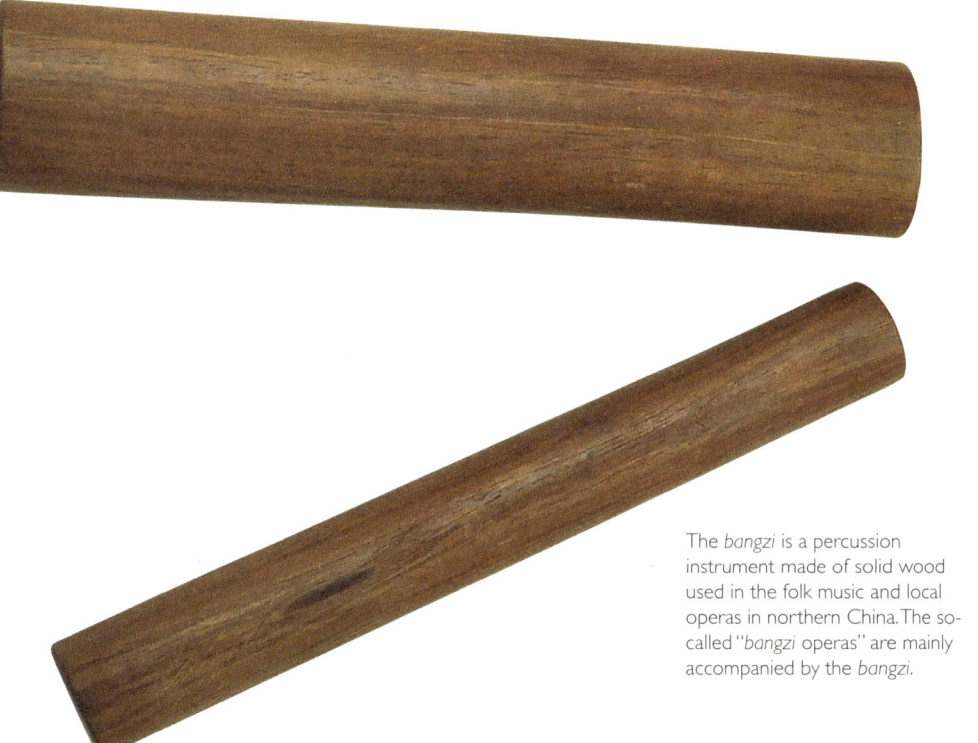

The *bangzi* is a percussion instrument made of solid wood used in the folk music and local operas in northern China. The so-called "*bangzi* operas" are mainly accompanied by the *bangzi*.

4 Bowed Stringed Instruments

The bowed instruments used in Chinese folk orchestras include the *gaohu*, *erhu*, *zhonghu*, *gehu* and *laruan*. This set of instruments, which produce sounds with the vibration of strings, are played by pulling a horsehair bow across the strings. With a melodious and pleasant timbre, the bowed stringed instruments can produce harmonies. The ensemble of a string section can

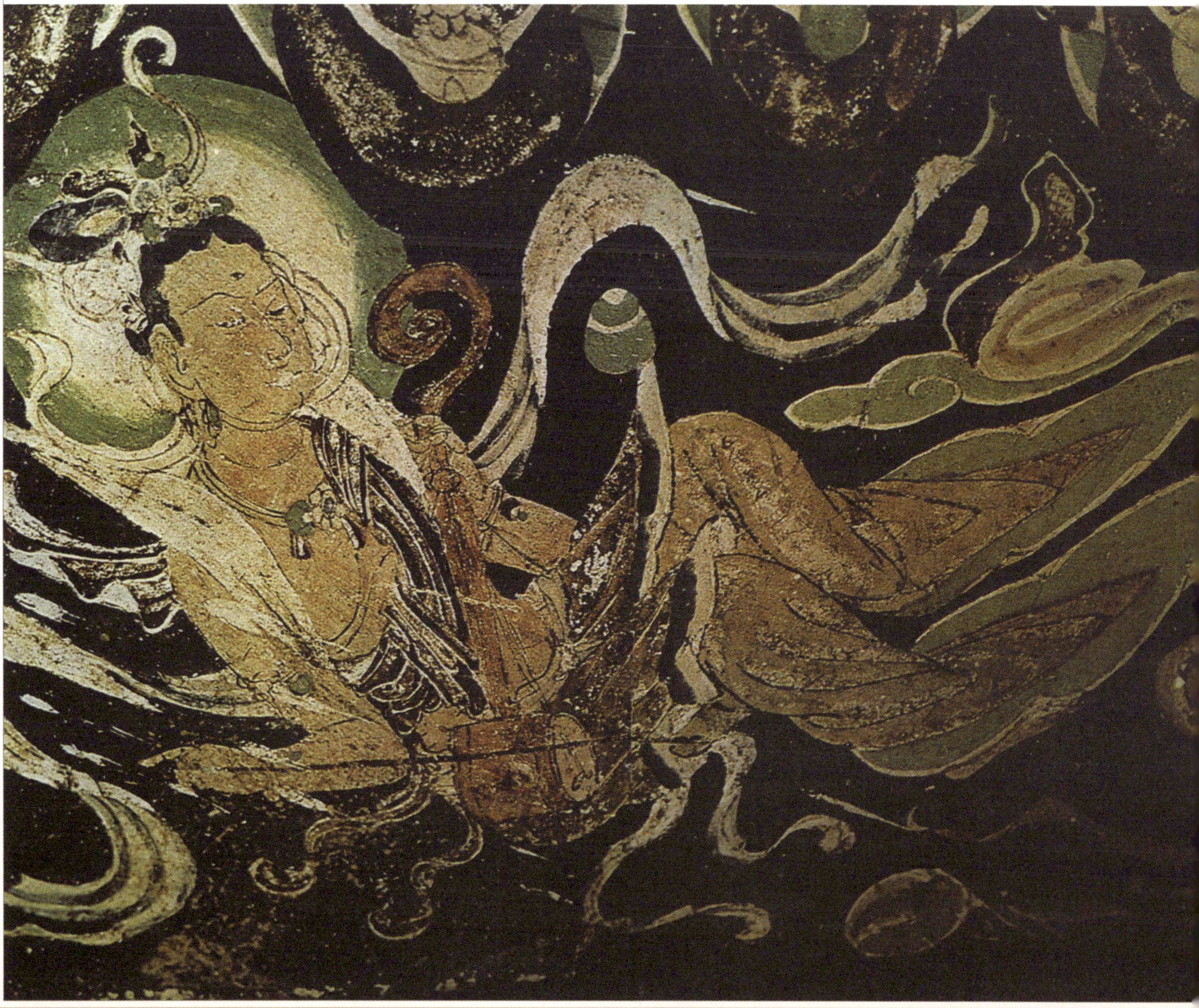

A performance of the *huqin* seen in a mural of the Yuan Dynasty in the No. 10 grotto of Yulin Grottoes in Gansu Province

show a variation in the breadth and intensity of the music. A bowed stringed instrument is usually played solo in an instrumental ensemble.

The composition of bowed stringed instruments is decided by their different tone colors. The *erhu* is an alto instrument whereas the *gaohu* is a melodious high-pitched instrument. With its deep and solid timbre, the *zhonghu* plays the role of harmonizing the *erhu* and the *gaohu*.

The section of bowed stringed instruments in a Chinese folk orchestra is a section typical of the Chinese national style. It is most suited for playing joyful and harmonious tunes.

Erhu

A fairly large Chinese folk orchestra is usually equipped with 20 *erhu* while a medium-sized orchestra consists of 6 to 12 *erhu*. This section of the *huqin* family is composed of high-pitched, alto and bass *erhu* and makes a deep and gentle sound. It is often used to play a harmonic melody. In a seated position the *erhu* player puts the base of the *erhu* on the lap of his left leg and holds the *erhu* upright with his left hand. The player plays the *erhu* by pushing and pulling the bow and the bowstring across the strings with their right hand.

> **Varieties of the *Huqin***
>
> After more than 300 years of development the *huqin* has become a bowed stringed instrument of great variety. According to their difference in structure, the *huqin* family is divided into two main types: those sounded with the vibration of a skin and those sounded with the vibration of a board surface. The first type consists of the *erhu*, *gaohu*, *jinghu*, *zhonghu*, *gehu*, *guanghu*, *zhuihu*, *datong* and *sihu*. The second type includes the *banhu*, *gaibanzi*, *erguxuan*, *zhutiqin*, *laohu*, *leiqin*, *qiaozixian* and *yehu*.
>
> Section of a scroll painting showcasing *A Mid-autumn Festival Banquet Held at Lin Hall* of the Ming Dynsaty. The whole painting depicts the scholars' lifestyle—playing chess and music, talking about archery and other activities. This section is about playing music. In the painting three scholars are having a dinner in celebration of the mid-autumn festival. One scholar is playing the *xiao* while two boy servants are playing the *erhu* and the *kuaiban* respectively by his side. The other two scholars are enjoying their performance. This painting records the lifestyle of scholars during the Ming Dynasty.

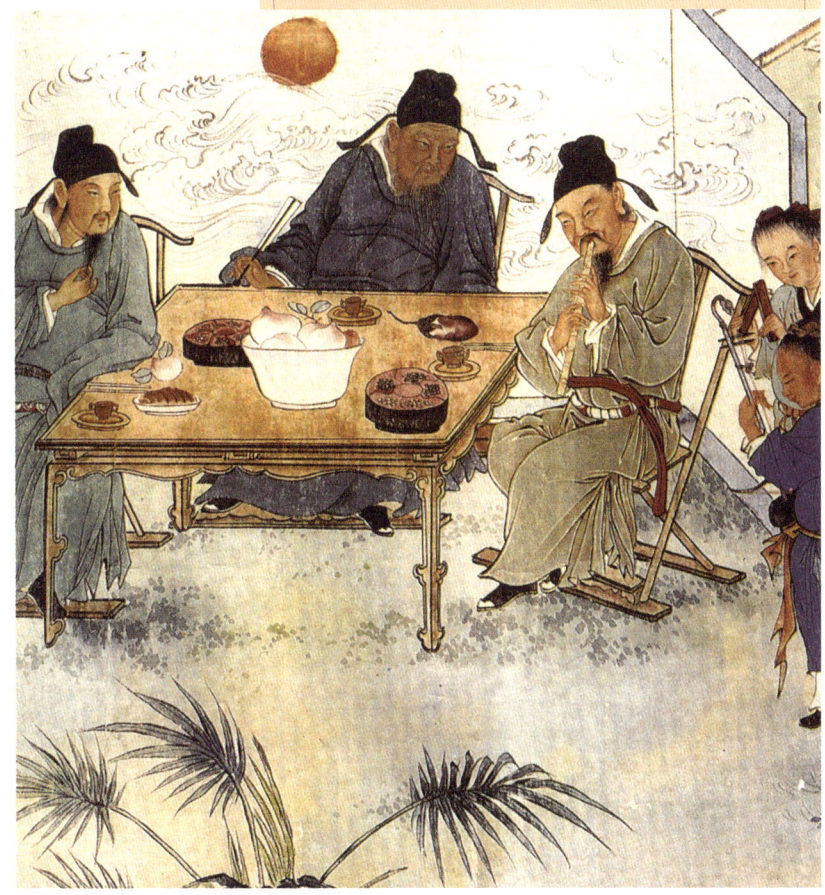

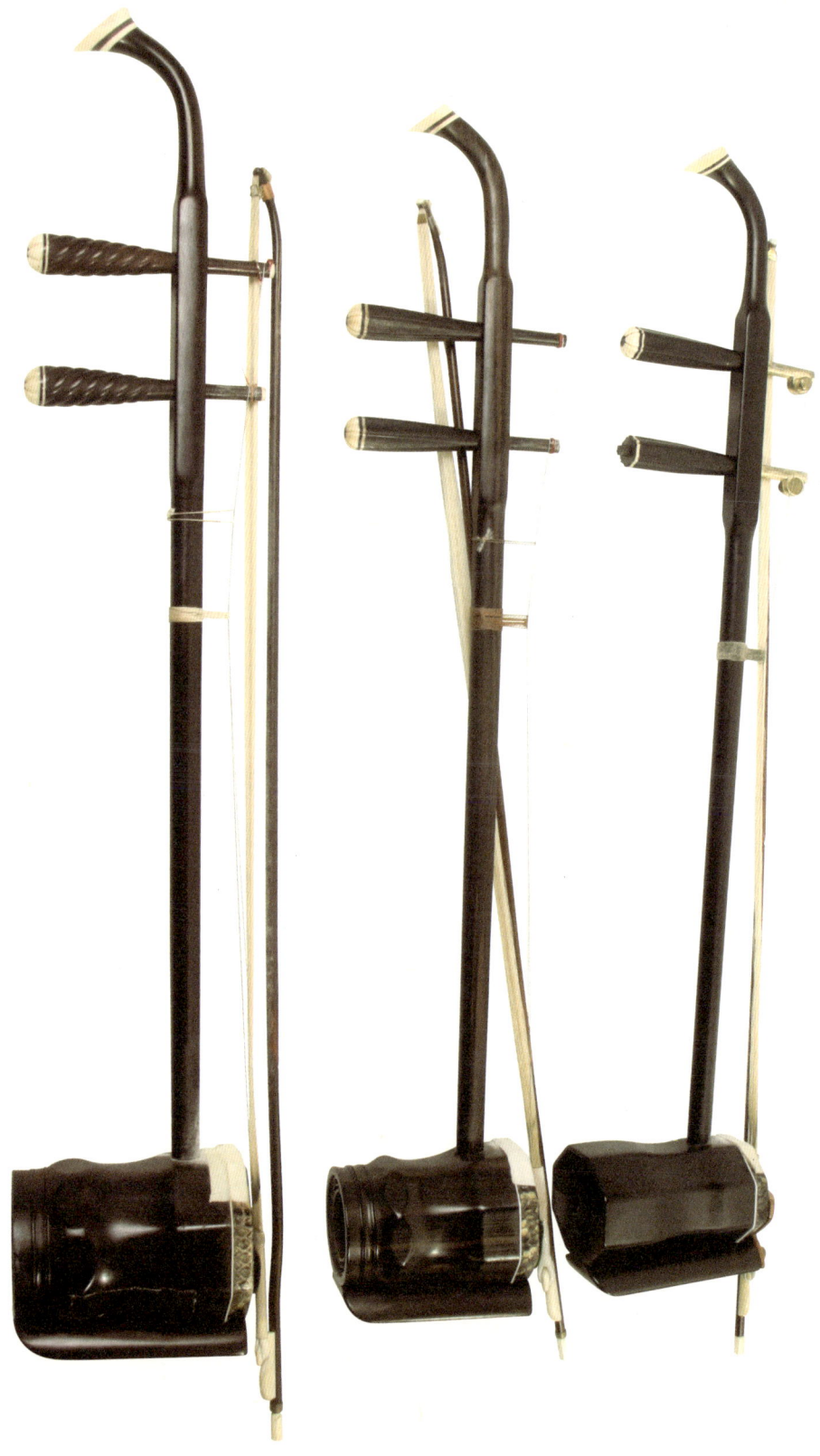

The *erhu*, *zhonghu* and *gaohu*

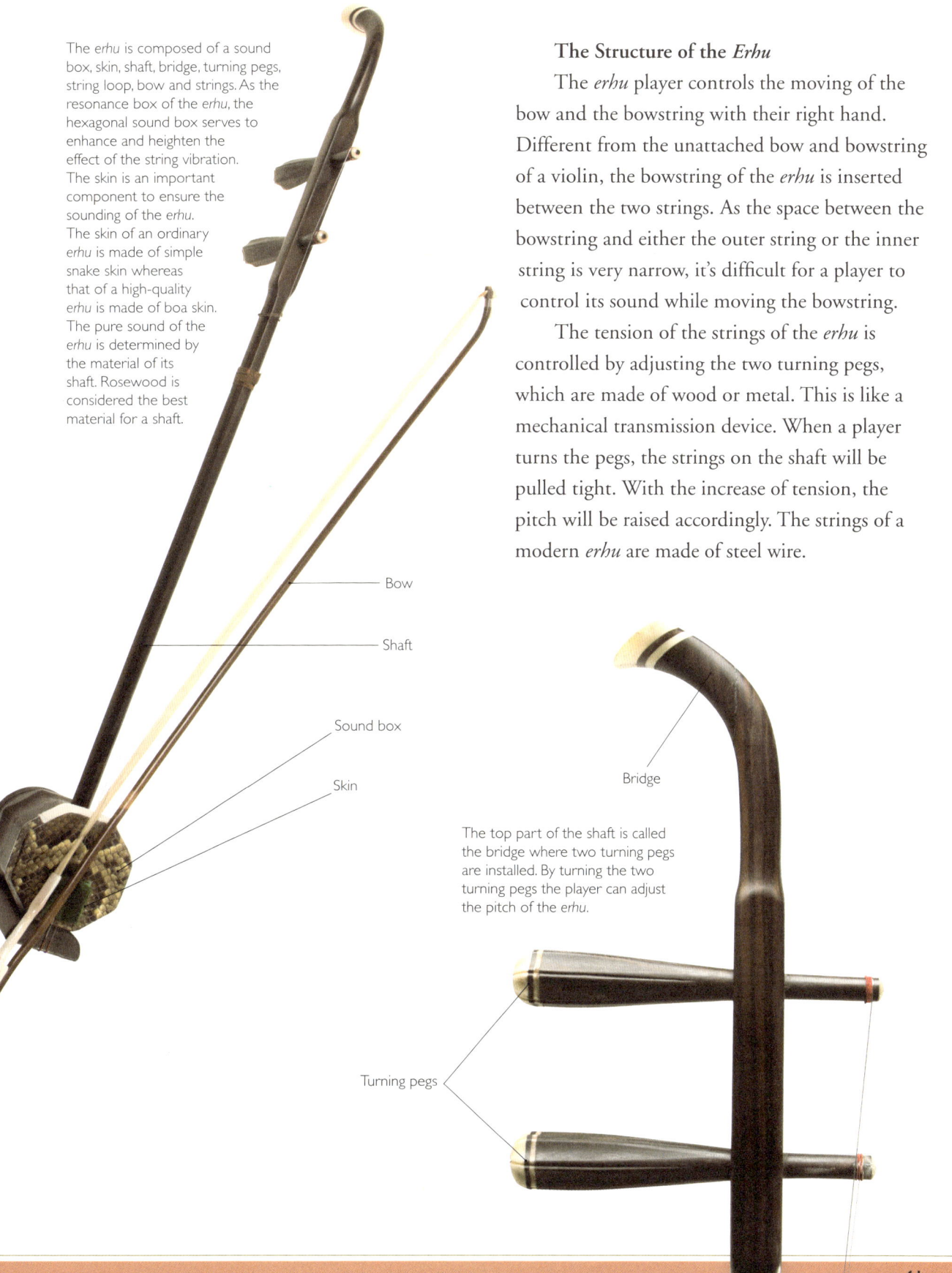

The *erhu* is composed of a sound box, skin, shaft, bridge, turning pegs, string loop, bow and strings. As the resonance box of the *erhu*, the hexagonal sound box serves to enhance and heighten the effect of the string vibration. The skin is an important component to ensure the sounding of the *erhu*. The skin of an ordinary *erhu* is made of simple snake skin whereas that of a high-quality *erhu* is made of boa skin. The pure sound of the *erhu* is determined by the material of its shaft. Rosewood is considered the best material for a shaft.

The Structure of the *Erhu*

The *erhu* player controls the moving of the bow and the bowstring with their right hand. Different from the unattached bow and bowstring of a violin, the bowstring of the *erhu* is inserted between the two strings. As the space between the bowstring and either the outer string or the inner string is very narrow, it's difficult for a player to control its sound while moving the bowstring.

The tension of the strings of the *erhu* is controlled by adjusting the two turning pegs, which are made of wood or metal. This is like a mechanical transmission device. When a player turns the pegs, the strings on the shaft will be pulled tight. With the increase of tension, the pitch will be raised accordingly. The strings of a modern *erhu* are made of steel wire.

The top part of the shaft is called the bridge where two turning pegs are installed. By turning the two turning pegs the player can adjust the pitch of the *erhu*.

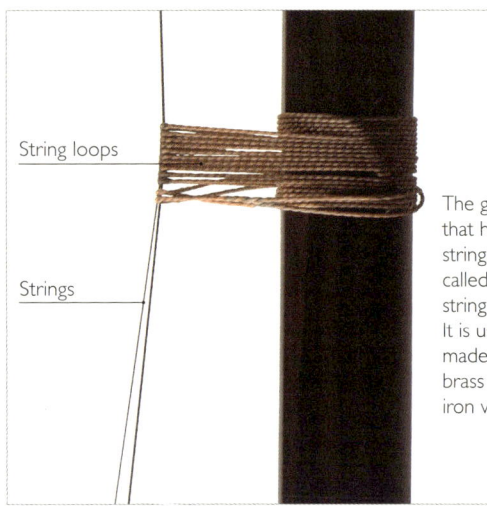

String loops

Strings

The gadget that holds strings is called the string loop. It is usually made from brass wire or iron wire.

The Sounding of the *Erhu*

The *erhu*'s sound is produced with the physical vibration caused by the friction between the bowstring and the strings. The length of the strings between the bridge and a tight loop of string is the range of vibration. The inner string is thicker than the outer one. Starting from the empty string sound (basic pitch) at the tight loop of string and moving fingers downward from the upper grip (the original grip) to the lower grip, the pitch of the musical sound is made as the strings ascend gradually.

The bowstring of the *erhu* and the fingering of the player combine to make a variety of musical notes. In his *erhu* solo piece *Kongshanniaoyu*, the *erhu* musician Liu Tianhua mimicked a great variety of birdsongs with a slide of his left hand in a portamento style. The hopping of the bowstring between the two strings can make a series of water dripping notes, thus producing light-hearted and dynamic sound effects.

A'bing and his *Erquanyingyue*

There is a tourist attraction at the foot of the Huishan Hill in Wuxi, Jiangsu Province known as "9 Dragons and 13 Springs". The most picturesque second spring is the birthplace of Hua Yanjun (also known as A'bing).

After his parents passed away, the young A'bing was adopted by Hua Qinghe, a Taoist priest, and lived with his adoptive father in the local Taoist temple. Hua Qinghe was an amateur musician especially good at playing the *pipa* and the *erhu*. The gifted A'bing acquired the skill of *erhu*-playing from him and quickly became an *erhu* performer on the streets. When the middle-aged A'bing lost his sight, people started to call him "Blind A'bing".

"*Erquanyingyue*" (which literally means "the moon mirrored on the second spring") is A'bing's representative composition. This moving and heart-stirring tune is more an expression of the composer's unfortunate lot in life than a depiction of the picturesque scene.

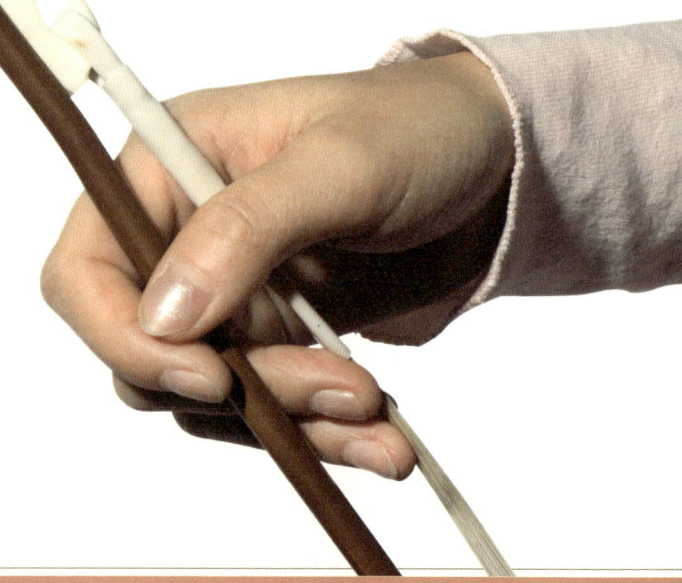

A player is required to use both their thumb and index finger to control the movement and balance of the bow the way one uses chopsticks. That's why someone said, "If you know how to hold chopsticks, you will certainly know how to hold a bow."

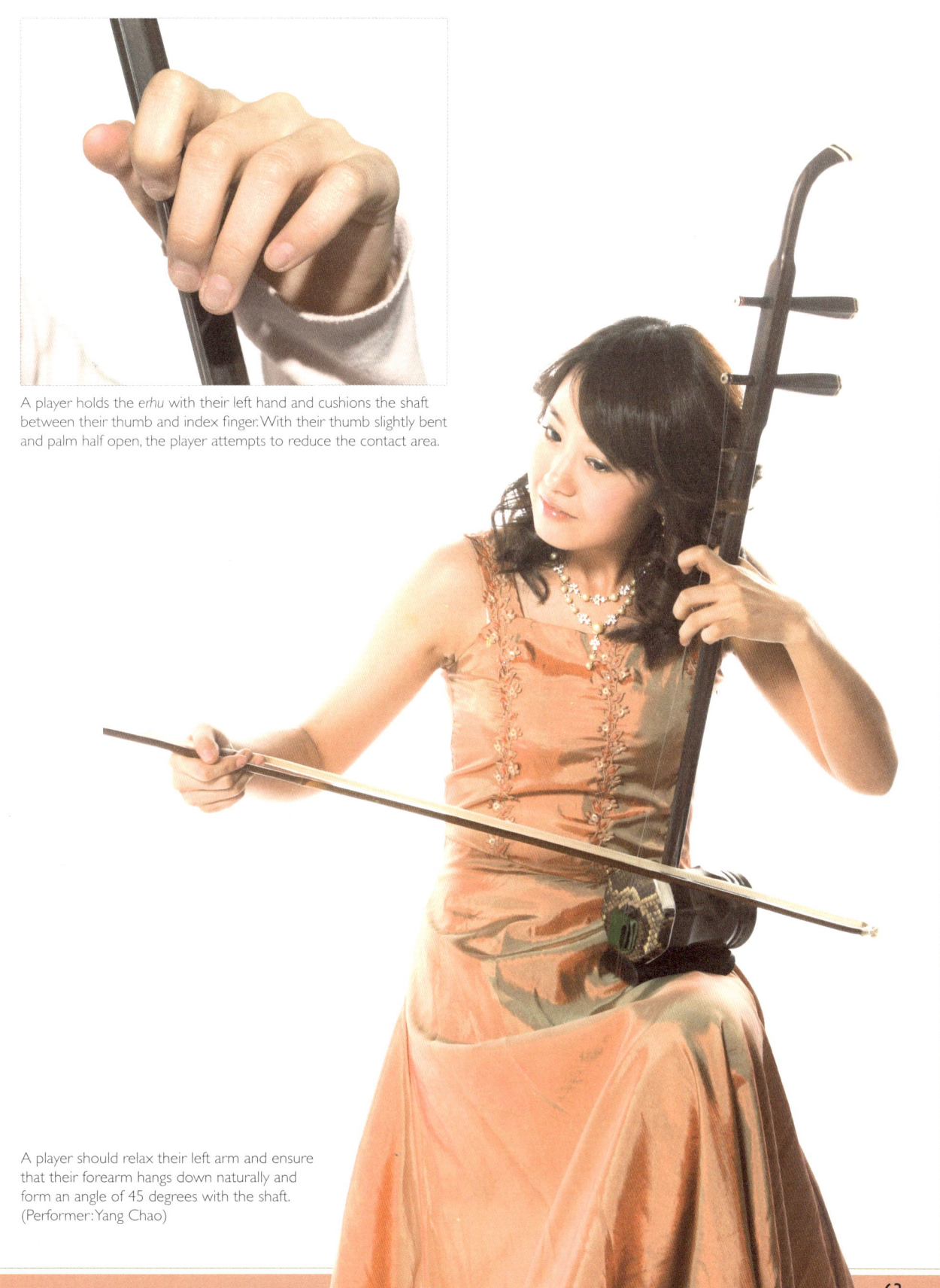

A player holds the *erhu* with their left hand and cushions the shaft between their thumb and index finger. With their thumb slightly bent and palm half open, the player attempts to reduce the contact area.

A player should relax their left arm and ensure that their forearm hangs down naturally and form an angle of 45 degrees with the shaft. (Performer: Yang Chao)

Gaohu

The *gaohu* is a high-pitched *erhu*. As one of the high-pitched instruments in a Chinese folk orchestra, the *gaohu* is known for its bright, soft and exquisite timbre and sweet and melodious tunes. Slightly smaller in size, the structure of the *gaohu* is the same as that of the *erhu*. In a seated position, the player puts the body of the *gaohu* between their knees so as to adjust its volume and timbre at any time.

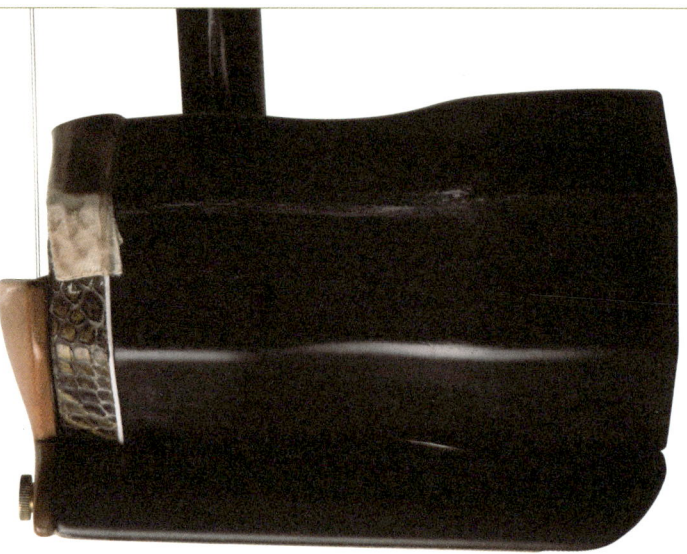

The sound box of the *gaohu* (the flank)

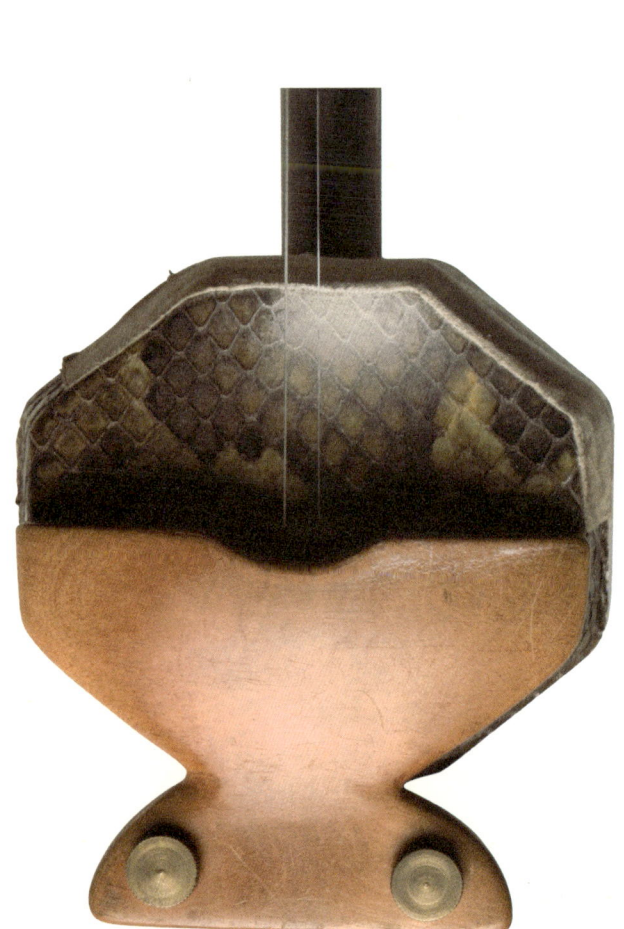

The sound box of the *gaohu* (the front)

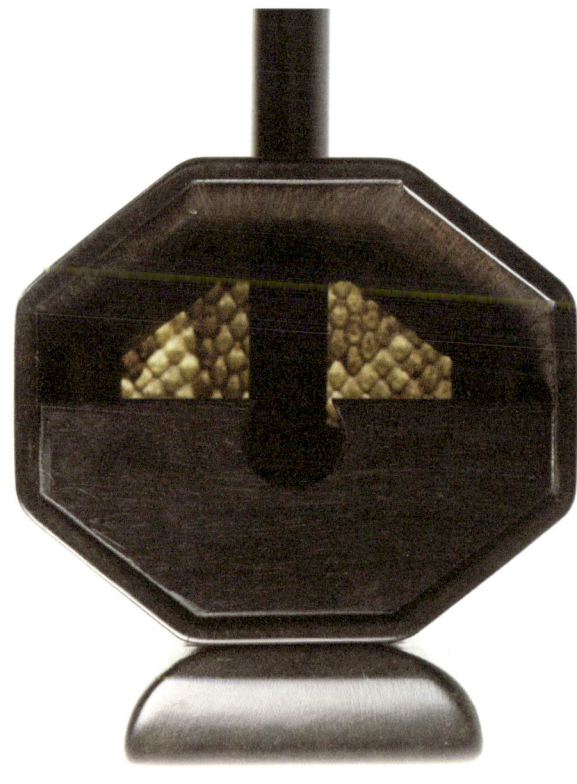

The sound box of the *gaohu* (the back side)

Zhonghu

Slightly bigger in size and lower in pitch, the *zhonghu* is used in the same way as the *erhu*. While the technique of playing is similar, the *zhonghu* player is required to exert greater strength when moving the bowstring with their right hand since the distance between grips is greater than that of the *erhu*. As a result, the *zhonghu* makes a deep, soft and melodious sound.

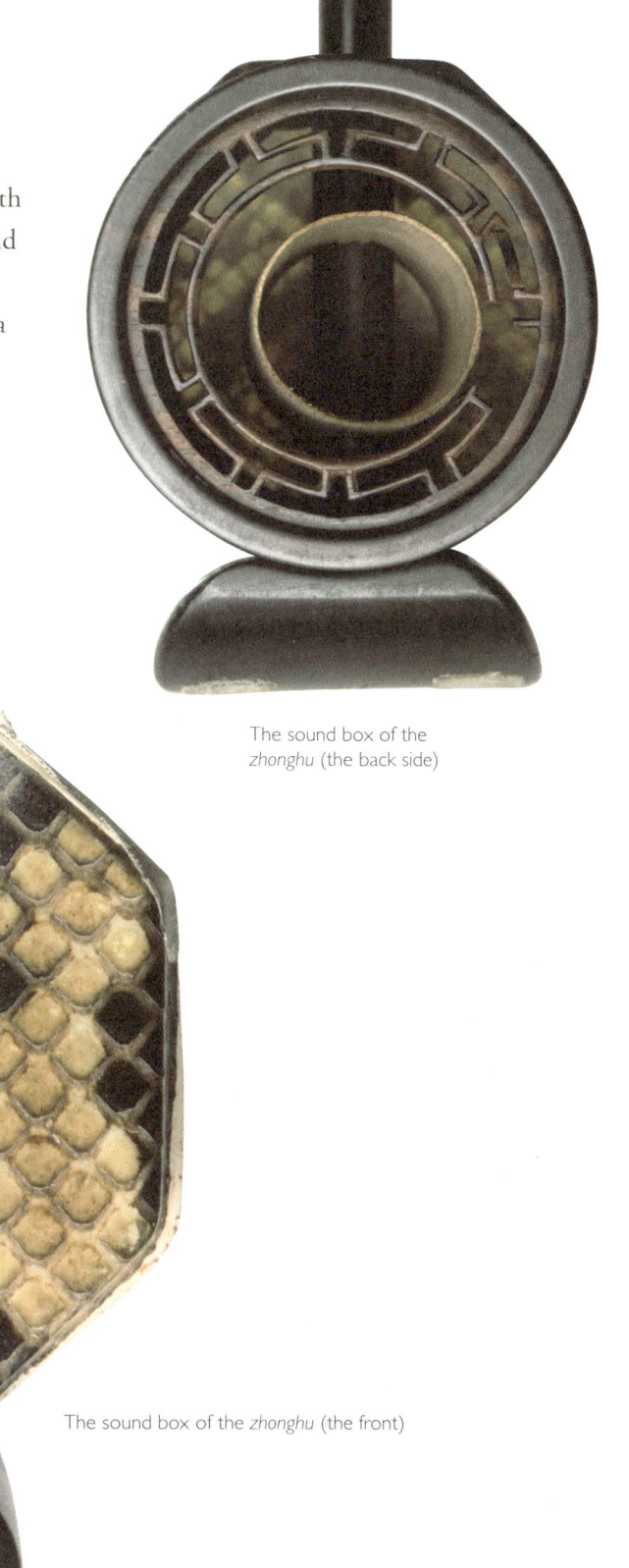

The sound box of the *zhonghu* (the back side)

The sound box of the *zhonghu* (the front)

Laruan

The *laruan* is a Chinese bowed stringed instrument similar to a cello. It combines the special features of bowed stringed instruments and plucked stringed instruments. It was specially invented as a bass stringed instrument for a Chinese folk orchestra. The *laruan* is distinguished by its loud, broad and sonorous tone colors.

In performances the *laruan* is supported by a steel frame at the bottom to ensure its stability.

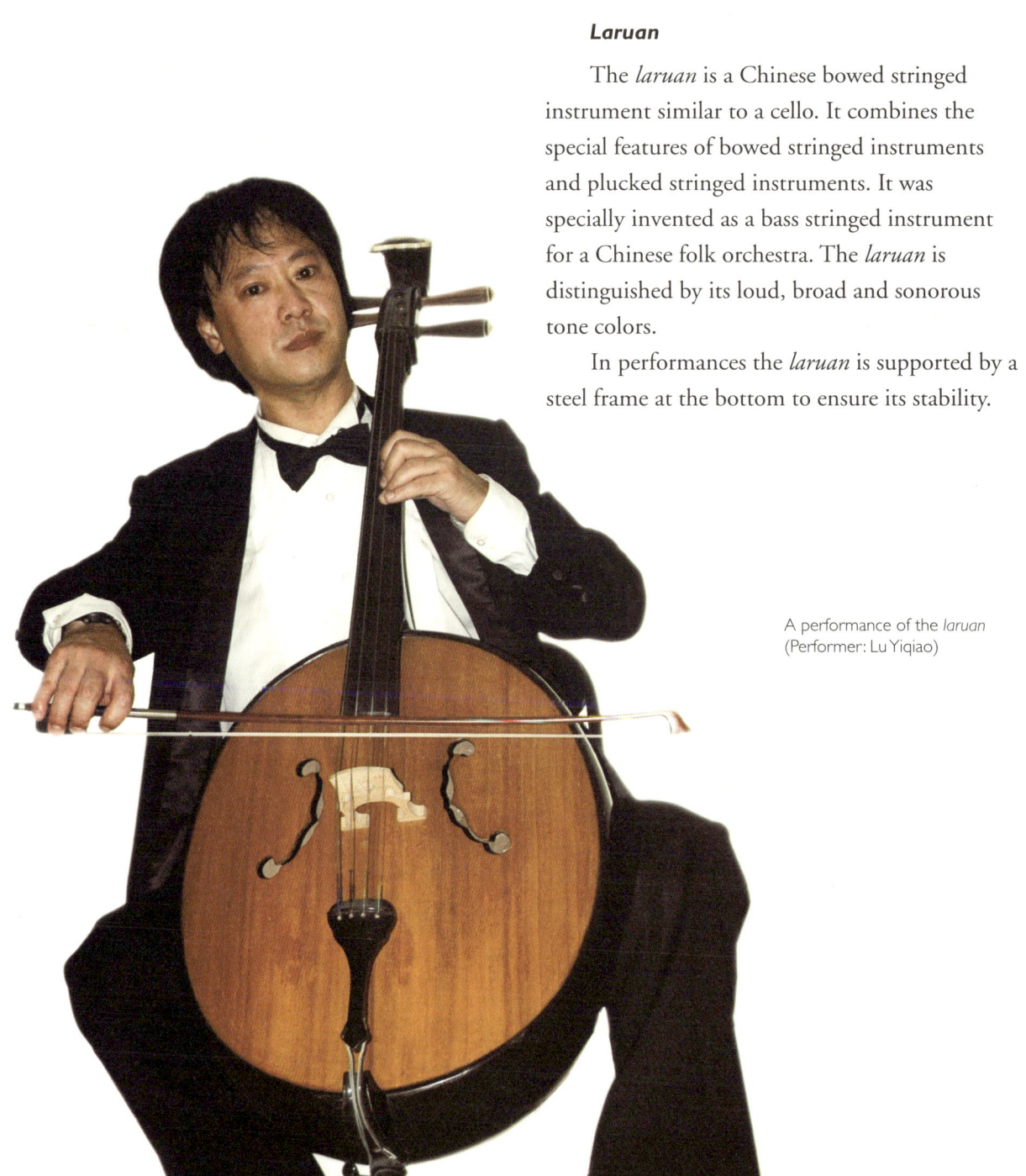

A performance of the *laruan*
(Performer: Lu Yiqiao)

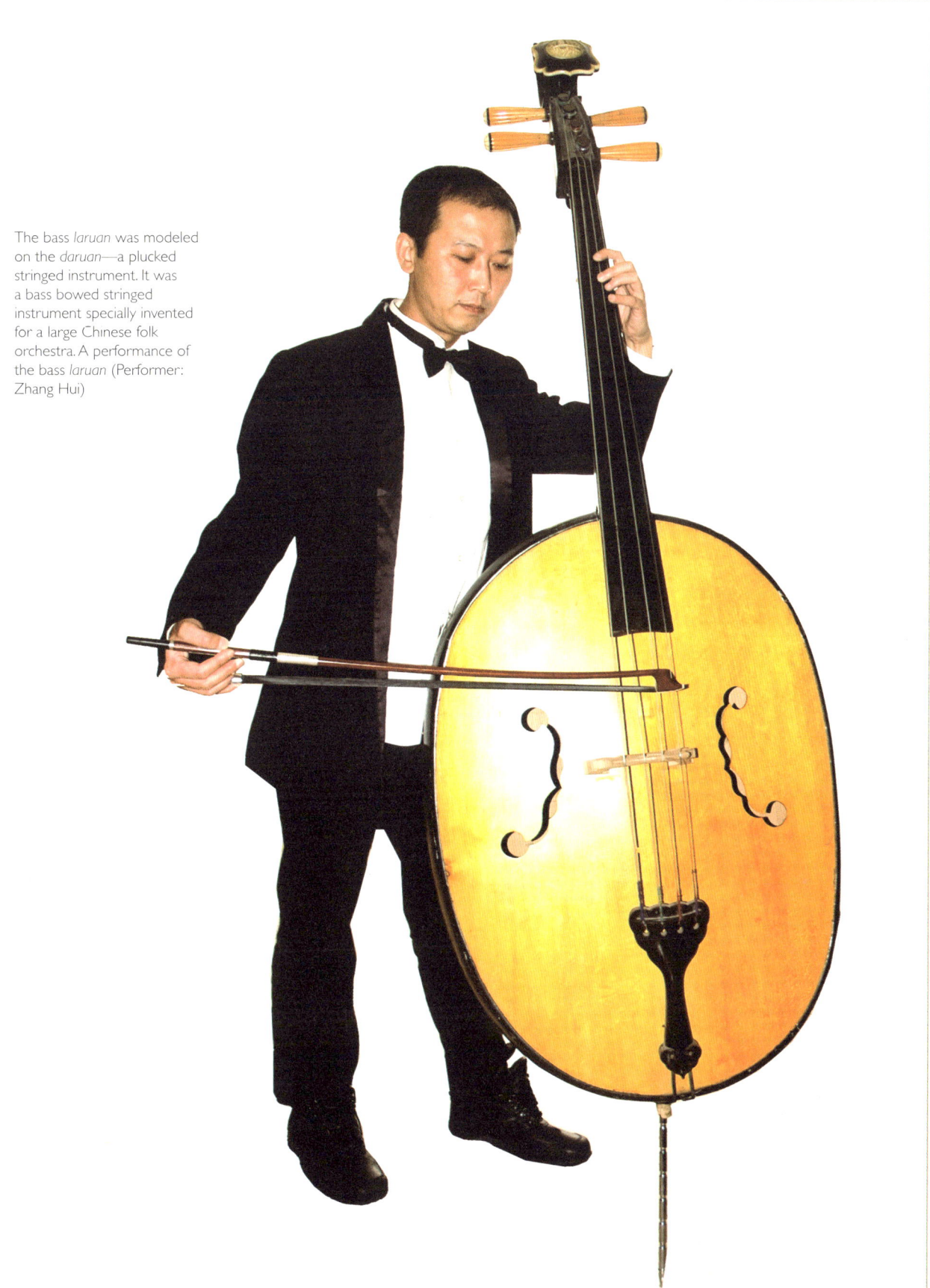

The bass *laruan* was modeled on the *daruan*—a plucked stringed instrument. It was a bass bowed stringed instrument specially invented for a large Chinese folk orchestra. A performance of the bass *laruan* (Performer: Zhang Hui)

CHAPTER TWO
The History of Chinese Music

Chinese music is a big family composed of various distinctive types of music, ranging from the *taoxun*, *gudi*, *zhong* and *qing* in the Western Zhou Dynasty, the *konghou* and *pipa* in the Sui, Tang and Five dynasties to the local music and *huqin* of the Ming and Qing dynasties. Each type of music reflects one facet of musical achievement made during various stages of Chinese history. Chinese music has always played an active role in imperial palaces, religious ceremonies and in the daily life of the average citizen.

Chinese folk music played at weddings, funerals or in festivals and fairs, uses particular musical instruments to bring into full play their distinctive features in order to create the perfect atmosphere for the occasion. The religious music played in religious services conducted in Buddhist and Taoist temples, utilizing musical instruments such as the *di* (flute), *sheng* (free reed instrument), *zhong* and *qing* (variations of bells), produces a peaceful and solemn atmosphere. Court music, which reached its zenith during the Tang Dynasty, is immortalized by the Five Dynasties painter Gu Hongzhong in his painting *The Night Revels of Han Xizai* which illustrates a performance of court music at an official's banquet. After the Song Dynasty, Chinese music became more secular. As it followed a more orthodox mode of expression, it failed to immerse itself in everyday life, causing

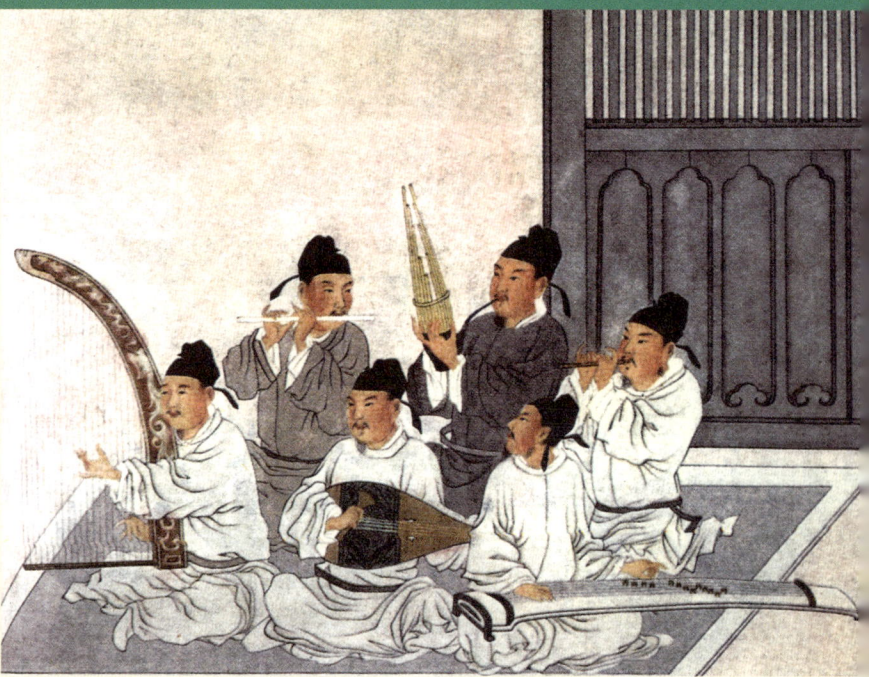

A painting of a performance from the Song Dynasty copied by Qiu Ying of the Ming Dynasty

court music's decline in popularity. The scholars' music was based on Confucian thinking. This kind of music, usually played with such instruments as the *guqin* (similar to a zither), *pipa* (similar to a lute), *zheng* (a type of plucked zither), *xiao* (a type of flute) and *xun* (similar to an ocarina), was the embodiment of the musical life of academia. Refined music of this kind is still prevalent in today's society.

In accordance with its course of change and development, the history of Chinese music can be divided into the following four stages: the Rudimentary Stage (from the 21st century BC to 221 BC), the Thriving Stage (from 221 BC to 960 AD), the Mature Stage (from 960 AD to 1840) and the Modern and Contemporary Stage (from 1840 to present).

1 The Rudimentary Stage
(From the 2100 BC to 221 BC)

Music was ushered in during this stage with the appearance of various percussion instruments. Big bands of court musicians were beginning to appear. This along with the publication of *The Book of Songs* and *The Poetry of Chu*, meant that Chinese music was beginning to take shape.

Archeological finds indicate that different kinds of musical instruments appeared as early as the remote antiquity and pre-Qin dynasty, for example, the bone whistle and bone flute unearthed at the Hemudu ruins of the Neolithic Age in Zhejiang Province, the *xun* unearthed at the Banpo site of the Neolithic Yangshao culture near Xi'an, the stone *qing* (a type of bell) unearthed at the Yin ruins in Anyang, Henan Province and the *bianzhong* and *bianqing* (types of bells or chimes) unearthed from the grave of Duke Yi of the Zeng State in Sui county, Hubei Province. All of the instruments listed are of excellent workmanship yet differ in tone quality. The unearthed musical instruments at the Yin ruins and the oracle bone inscriptions of the Shang Dynasty, show us that a dozen varieties of musical instruments appeared during that period, for example the *zhong* (a type of bell), *qing*, *taoxun*, *tonggu* (a type of drum), *ling* (small type of bell) and *yue* (a type of flute). All of which show much care and thought in their designs.

Starting from the Zhou Dynasty musical instruments began to take the combined form of blowing, striking and plucking. Both solo performances of single instruments and concert

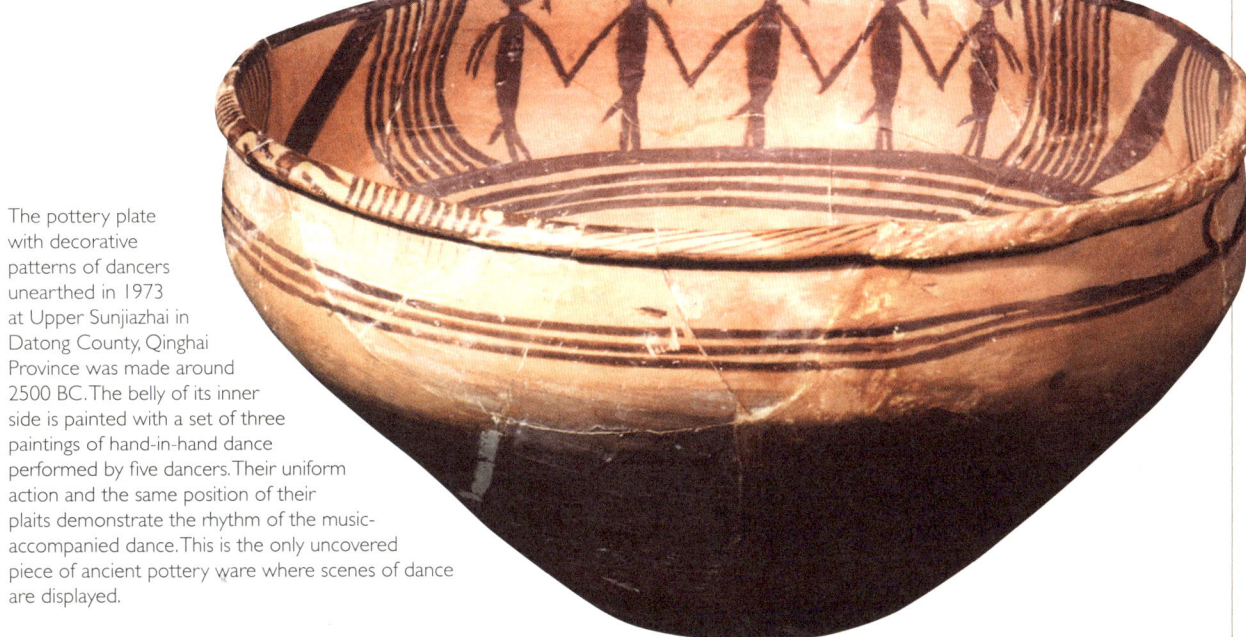

The pottery plate with decorative patterns of dancers unearthed in 1973 at Upper Sunjiazhai in Datong County, Qinghai Province was made around 2500 BC. The belly of its inner side is painted with a set of three paintings of hand-in-hand dance performed by five dancers. Their uniform action and the same position of their plaits demonstrate the rhythm of the music-accompanied dance. This is the only uncovered piece of ancient pottery ware where scenes of dance are displayed.

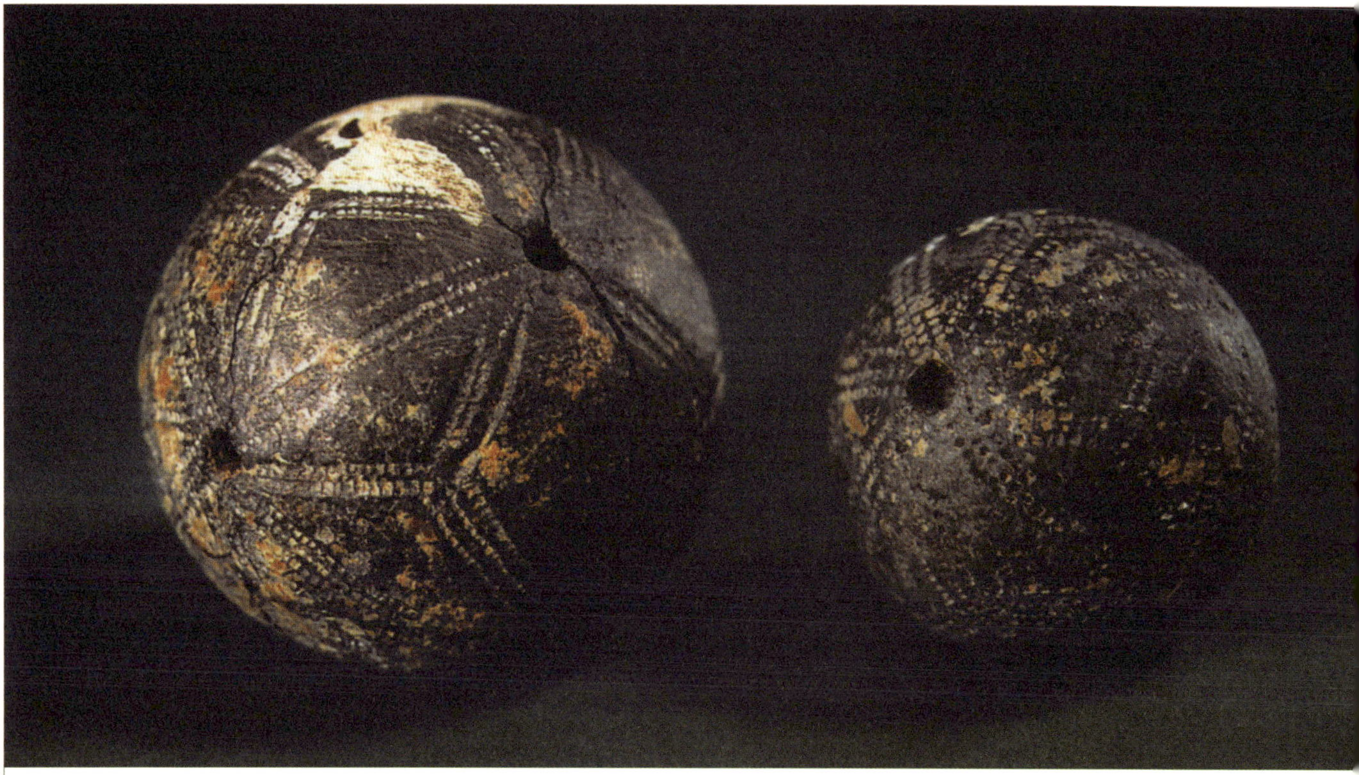

The pottery *xiangling* unearthed at Zhujiazui, Jingshan County, Hubei Province in the 1950s is part of the 5,000-year-old Qujialing culture which was prevalent in the Jianghan plains at the middle reaches of the Yangtse River. The ball-shaped *xiangling* is divided into two varieties depending on their different sizes. The black or grey hollow *xiangling*, which has 6 symmetrical holes, are filled with 15 or more small pottery balls. Similar to a maraca, the *xiangling* is sounded by shaking.

performances of palace bands were prevalent at this same time (imperial ceremonial music being a typical example of the latter). The chief instruments adopted by a palace band were the *bianzhong* and *bianqing*. The *zhong* and *qing* in different sizes were hung in two layers and the striking of these instruments produced musical notes of different pitches. The Zhou Dynasty adopted the system of ruling by rites and music, and employed 1,463 musicians in the palace. Their performances entailed not only music, but poetry and dancing. The popular dances, and their musical accompaniment, employed during the following six dynasties—*Yunmen*, *Xianchi*, *Xiaoshao*, *Daxia*, *Dahuo* and *Dawu*—are each a manifestation of the most influential music, songs and dance from the time of their conception, ranging from the time of the Yellow Emporer to the Zhou Dynasty.

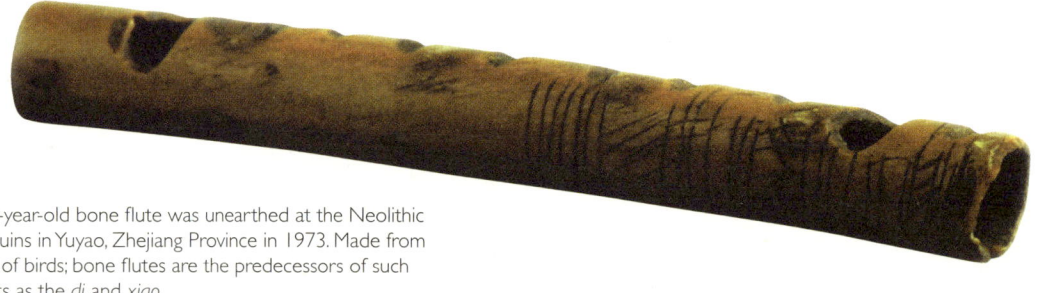

The 7,000-year-old bone flute was unearthed at the Neolithic Hemudu ruins in Yuyao, Zhejiang Province in 1973. Made from the bones of birds; bone flutes are the predecessors of such instruments as the *di* and *xiao*.

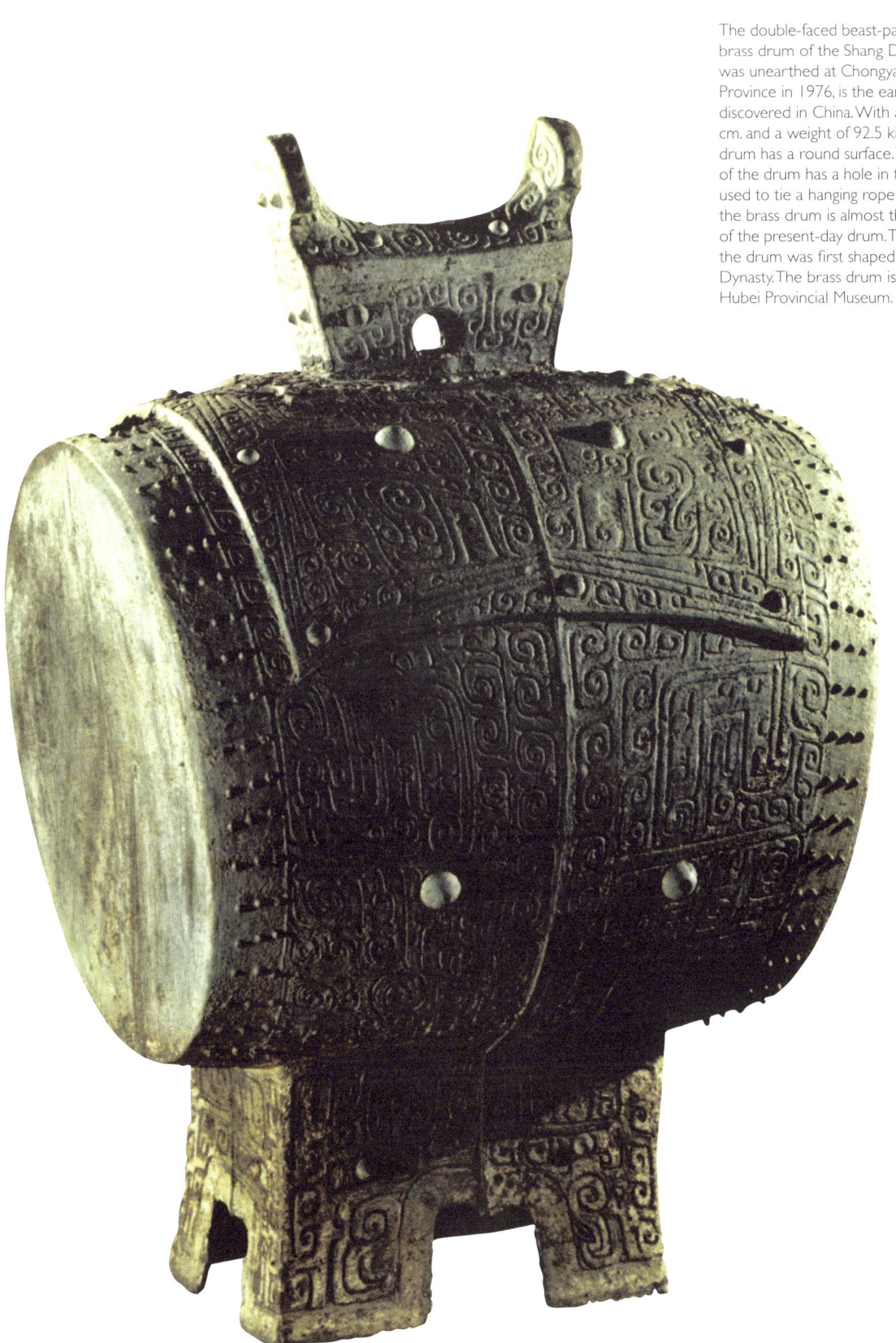

The double-faced beast-pattern-decorated brass drum of the Shang Dynasty, which was unearthed at Chongyang County, Hubei Province in 1976, is the earliest brass drum discovered in China. With a height of 75.5 cm. and a weight of 92.5 kilograms, the drum has a round surface. The upper part of the drum has a hole in the center that is used to tie a hanging rope. The structure of the brass drum is almost the same as that of the present-day drum. This is proof that the drum was first shaped during the Shang Dynasty. The brass drum is displayed in the Hubei Provincial Museum.

Xun

It is said that the *xun* was a round stone used, initially, as a tool to throw at one's prey and later refined to imitate birdsongs as a hunting tool. After the Qin and Han dynasties the *xun* was used in the palace and also among scholars as a chief wind instrument in the performance of imperial ceremonial music. With its hollow, thick and solemn sound of primitive simplicity, the *xun* is suited for expressing grief. There are two types of *xun*. One type is made of clay and fired. It is possible to preserve this type of *xun* for a long time because it does not decay easily. The second type is made of stone with holes bored into it. The performer plays the *xun* by blowing through it. The *xun* is an example of the musical culture of the Neolithic Age.

The earliest *xun* has only one blowing hole. With the increase of finger holes, the *xun* was used to play tunes. The *xun* looks like a flat fish with the blowing hole at the top or at the fish's mouth. The shoulder parts on both sides have finger holes. The surface of the *xun* is decorated with painted or carved net-shaped and striped patterns.

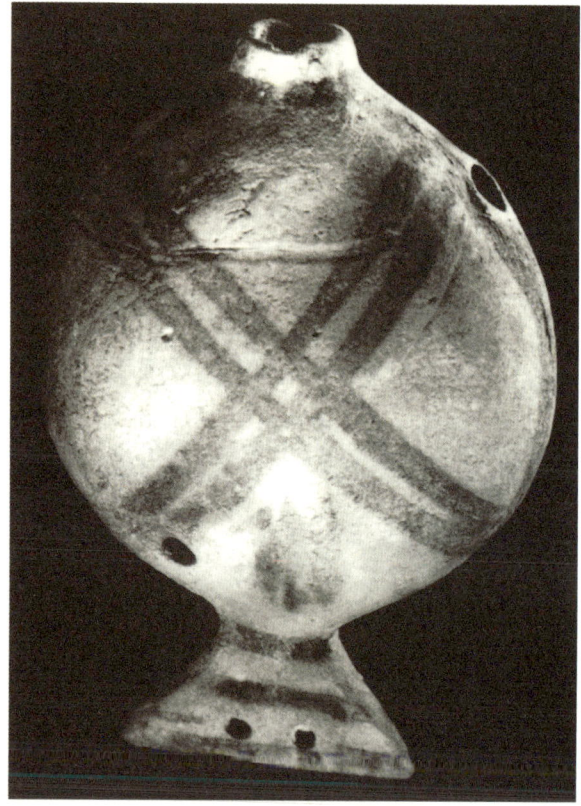

The *xun* unearthed at the Huoshaogou ruins in Yumen, Gansu Province assumes the shape of a flat round fish. The body of the *xun* is decorated with stripes.

This pottery *xun* was unearthed in the Fuhao grave of the Yin ruins in 1976 at Anyang, Henan Province. The three pottery *xun* are made of grey pottery clay and have a smooth surface. With one piece smaller than the other two, they all come in the shape of an upside-down top. This demonstrates that the pottery *xun*—the most advanced musical instrument of the Neolithic Age—was mature during the Shang Dynasty.

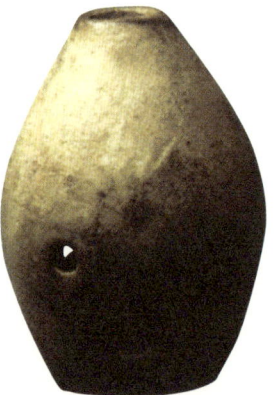 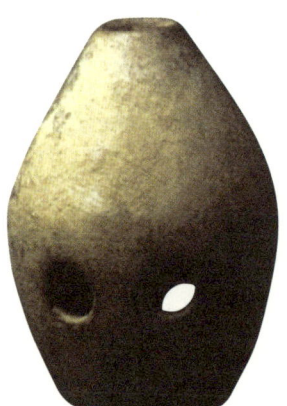 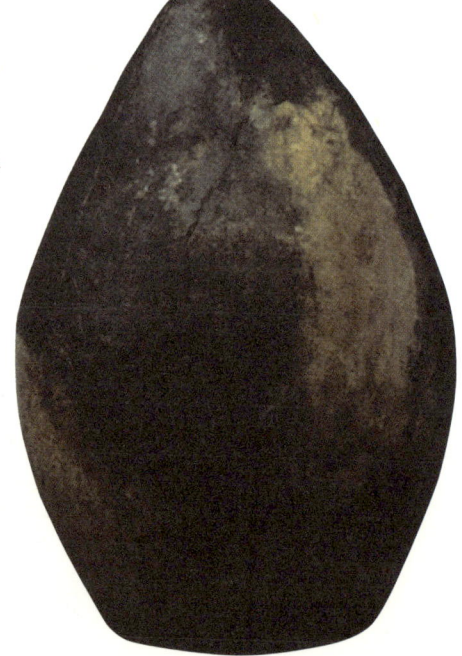

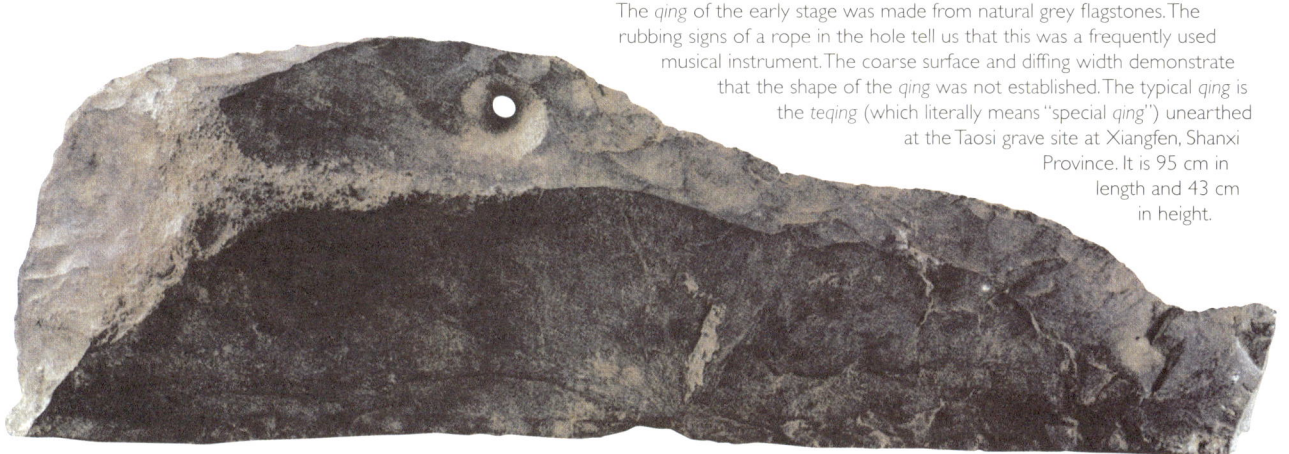

The *qing* of the early stage was made from natural grey flagstones. The rubbing signs of a rope in the hole tell us that this was a frequently used musical instrument. The coarse surface and diffing width demonstrate that the shape of the *qing* was not established. The typical *qing* is the *teqing* (which literally means "special *qing*") unearthed at the Taosi grave site at Xiangfen, Shanxi Province. It is 95 cm in length and 43 cm in height.

Qing

When people work in the fields, they are attracted by the melodious sound of rocks being struck. As a result, when they celebrate a good harvest, they will strike the stoneware and dance merrily by imitating the actions of birds and animals. The stoneware can be considered as the prototype of the *qing*.

The *qing* was an ancient percussion instrument. The different shapes of *qing* were made of natural rocks through cutting and grinding. The *qing* was used as a musical instrument 4,400 years ago. The single-*qing* performance was developed into the multi-*qing* performance, hence the *bianqing* (or serial *qing*). It was widely used by the palace band to perform imperial ceremonial music. A huge-size *qing*, when hung on its own, could make a very special sound. This kind of huge *qing* was only used in the sacrificial rites to Heaven attended by the emperor himself or in important religious activities. You can still find this kind of "special *qing*" at the Temple of Heaven in Beijing. The sound produced by the "special *qing*" is deep, sonorous and melodious. Though the *qing* was only a court musical instrument, its use on special occasions indicated its high status.

The *teqing* unearthed at Erlitou, Yanshi, Henan Province is 58 cm long, 27 cm high and 3.45-4.50 cm thick. The 3,800-year-old *qing*, which was unearthed in 1975, is the product of the mid-Xia Dynasty.

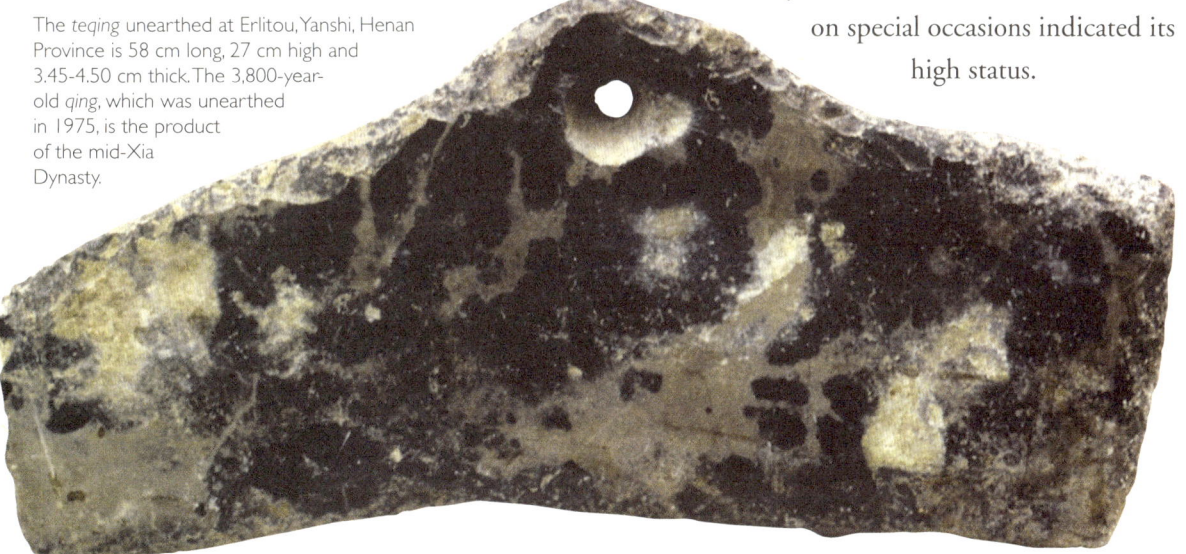

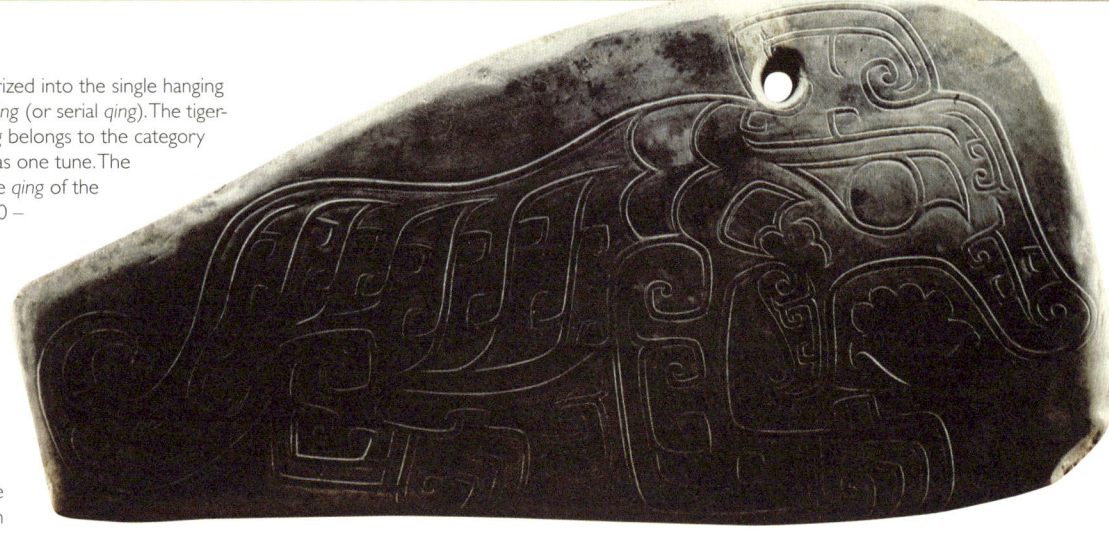

The *qing* are categorized into the single hanging *teqing* and the *bianqing* (or serial *qing*). The tiger-patterned stone *qing* belongs to the category of *teqing* normally has one tune. The tiger-patterned stone *qing* of the Shang Dynasty (1600 – 1046 BC) is 84 cm long, 42 cm wide and 2.5 cm. thick. Unearthed at Wuguan Village, Anyang, Henan Province in 1950, the tiger-patterned *qing* is the biggest *qing* of the Shang Dynasty. An example of artistic expression from the Shang Dynasty, the tiger-patterned *qing* is displayed at the National Museum. The tiger-patterned *teqing* is made of greenish grey stone that is grinded and carved. The surface of the *qing* is carved with a pattern of a tiger lying flat. The distinct carving shows how sophisticated the art of stone carving was at that time. At the top of the tiger head there is a hole for hanging a rope. The signs of rubbing are obvious. During the Xia and Shang dynasties the stone *qing* gradually became an important instrument for rites and music. Recorded in ancient literature, the *teqing* was used at palace banquets hosted by the emperor and princes, sacrificial ceremonies held in temples and ancestral halls, and at court ceremonies.

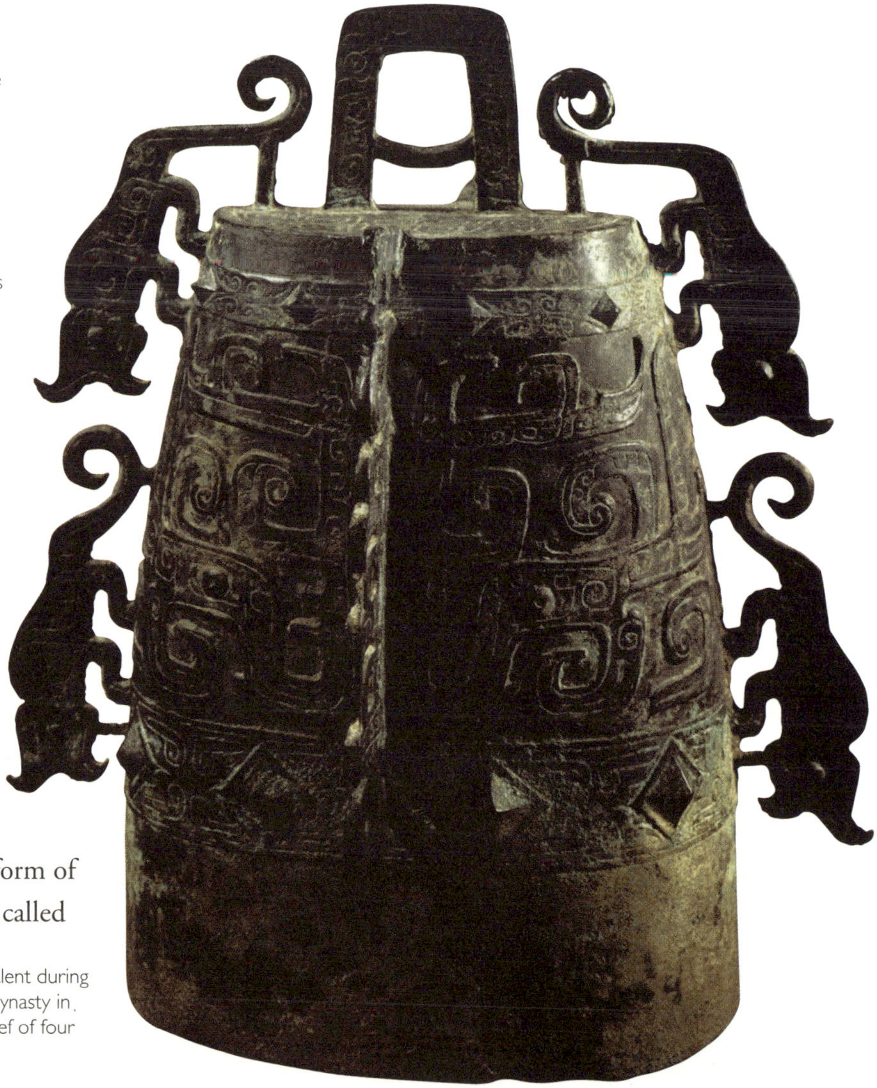

The *Bianzhong* Unearthed from the Grave of Duke Yi of the Zeng State in Sui County, Hubei Province

The *bianzhong* were unearthed in 1978 from the ancient grave of Duke Yi of the Zeng State in Leigudun, Sui County, Hubei Province. Many musical instruments were unearthed in Duke Yi's grave and a form of dance with musical accompaniment called

The *fuzhong* is a bronze musical instrument prevalent during the late Shang Dynasty and the Western Zhou Dynasty in present-day Hunan and Guangxi provinces. A relief of four tigers is featured on its body.

"happiness at home" was discovered there, which vividly reproduced a scene where the lord held a banquet at his residence. The use of the *bianzhong* demonstrates the large size of such a band needed to perform such a piece.

Each piece of the three-layer chime bells can produce two different pitches (Scale 3). The chime bells are based on *guxi*—one of the tones of the ancient Chinese twelve-tone scale. The astonishing fact is that the tone which registers 256.4 on the sound range corresponds to the pitch of Central C of the piano. Thus the chime bells can be used to play a five-, six- or seven-tone musical piece.

Huge in structure, the chime bells are played by three musicians holding two mallets each. The sound, when harmonized, can produce harmonious musical effects. The set of chime bells possesses a fairly complete pitch variation system. Taking into consideration the history of musical development in the world, the chime bells appeared 2,000 years earlier than musical instruments with an equal twelve-tone temperament in Europe. The fine workmanship of the chime bells proved that China's smelting technique of bronze had reached a very high standard early in its history.

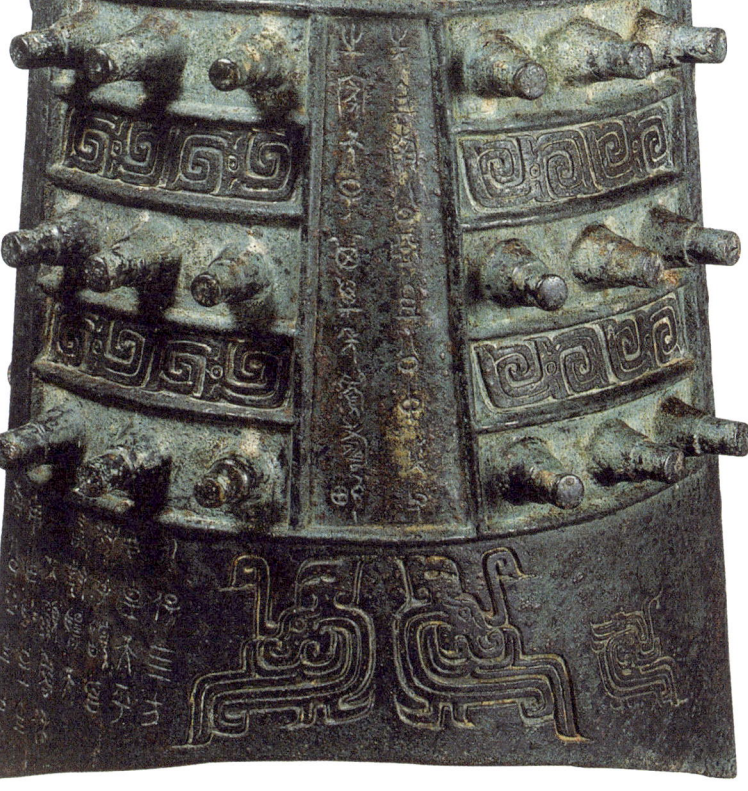

Bell and music
Bells like this played an important role in the activities of worship and warfare in ancient China. In the Western Zhou Period, music and ceremonies were very sophisticated, but by the Spring and Autumn Period in which Confucius lived, all previous social orders and moral standards were falling apart. When confronted with the demise of propriety and music, Confucius sought to reinstate ceremonies (or propriety) and music that were considered to have an exemplary effect in society. He believed that "ceremonies (or propriety)" could instill order and that "music" could create harmony. Ceremonies and music were a driving force behind a harmonious society.

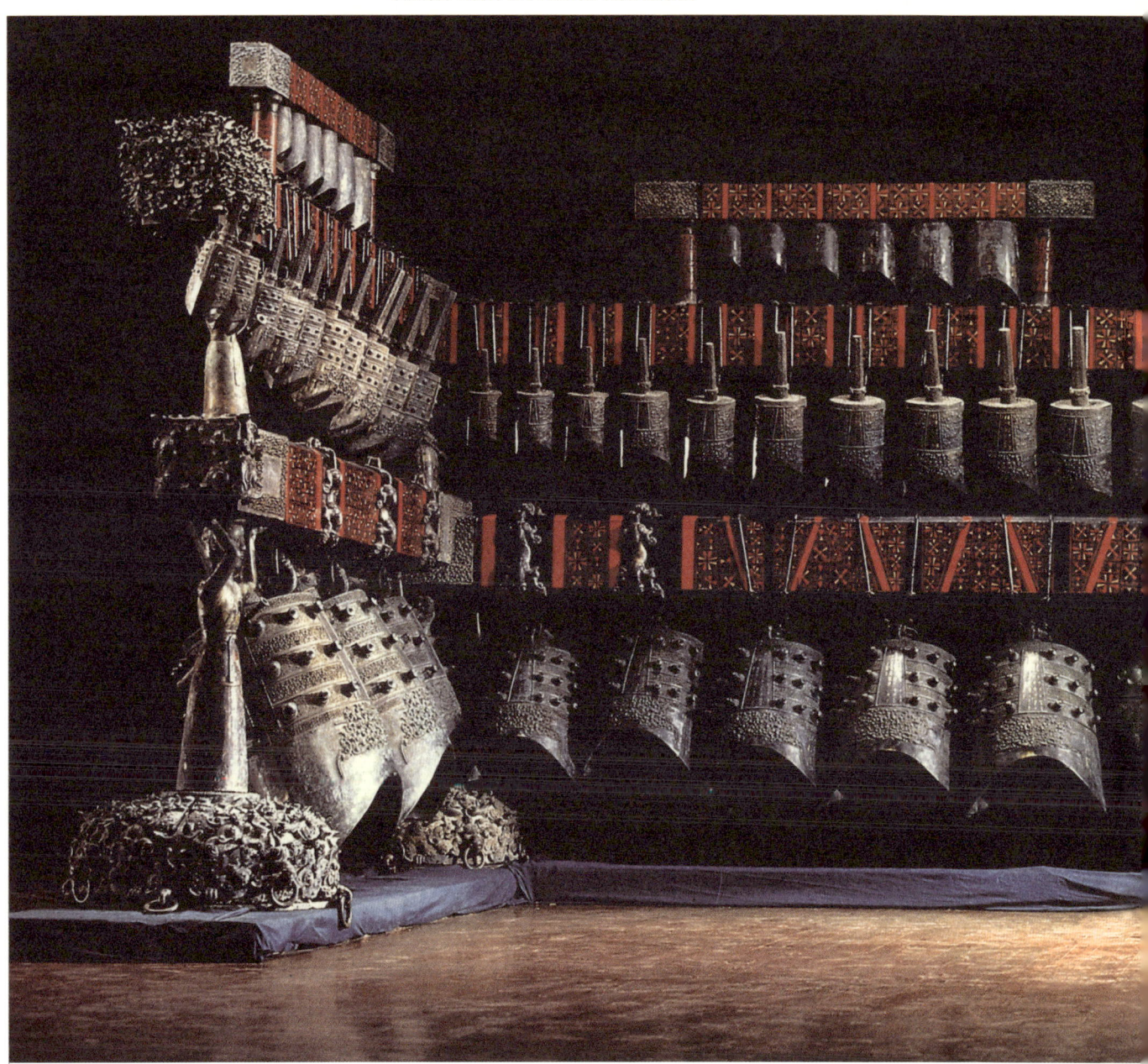

Chapter Two The History of Chinese Music   The Rudimentary Stage (From the 2100 BC to 221 BC)

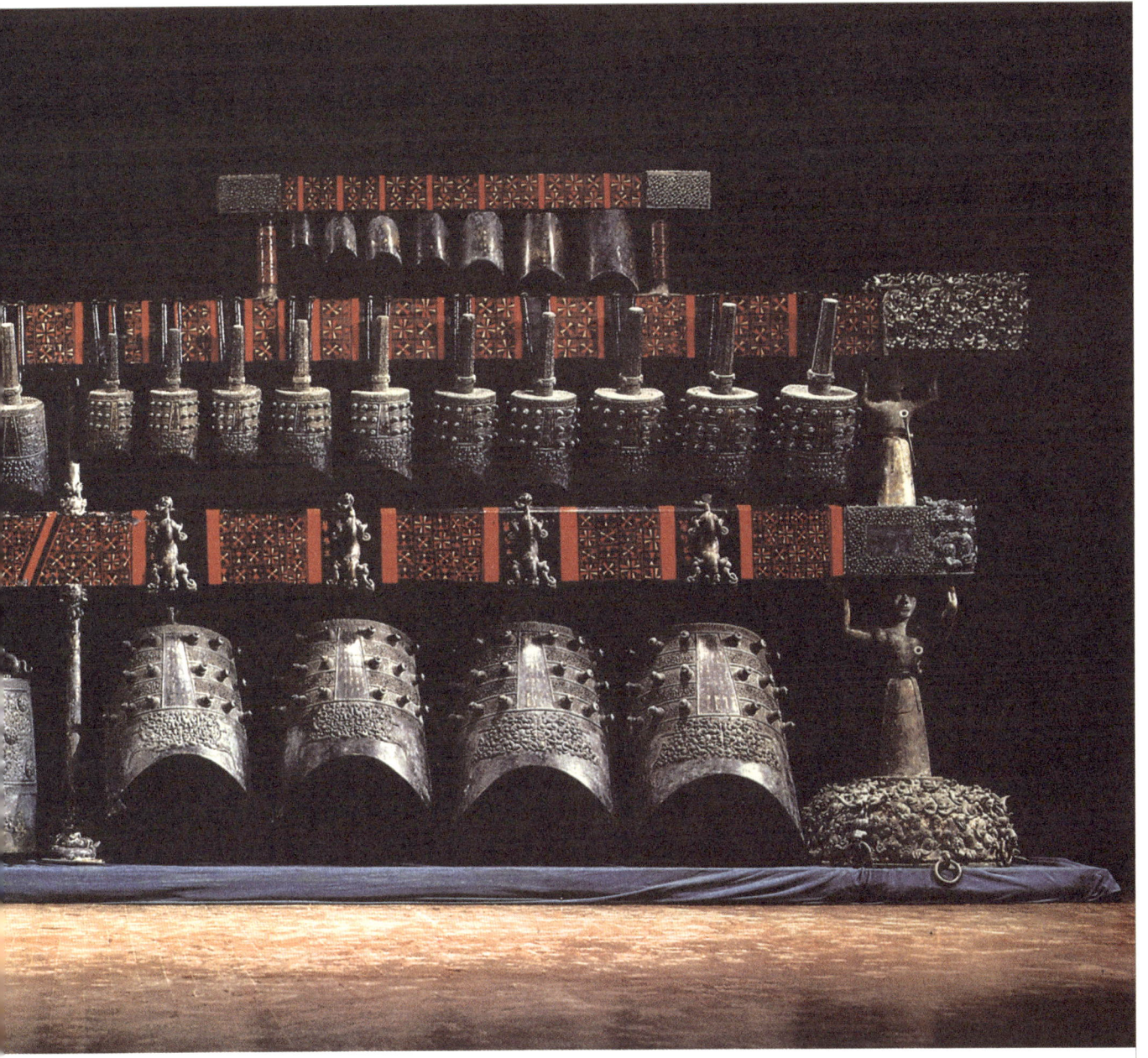

The *bianzhong* unearthed from the Grave of Duke Yi of the Zeng State in Sui County, Hubei Province

The Book of Songs

The Book of Songs is comprised of works of poetry, music and dance. It can be regarded as the earliest songbook in China. The original work contains 311 pieces. Of these 305 pieces are still kept intact. They include poems written from during the Western Zhou Dynasty until the Mid-Spring and Autumn Period (from the 11th century to the 7th century BC).

According to its contents, *The Book of Songs* consists of three sections: *feng* (folk songs), *ya* (court music)

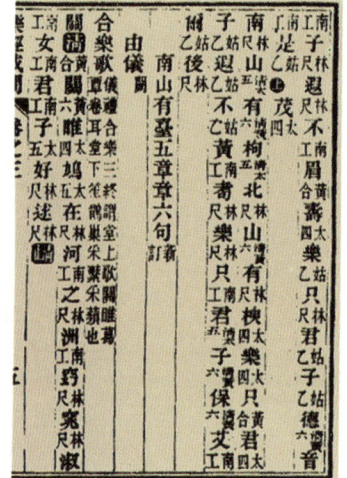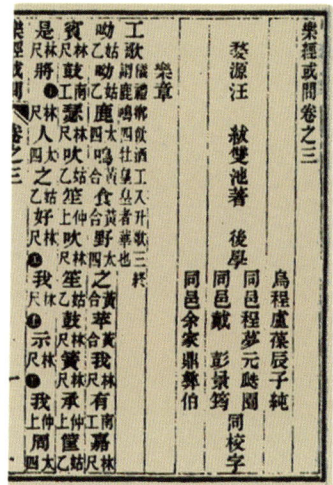

This is the musical score of a poem collected in *Yuejinghuowen* of *The Book of Songs* and the earliest worded score in Chinese history.

and *song* (religious music). *Feng* is a collection of ballads prevalent in the areas along the Yellow River and the Yangtze River, featuring mainly love songs. *Ya* is a collection of court hymns concerning enjoyment through drinking, singing and reciting poetry. *Song* is a collection of sacrificial songs sung to pay respects to one's ancestors and for praying to the gods for good fortune.

The certain style of the song determined the different form of the performance. Some are accompanied by musical instruments and others are accompanied by dance. Some vocal accompaniment supported by instruments has a charm of its own. Many of these popular songs are an honest depiction of people's lives at that time.

During the Spring and Autumn Period it was common practice to incorporate poetry into music. With the introduction of folk songs into the imperial palace, more and more musical instruments were used to accompany singing. *The Book of Songs* lists dozens of instruments, such as the *qin*, *se* (a stringed zither) and *xiao*.

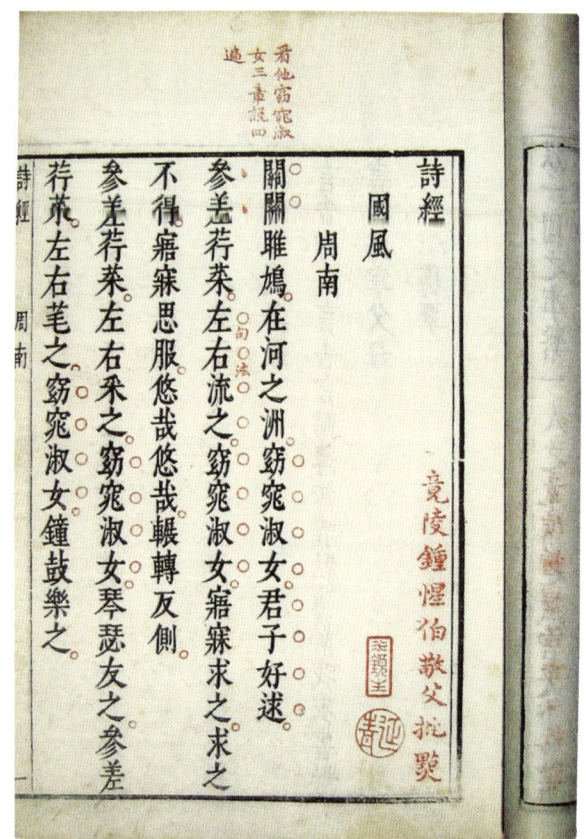

A page from *The Book of Songs*
Shi Jing, translated variously as the *Classic of Poetry*, the *Book of Songs* or the *Book of Odes*, is the earliest existing collection of Chinese poems. It comprises 305 poems, some possibly written as early as 1000 BC. It forms part of the Five Classics.

Lü's Spring and Autumn Annals— Ancient Music

This book is devoted to describing musical scales, musical instruments, musical pieces and musicians from the time period of Ruler Yandi to the early Spring and Autumn Period. It is a historical document on the early musical activities in China, and includes some legendary and mythological tales. Under the sponsorship of the great thinker and politician Lü Buwei, the Prime Minister of the Qin State, his followers compiled this book. In addition, this book illustrates the initial development of the aesthetic qualities of Chinese music. It also describes how ancient people used musical instruments to communicate and how certain ancient musical instruments were made.

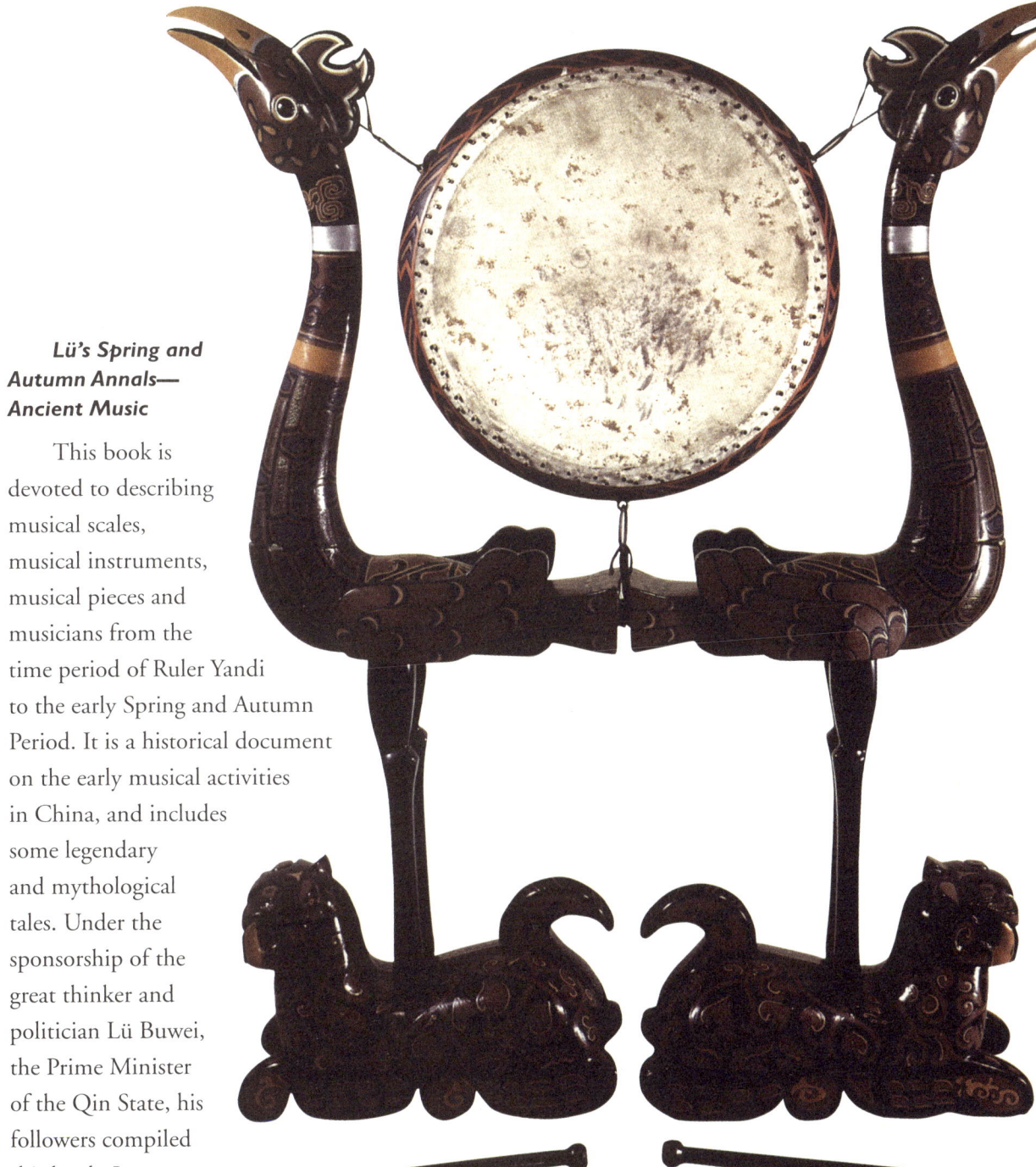

The 2,200-year-old drum with a tiger-patterned stand and a bird-patterned frame is a musical instrument of the Chu State during the Warring States Period. Its main body is composed of two tigers, two phoenixes and a flat drum. With a steady structure and a beautiful shape, the drum is known for its excellent artistic design and painting.

The Book of Music

The fairly complete system of rites and music was established in the Zhou Dynasty with emphasis laid on the concept of social status. In the mind of the ruling class, both "rites" and "music" were important parts of government. As a section of *The Book of Rites, The Book of Music* describes music as the harmonious unity of Heaven, Earth and Mother Nature. As music is closely related to moral principles and ethics, music is the refection of one's moral character in sound. "Rites" and "music" are used as norms of behavior to preserve the social system.

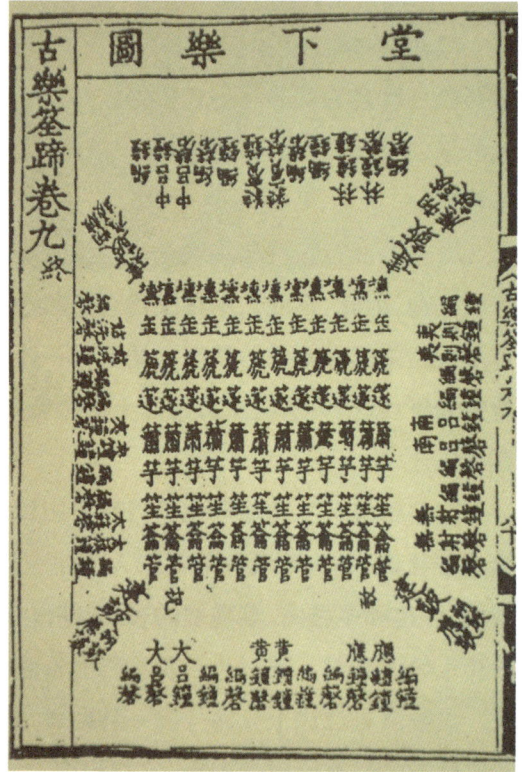

The formation of an ancient band as recorded in *The Book of Music*

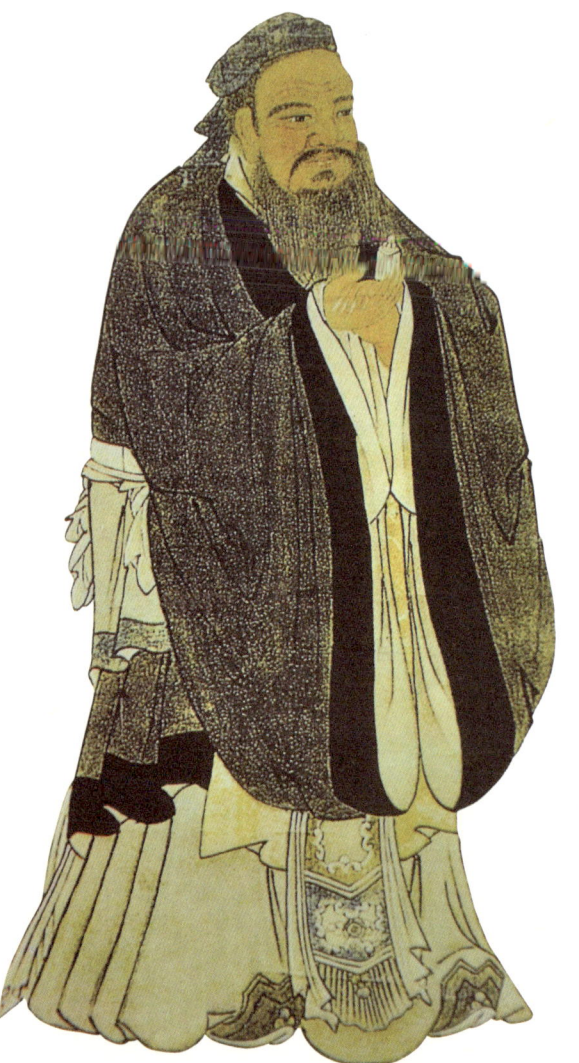

For example, hierarchy can be seen in the size and structure of a band. The emperor's band is positioned on four sides with 64 dancers in 8 groups. A duke's band is positioned on three sides with only 36 dancers in 6 groups. A minister or other senior official's band is composed of two groups while a junior official's band is restricted to one group only.

Confucius (551 BC – 479 BC), courtesy name Zhong Ni, a native of Lu State during the Spring and Autumn Period, was a great Chinese thinker, educator, founder of Confucianism in ancient China and a famous musician in Spring and Autumn Period as well.
The father of Chinese historiography Sima Qian wrote in his highly praised work *Records of the Grand Historian* (*Shiji*), there were originally 3,000 songs and poems in the *Book of Songs*, Confucius selected the three hundred and five songs (poems) that he felt best conformed to traditional ritual propriety and personally sang all of them and played the music on the string instrument to ensure that they fitted into the score. Through his efforts, the tradition of ancient rites and music was therefore rescued from oblivion and handed down to posterity, that they may help in carrying out the ideal of King's Way (*wang dao*) and in teaching the Six Arts.

Qu Yuan (340 – 278 BC) and *Jiuge*

Qu Yuan was a patriotic poet in the Warring States Period. After his years of strenuous effort to promote his political ideas failed, he committed suicide by drowning himself in the Miluo River. While in exile, he gained access to a great variety of folk music and wrote a lot of famous poems.

His most famous work *Jiuge* was characteristic of the culture of the Chu State which advocated witchcraft and sacrificial ceremonies and covered a wide range of subjects on ghosts, spirits and monstrous beasts. The 11 songs carried in this book were played by the instruments used for court music.

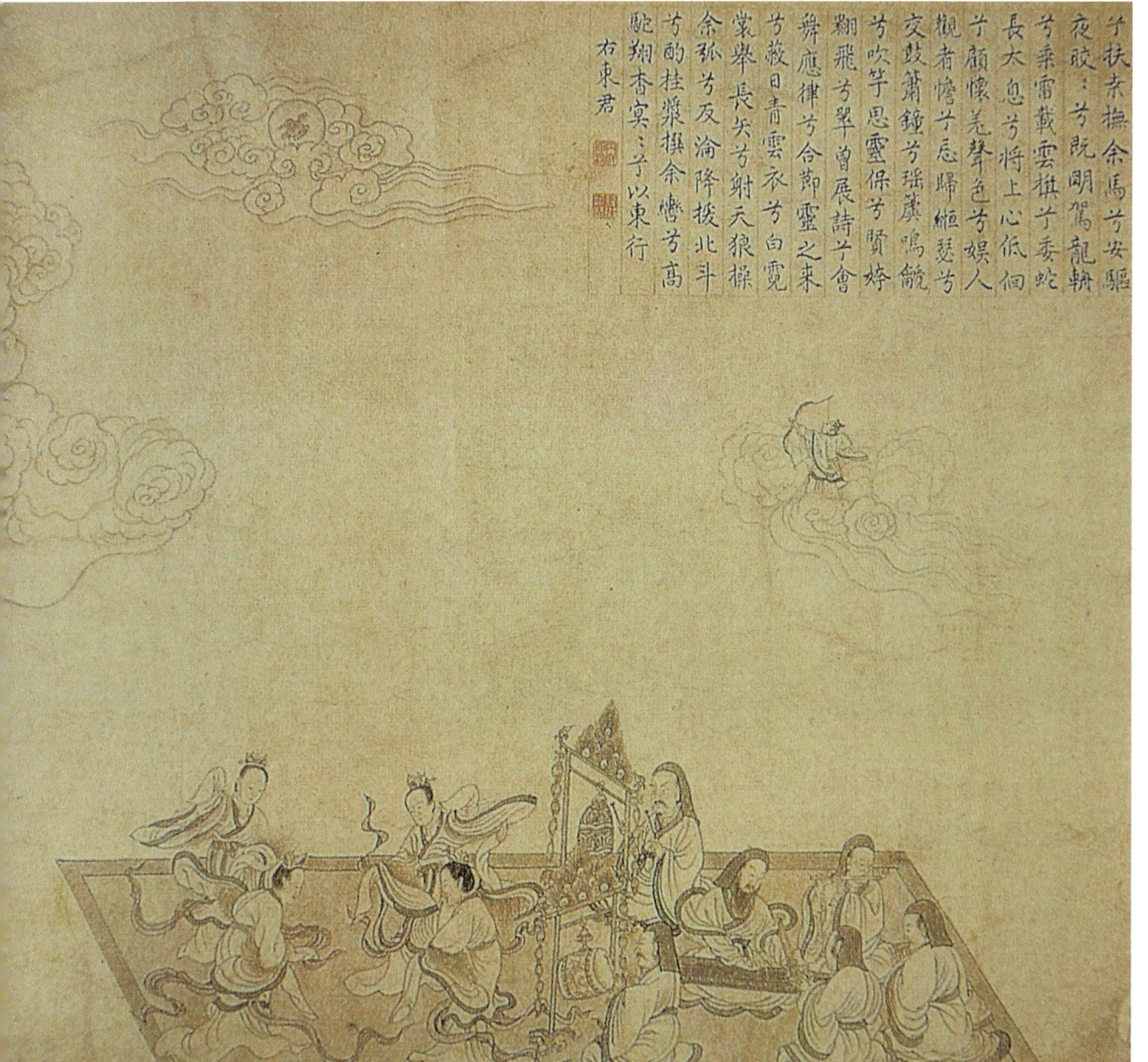

The scroll of *Jiuge* Painted by Painters of the Song Dynasty

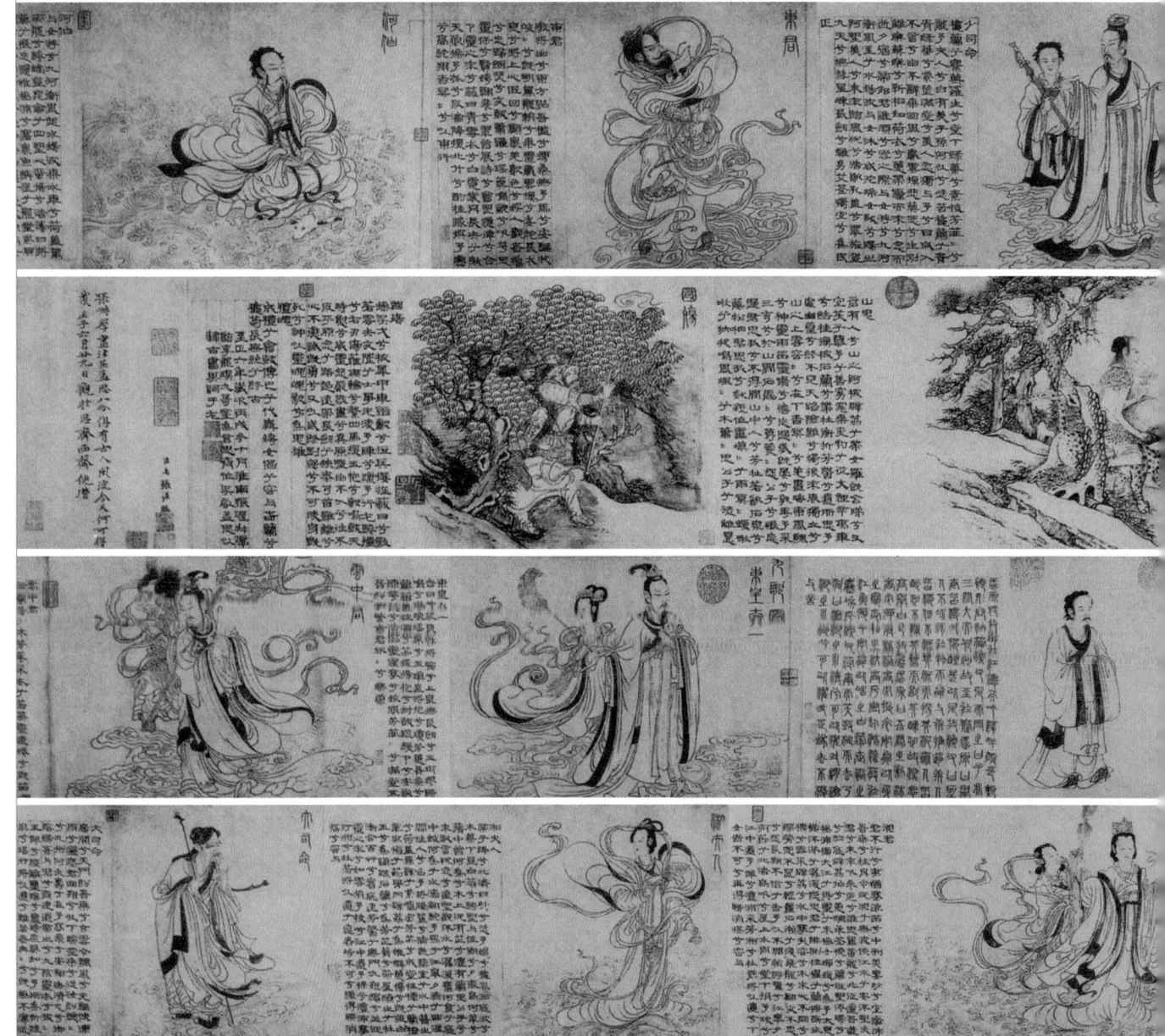

Jiuge was originally an ancient song. Tradition has it that Xia Qi stole it from Heaven. Qu Yuan transcribed this sacrificial song into a full-length song and dance drama to be performed at sacrificial ceremonies. This scroll painting, which consists of 11 sections, was made by Zhang Wo of the Yuan Dynasty.

2 The Thriving Stage
(From 221 BC to 960 AD)

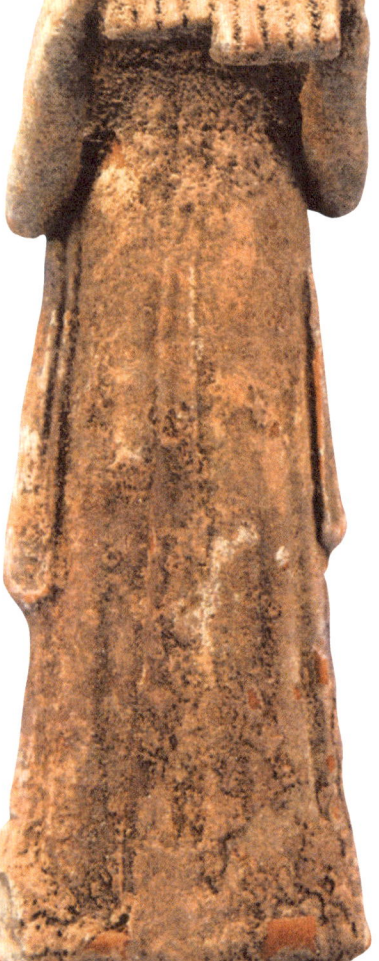

The 1,100-plus years witnessed the dynastic changes of the Qin, Western Han, Eastern Han, Three Kingdoms, Western Jin, Eastern Jin, Northern and Southern Dynasties and Sui. As far as the development of culture was concerned, the Tang Dynasty was perhaps its most prosperous time. This was also prime time for the development of music in Chinese history.

A fairly complete system of institutions in charge of music education, performance and research was formed during the Western Han Dynasty. Yuefu—an official conservatory—was staffed with "night readers" responsible for collecting and reading folk songs and "special listeners" responsible

Left: A tomb figurine of a *pipa* player of the Tang Dynasty

Right: A tomb figurine of a *paixiao* player of the Tang Dynasty

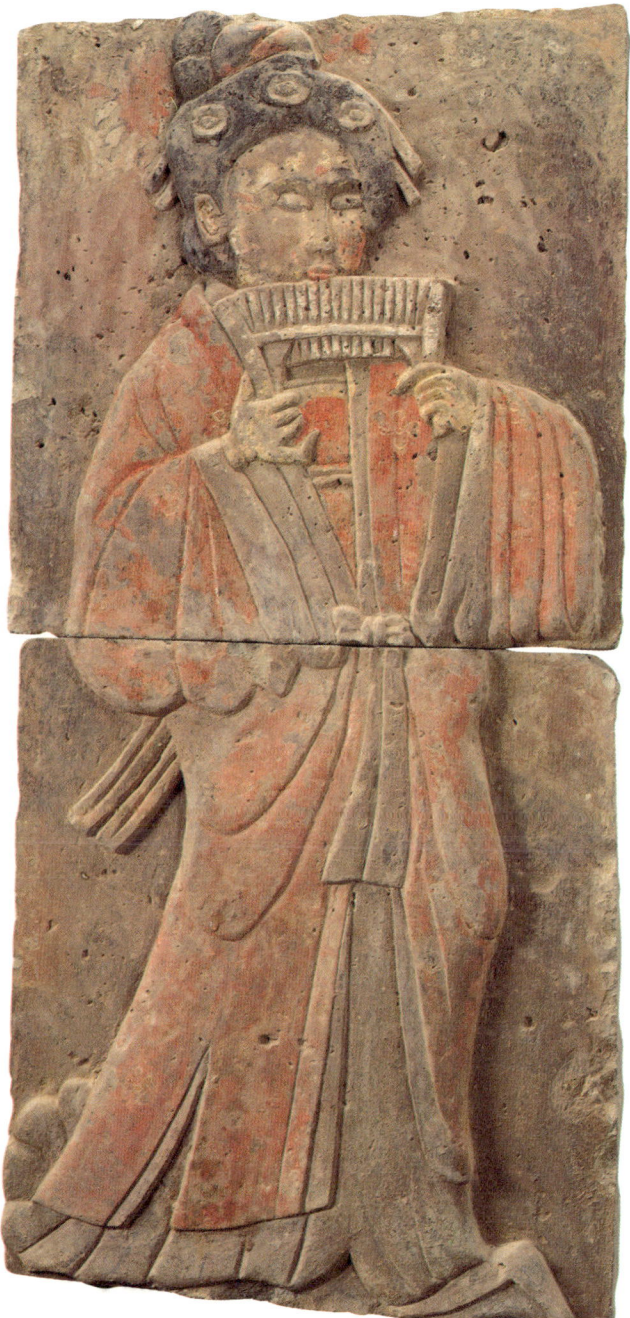

A lady playing the panpipe

for testing temperament. Most of them took part in musical performances. Those who played wind instruments in the guard of honor for the emperor or dukes were called "bugle players on horses". The other performers were given special titles such as "the *yu* player" and "the *qin* player". As the Han Dynasty was stable and prosperous, communication between different ethnic groups was frequent. During that period of time such ethnic instruments as the *hengchui*, *qiangdi*, *jia* and *konghou* (a type of harp) were introduced into the Central Plains, enriching Chinese music with new styles. The dominant artistic form of the Han Dynasty was *baixi*, which included acrobatics, singing, dancing and other folk music. The art of *baixi* enjoyed a great reputation in the imperial palace and in the residences of high officials and dignitaries.

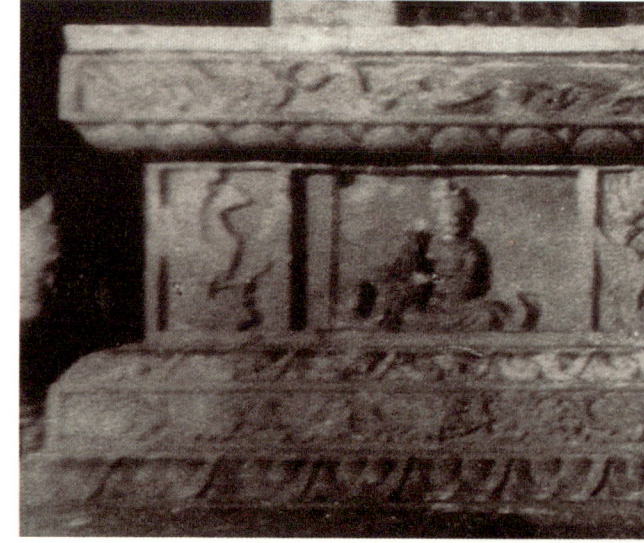

This relief was unearthed in Wang Jian's grave of the Five Dynasties at Chengdu, Sichuan Province. The relief is composed of 24 pieces of carved female musicians and dancers. The formation of the band demonstrates the harmonious combination of the music introduced from the Western Regions and the traditional music of the Han and Wei dynasties.

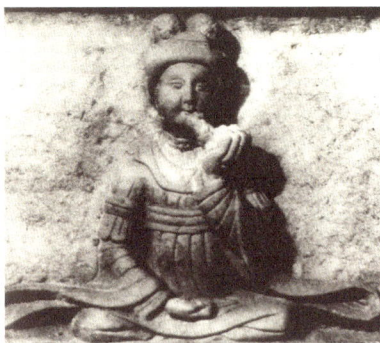
A female entertainer playing the *bei* (which means "conch").

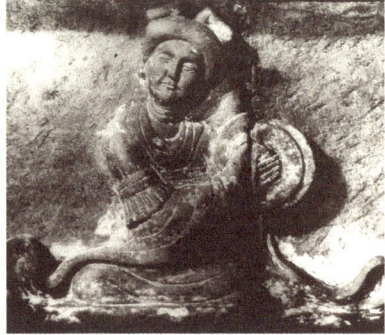
A female entertainer playing the brass *bo*. Originally from India, this instrument was commonly used during the Tang Dynasty.

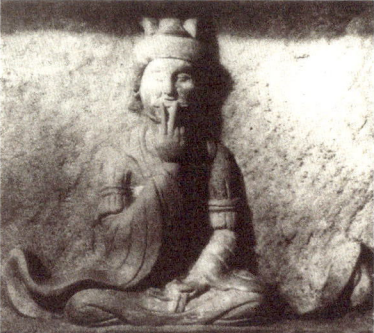
A female entertainer playing the leaf. Leaves used as musical instruments were popular in the south of China at this time. The entertainer is holding two spare leaves in her left hand.

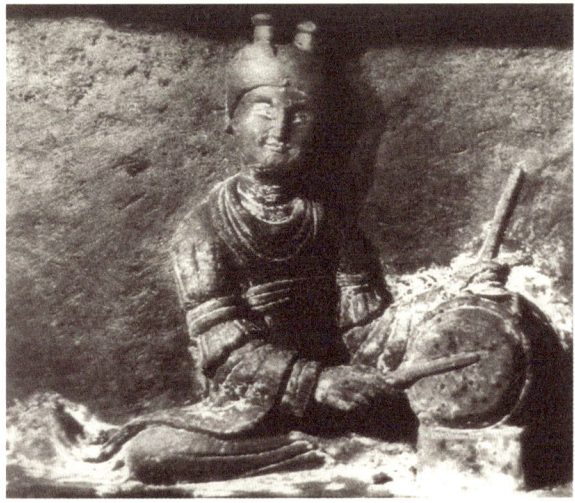
A female entertainer playing the *jiegu* (which is used to create a warm atmosphere).

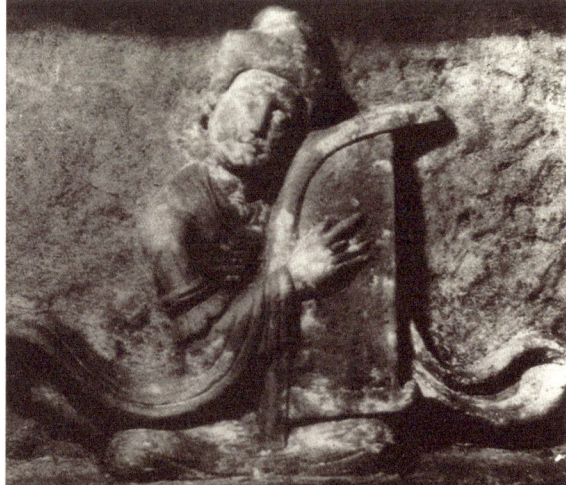
An attentive female entertainer playing the *konghou*.

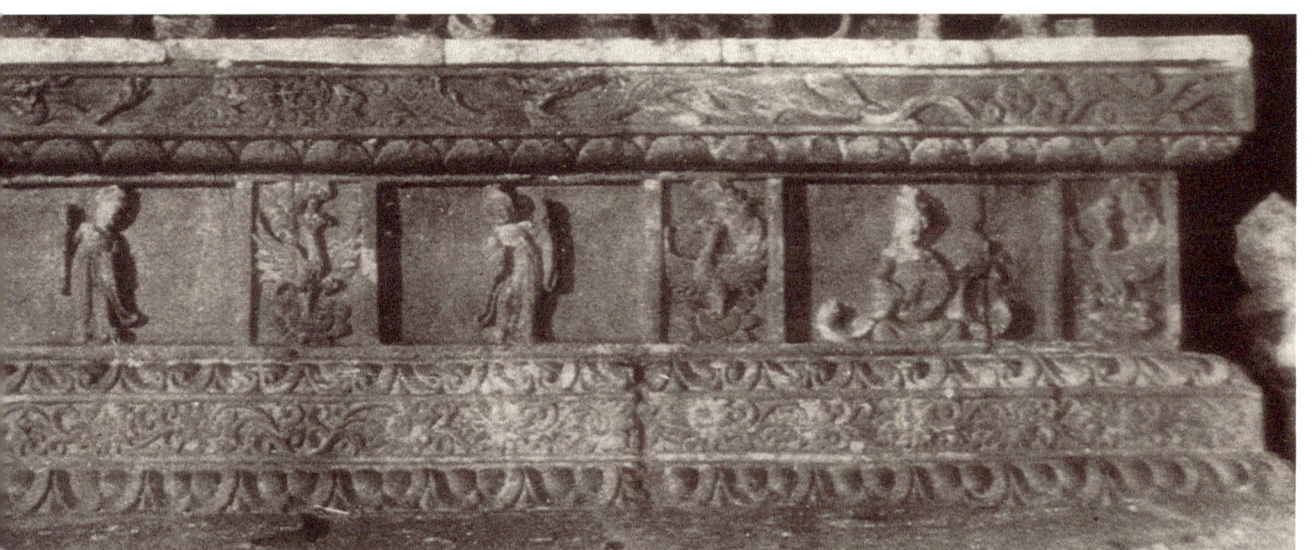

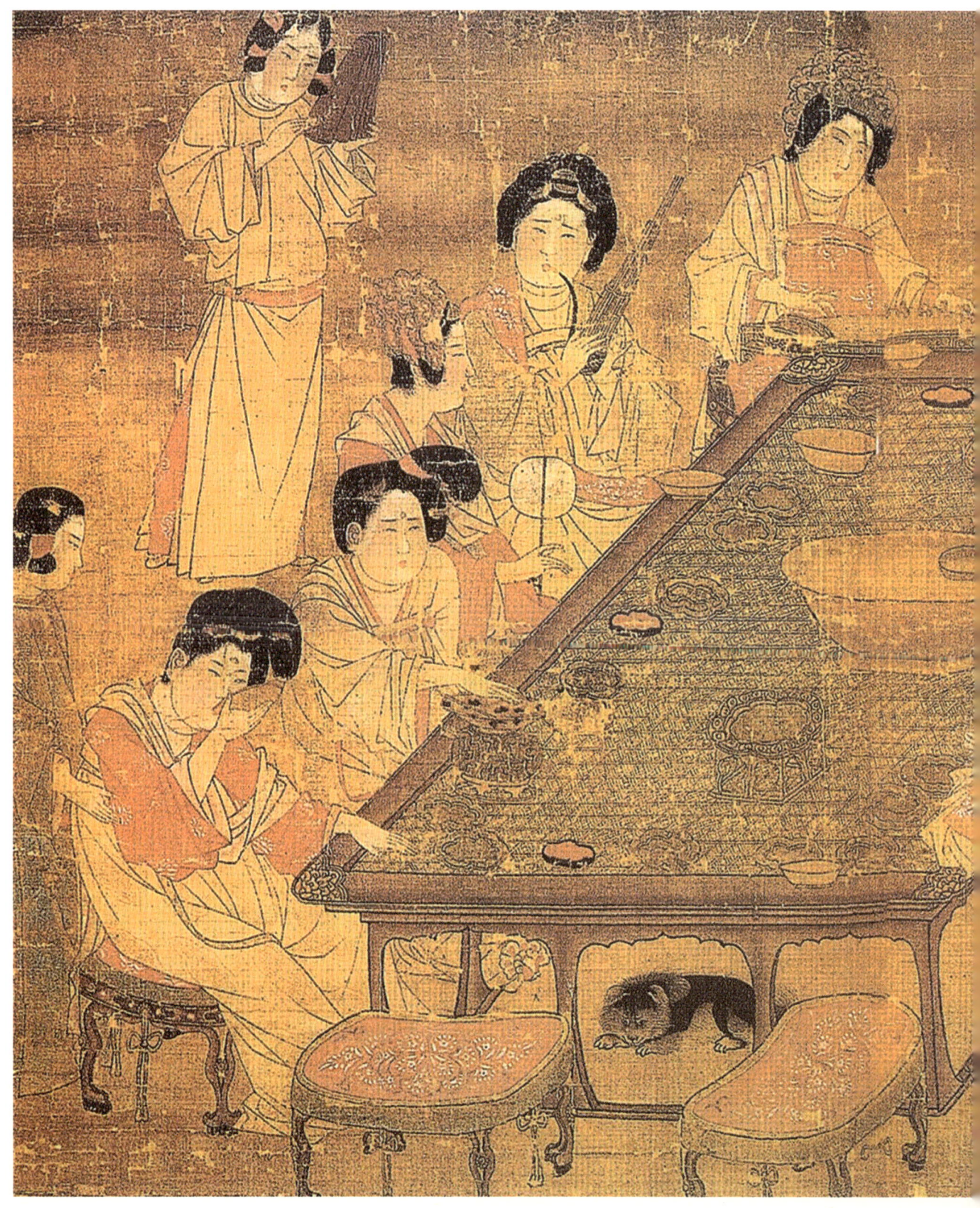

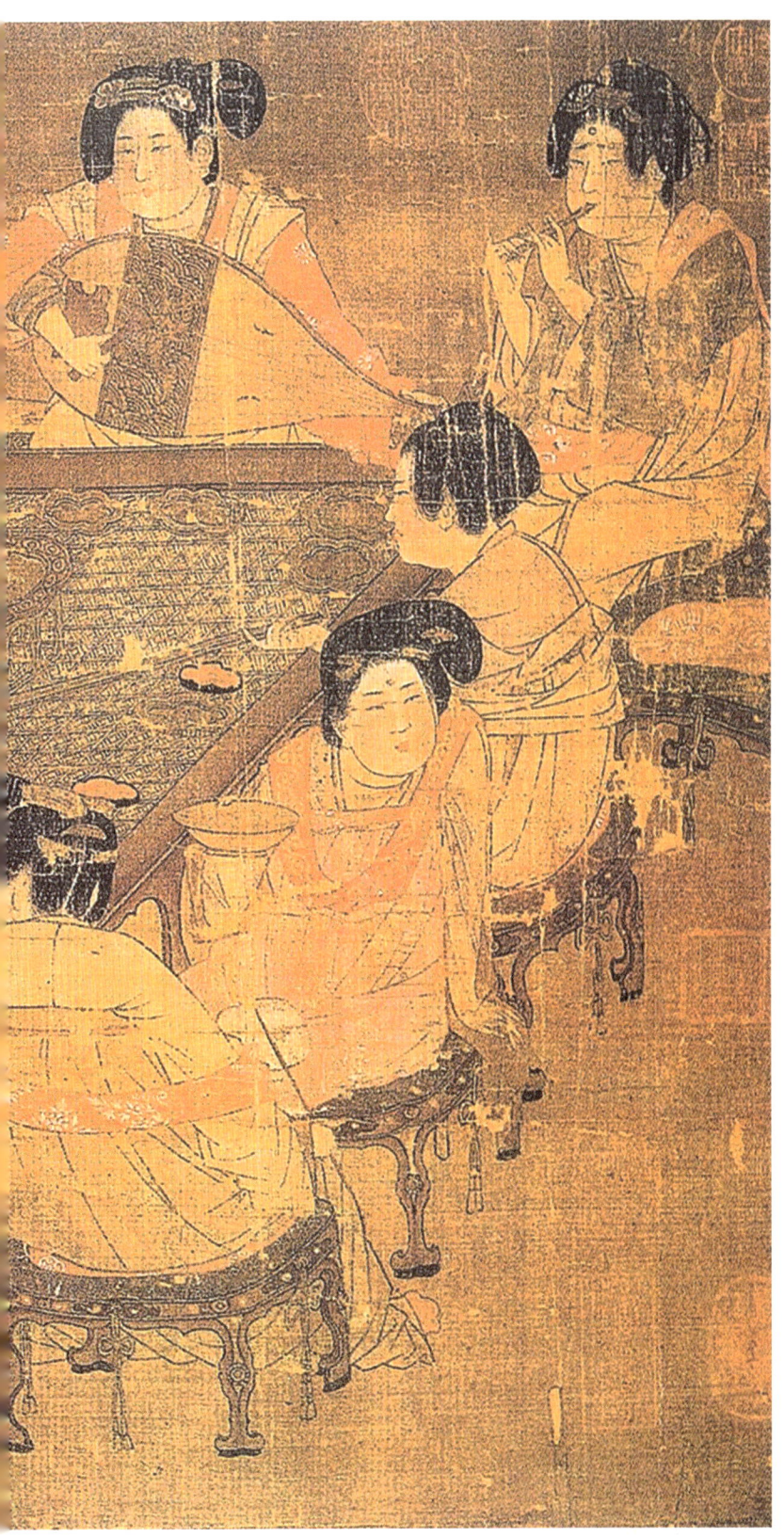

The Sui and Tang Dynasties witnessed an amazing development in ethnic musical instruments thanks to the exchange and integration of cultures between the Central Plains and other places in China as well as between the Han people and the ethnic minorities in the north. As the most popular form of music played at the court banquet, as well as for fun, the Yan music exerted great influence on neighboring countries. Japan, Korea and other countries sent a great many envoys to the Sui and Tang dynasties to learn more of China's culture, scientific knowledge and religion.

Revelry in Tang Court from the Tang Dynasty

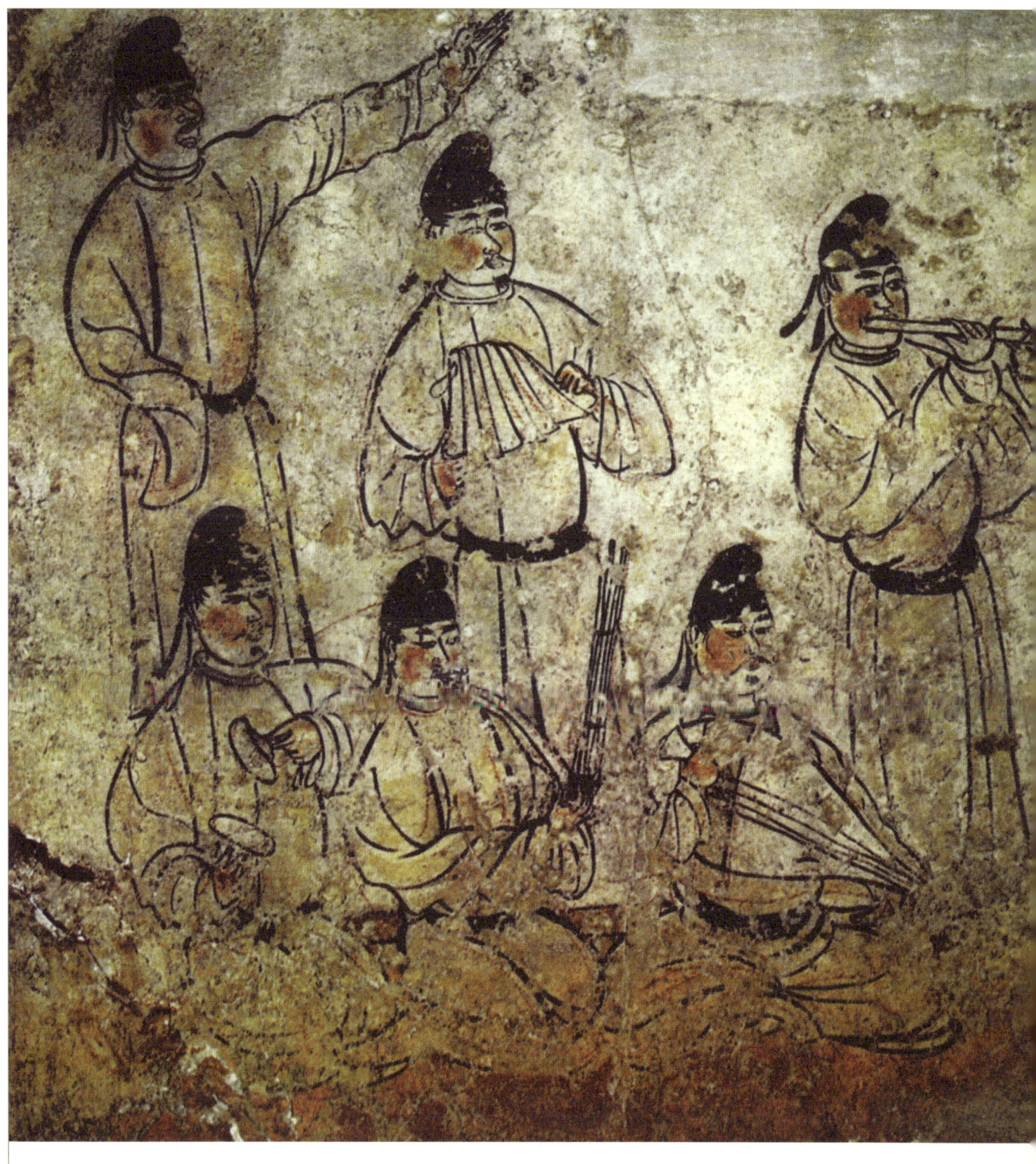

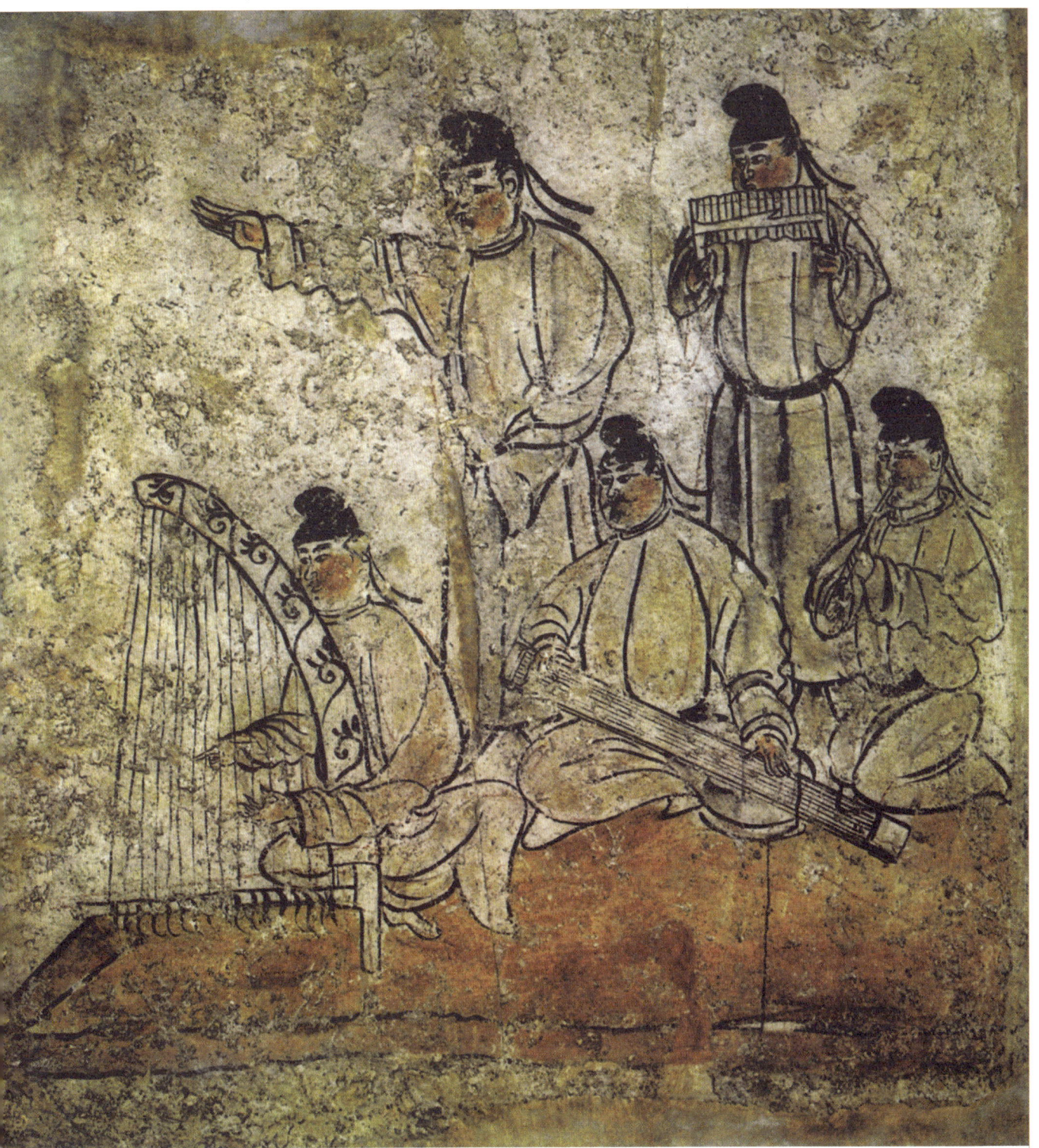

This mural section was unearthed in 1952 in Su Sixu's grave of the Tang Dynasty at Xi'an, and was painted in 745, the fourth year of the Tianbao period of the Tang Dynasty. The painting depicts a band of eleven male musicians. On the right in the first row are three performers playing the vertical *konghou*, *zheng* and *bili* (vertical flute) respectively. The two standing in the second row on the right are a *xiao* player and a singer. On the left, in the first row are three performers playing the *bo*, *sheng* and *pipa* respectively; the three standing in the second row are a singer, two performers playing *paiban* and flute.

A tri-colored glazed pottery from the Tang Dynasty depicting a band on a camel, unearthed in 1957 in Xi'an, Shaanxi Province. The camel stands at attention. Its humps are covered with a long felt, on which a band of 5 male performers are giving a performance. Their appearance is similar to that of people from the Westerner Regions. The singer is seen standing. Sitting around him are the musicians. One is holding a *pipa* while another appears to play a vertical flute. Another two appear to be beating drums. Unfortunately, only the *pipa* is kept intact whereas the other three instruments are missing.

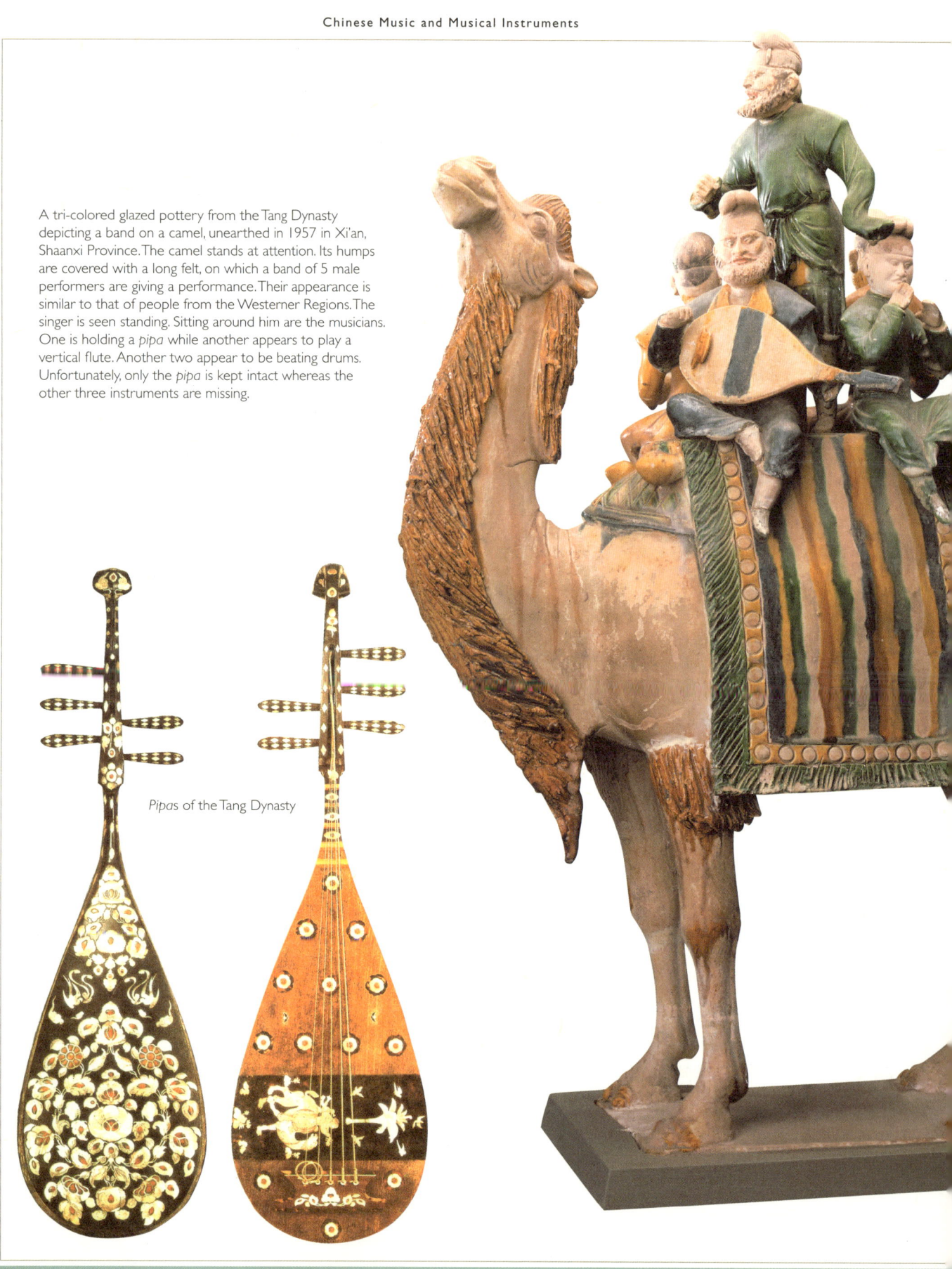

*Pipa*s of the Tang Dynasty

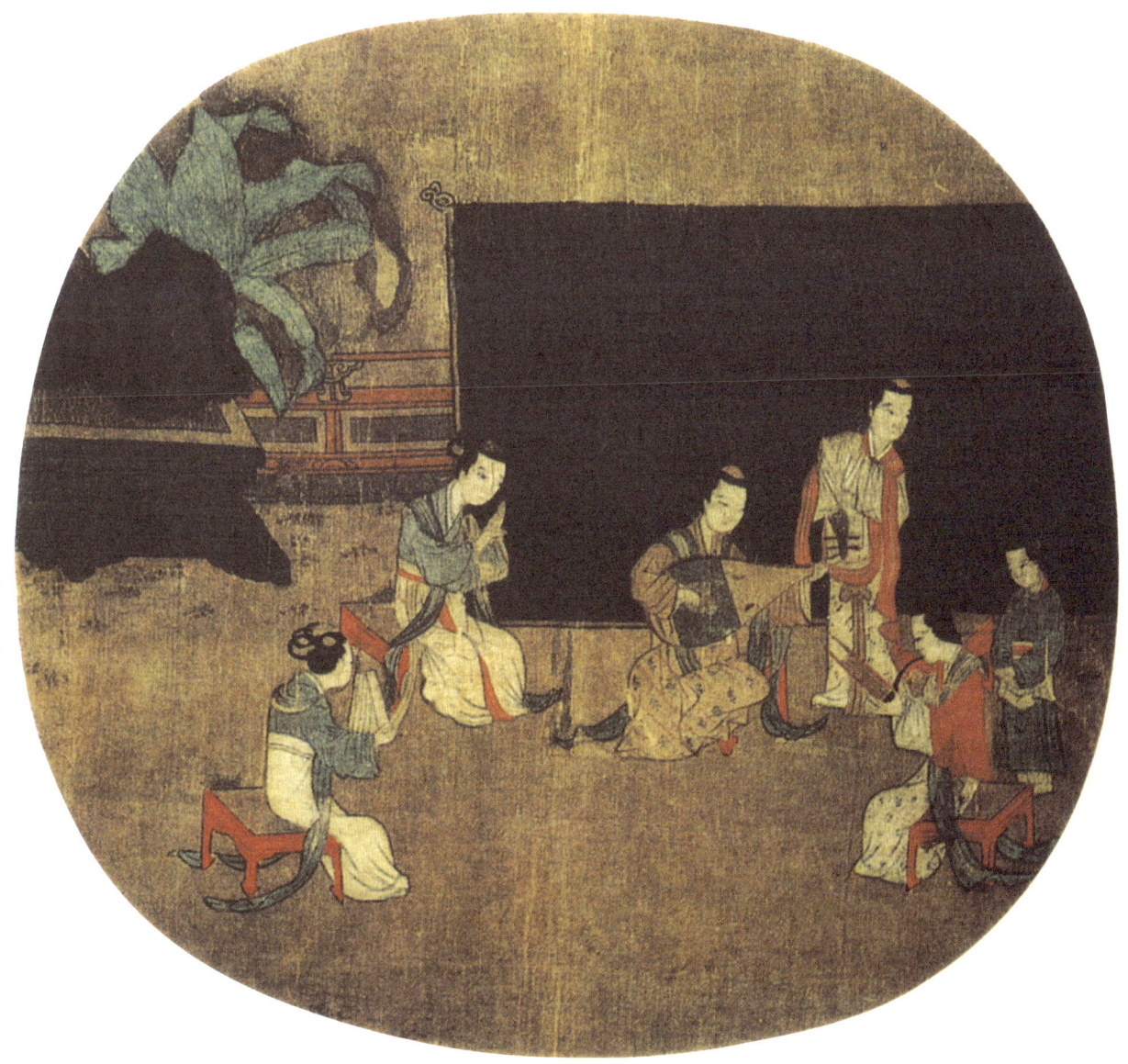

An ancient painting of a *pipa* performance

This "all-embracing" tradition was well kept up during the Tang Dynasty. As many as 300 different types of musical instruments were collected. Take the *pipa* for instance. People developed the *pipa* by combining the special features of the crooked-neck *pipa* and the five-stringed *pipa* introduced from the Western Regions. The frescoes of the Dunhuang Grottoes show that the *pipa* played a very important role at that time.

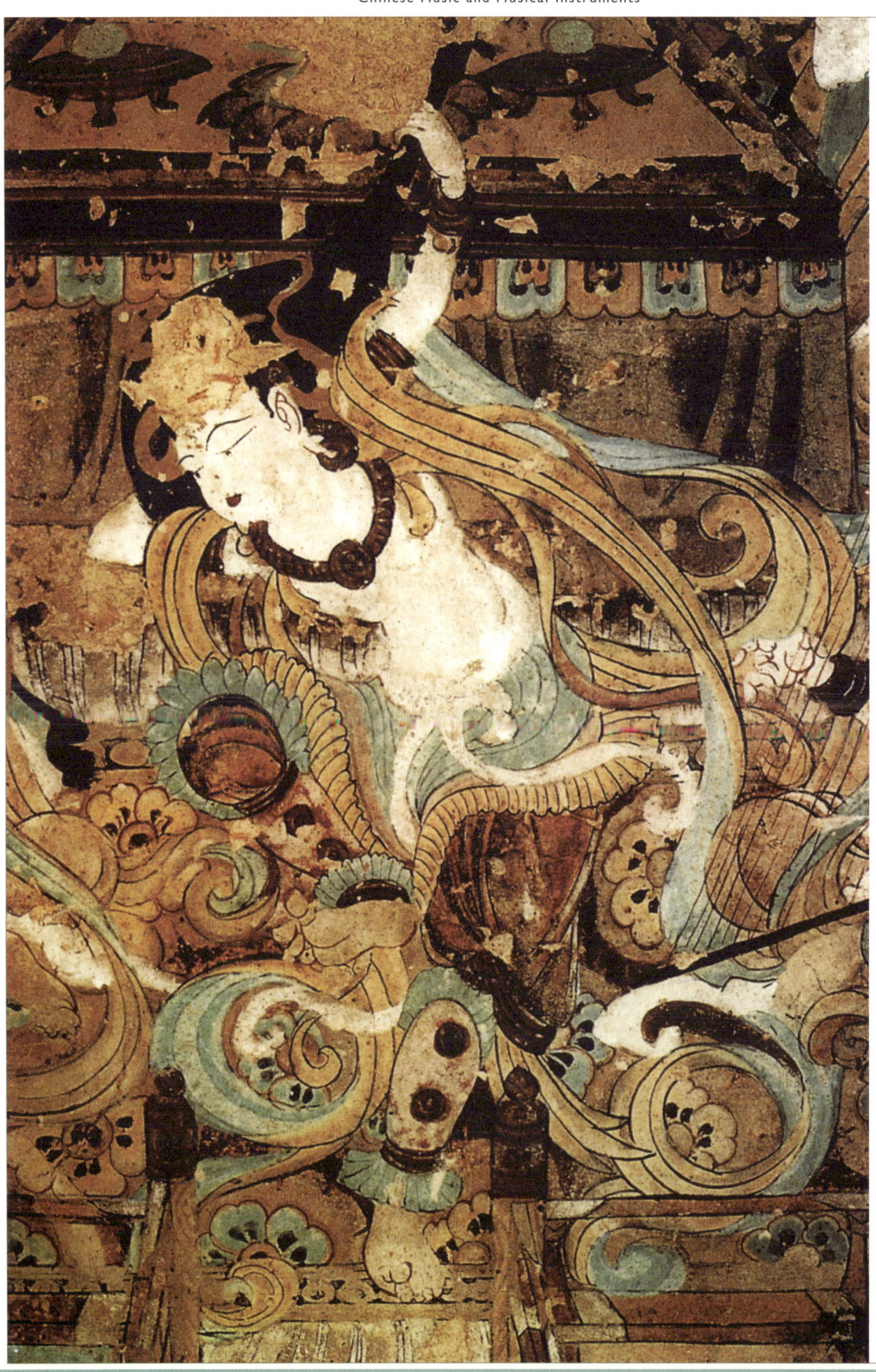

Playing the *pipa* from behind the player's back

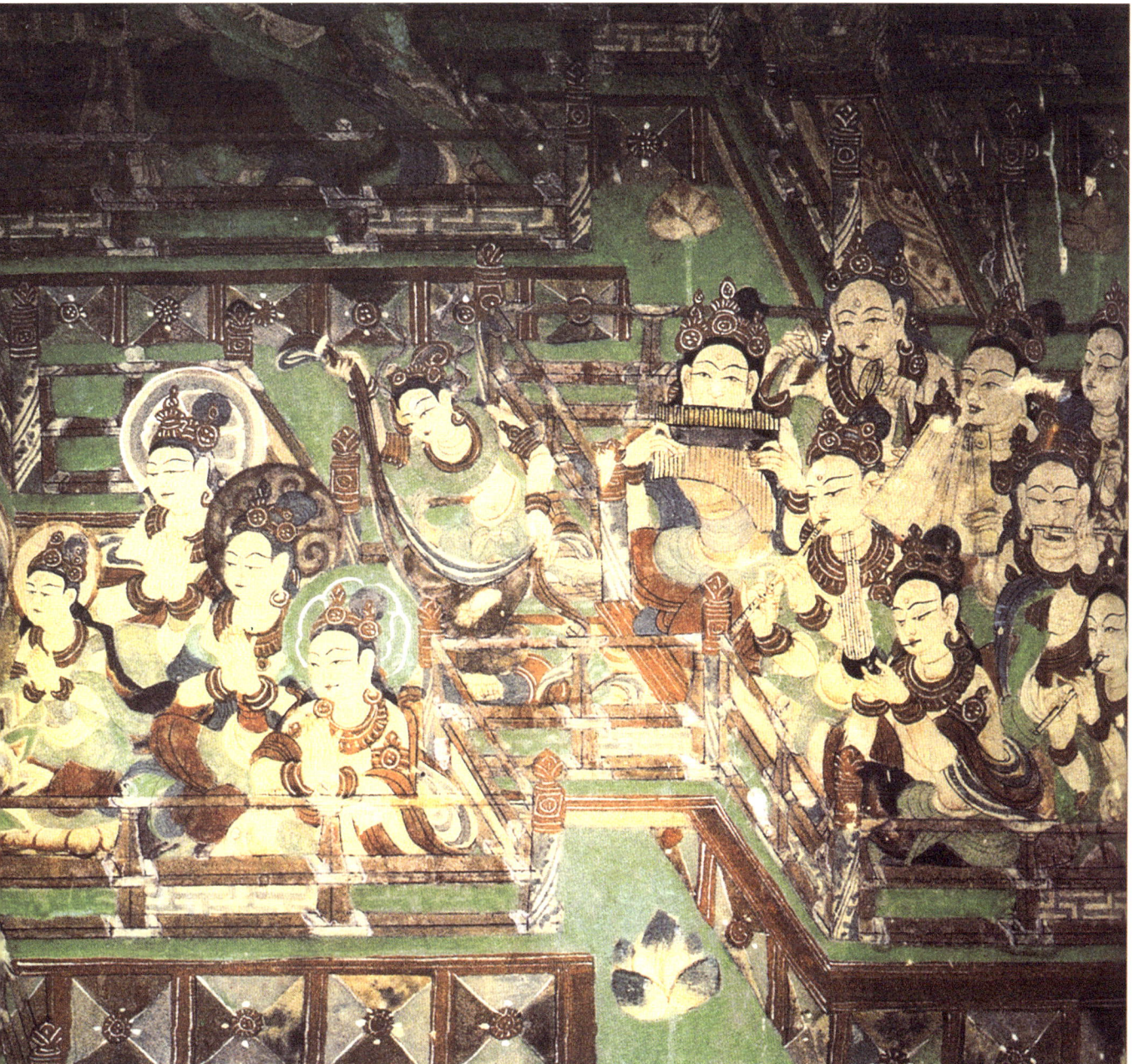

Entertainers shown in the mural of the northern wall of Cave #154 of the Dunhuang frescoes in Gansu Province

"Buddhist music" was played in temples during the Tang Dynasty. One fresco of the Dunhuang Grottoes depicts the performance of the *daqu*— Buddhist music—in the thriving Tang Dynasty. It was the usual practice of many temples to perform the *daqu* in the presence of Buddha statues and chant Buddhist scriptures to the accompaniment of music and dance. The performers of the Buddhist music including musicians, singers and dancers, became important jobs at that time. Their task was to rearrange the melody of the *daqu* and turn it into Buddhist music.

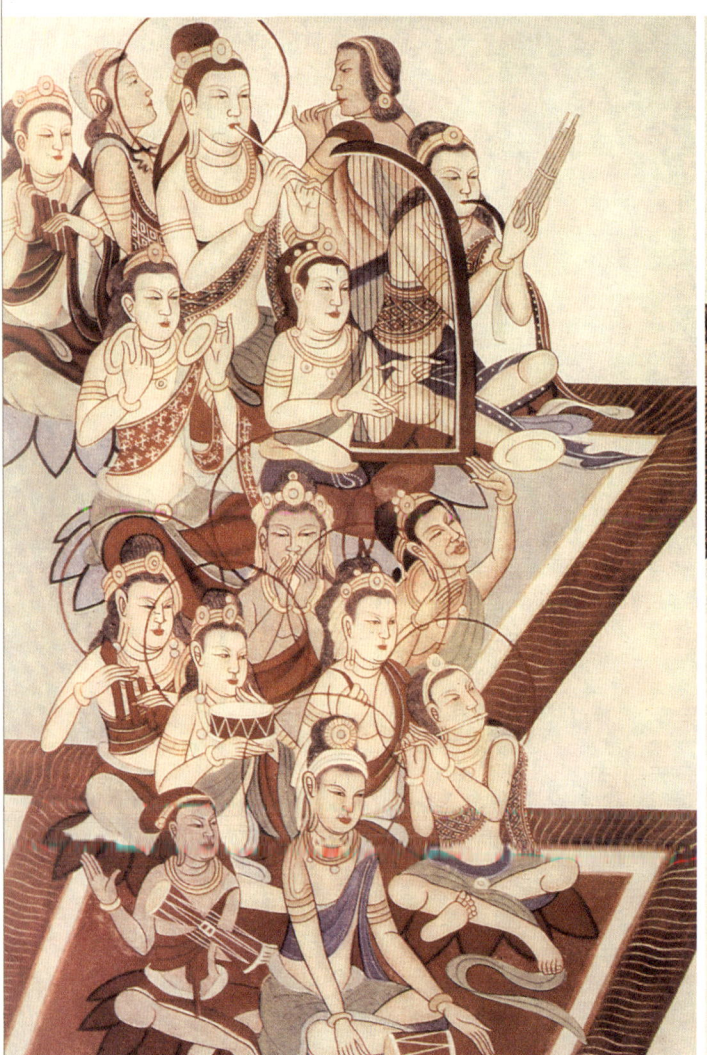
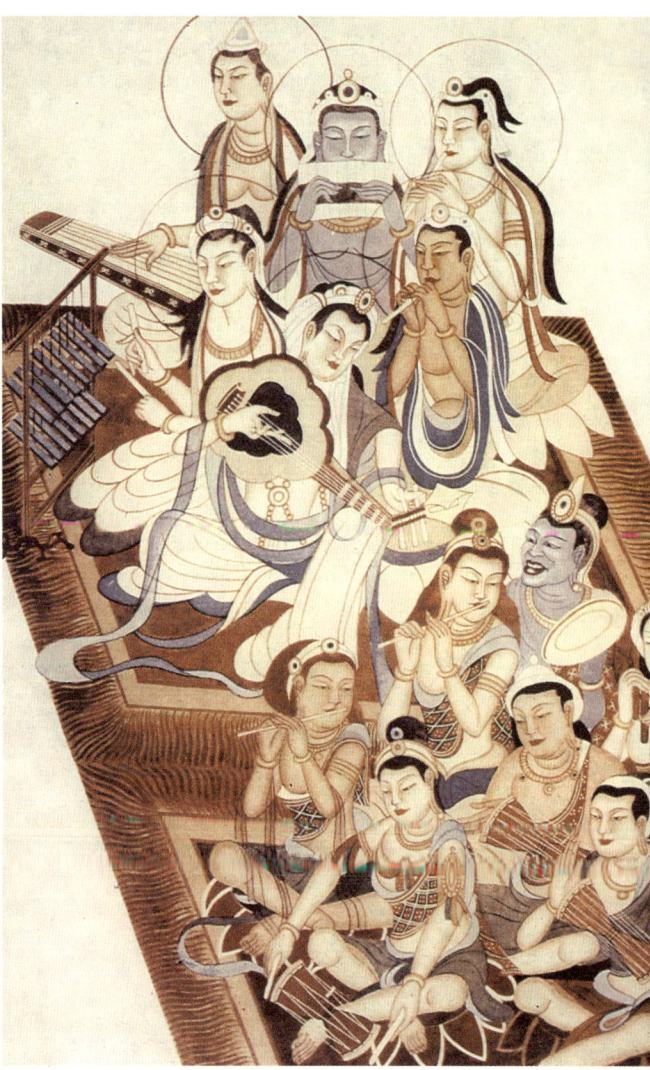

A band from the early Tang Dynasty shown in the mural entitled *Yaoshijingbian* of Cave # 220 of the Dunhuang frescoes. Sitting on the patterned carpet on the platform of each side is a band containing 28 musicians. Among the instruments played are the *guzheng, pipa, konghou, ruanxian, hengdi, paixiao, paiban, fangxiang, yaogu,* and *jiegu.* The mural depicts a carnival atmosphere.

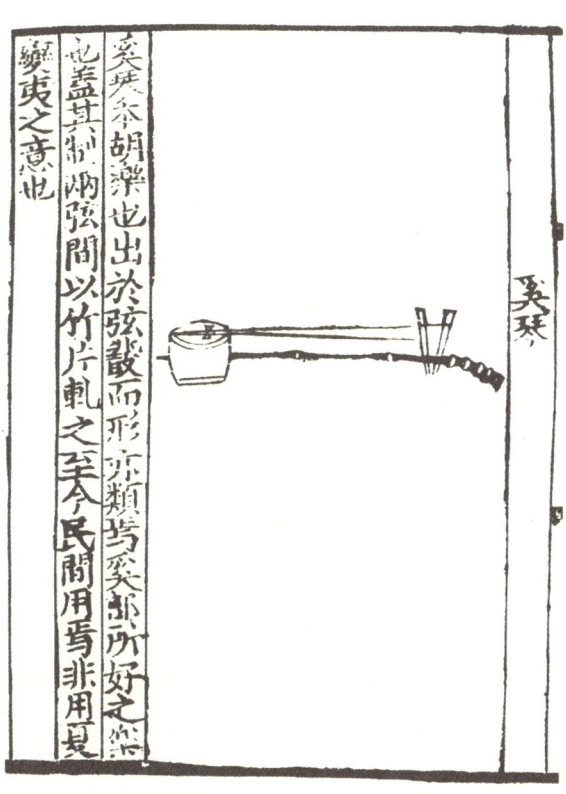

The shape of the *xiqin* appears simple and unsophisticated. The *xiqin* was first seen during the Tang Dynasty.

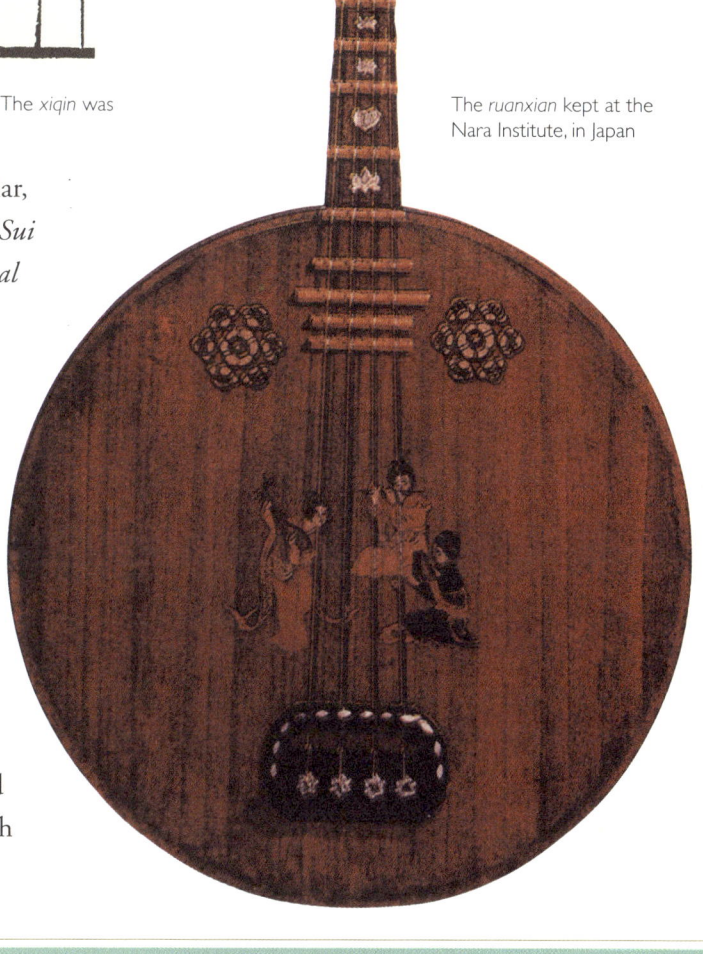

The *ruanxian* kept at the Nara Institute, in Japan

Kenzo Hayashi, a Japanese music scholar, writes in his works *On the Yan Music in the Sui and Tang Dynasties* and *A Research on Musical Instruments in East Asia* that there are still 100-plus pieces of Yan music left intact in Japan which were introduced from the Tang Dynasty. Some precious musical instruments and music scores are well preserved. Some popular bowed stringed instruments used in the Korean Peninsula today, such as the *xiqin* (haegeum), *jiayeqin* (gayageum) and *bili*, were introduced from the Sui and Tang dynasties. After their constant use of these instruments, the Korean people have turned them into their own ethnic instruments with their own local characteristics.

Guqin

With a history of 3,000-plus years, Chinese *guqin* (or ancient *qin*) is known as one of the most ancient plucked stringed instruments in the world. Similar to a zither its sound is produced by its strings and wooden resonator. The art of the *guqin* constitutes an essential part in the history of Chinese music, aesthetics, social culture and thought. This musical instrument is one of the leading representatives of ancient Chinese music. In November 2003 the art of Chinese *guqin* was on the "Masterpieces of the Oraland Intangible Heritage of Humanity" by UNESCO.

The art of the *guqin* witnessed a dramatic development in the Wei Kingdom and the Jin Dynasty. The well-known "seven wise scholars in the bamboo grove" in Chinese history refer to a group of seven dignitaries who shared an interest in drinking, singing poems and playing the *guqin*. Over a cup of liquor they talked heatedly about art, thought and politics. Ruan Ji of the Eastern Han Dynasty was known as a "crazy drunkard". However, the tunes of the *guqin* which he composed are well organized and modulated. The undulating rhythm of his lively musical arrangement faithfully describes the mentality of a crazy drunkard.

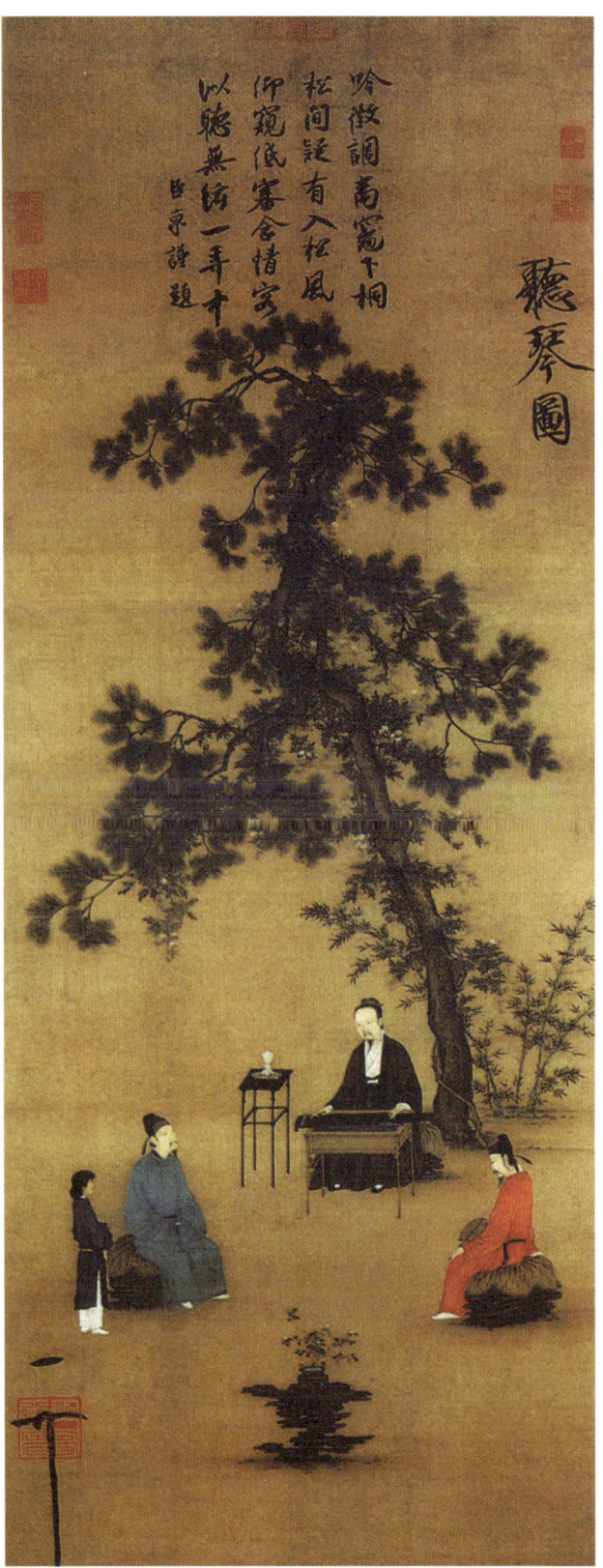

Scroll Painting of Enjoying the Qin Performance was done by Zhao Ji (1082 – 1135) from the Northern Song Dynasty. You can see a seated man in a Taoist robe playing the *qin* beside a grove of pine and bamboo. Sitting on each side are two men wearing official attire and black gauze caps. The officials in red and green respectively are listening attentively. A young servant is standing in a submissive manner. The painting reflects the order of seniority in a court.

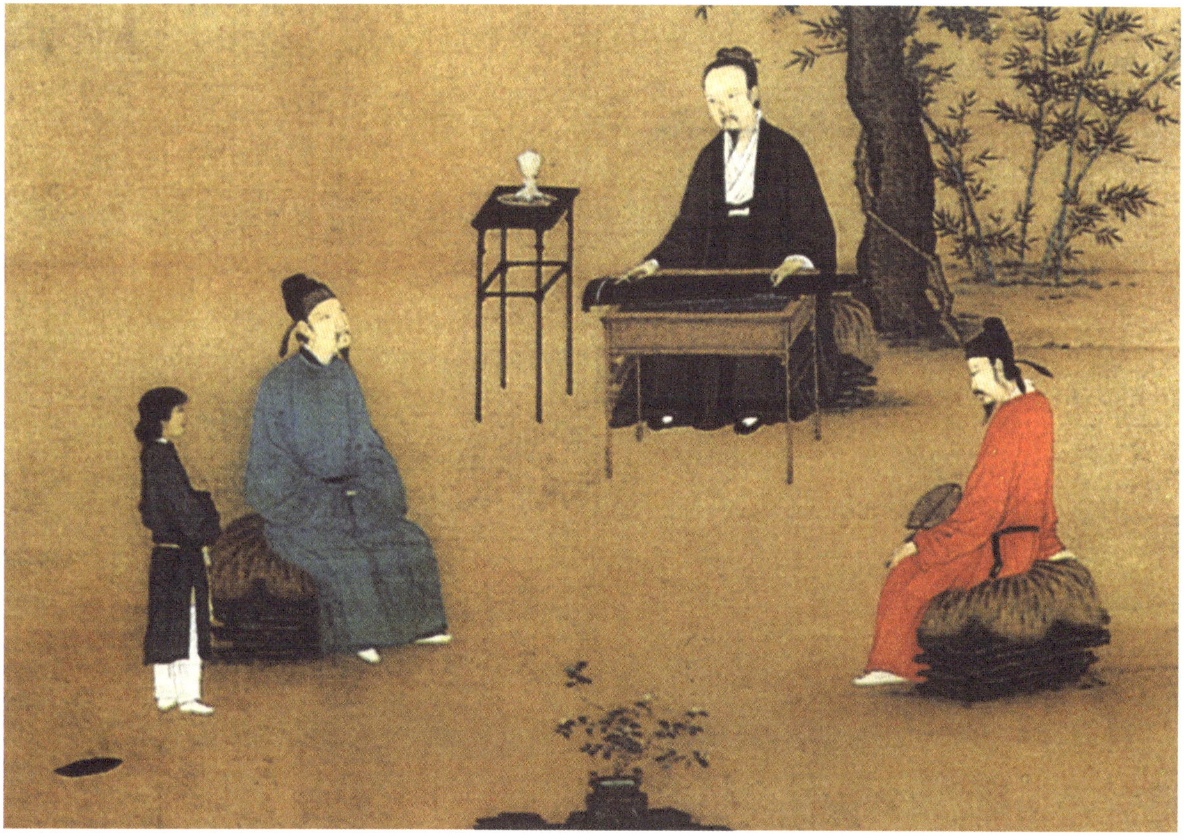

Scroll Painting of Enjoying the Qin Performance (detail)

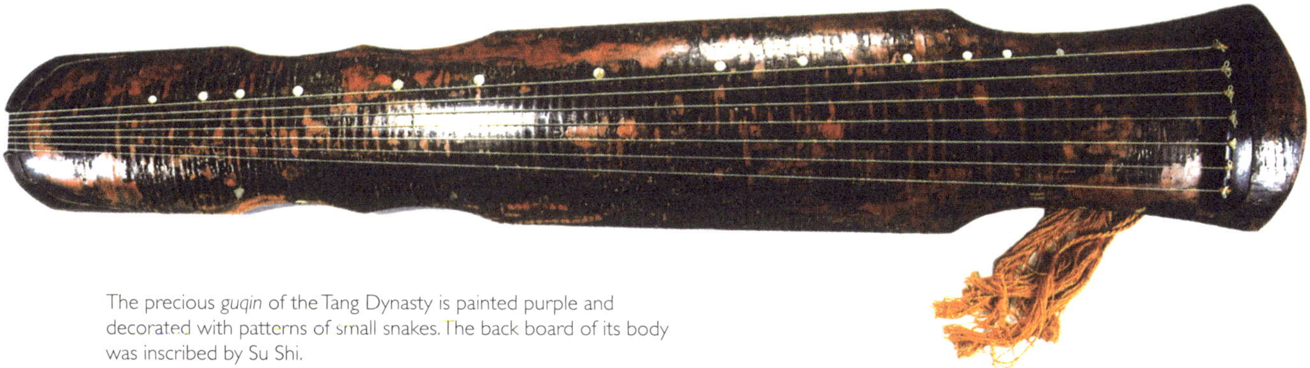

The precious *guqin* of the Tang Dynasty is painted purple and decorated with patterns of small snakes. The back board of its body was inscribed by Su Shi.

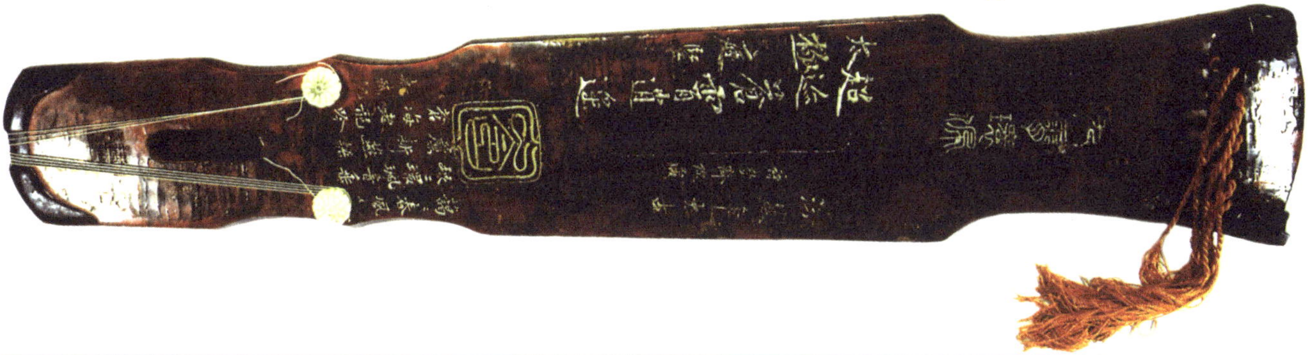

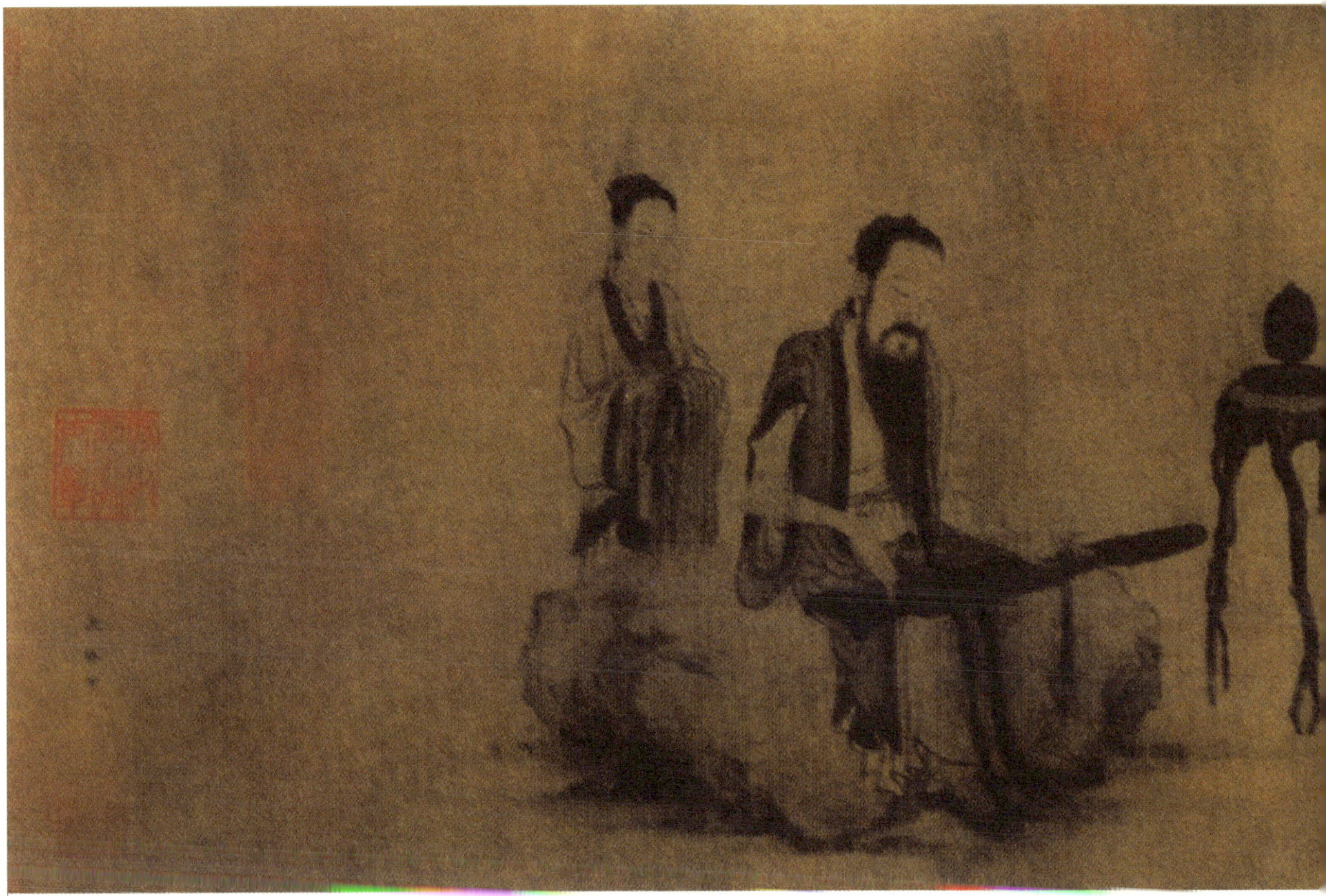

Painting of Bo Ya Playing the Qin is an ink painting on a silk scroll by Wang Zhenpeng, a famous painter from the Yuan Dynasty. The painting depicts the scene where Bo Ya is playing the *qin* for his soul mate Zhong Ziqi. The player's attentiveness and the listener's entrancement are vividly revealed. This illustrative painting tells the story of historical figures, which was first carried in *Lü's Spring and Autumn Annals*.

Guanglinsan

Guanglinsan is a famous *guqin* verse which has a great impact on ancient Chinese music. Ji Kang (224 – 263 AD), an outstanding prose writer and poet during the period of the Wei Kingdom and the Jin Dynasty is one of the well-known "seven wise scholars in the bamboo grove". He was especially good at playing this verse. He was sentenced to death for giving offence to other dignitaries. As a result, *Guanglinsan* was lost. Since then this famous verse has been wrapped in mystery and has become a popular topic of discussion throughout history.

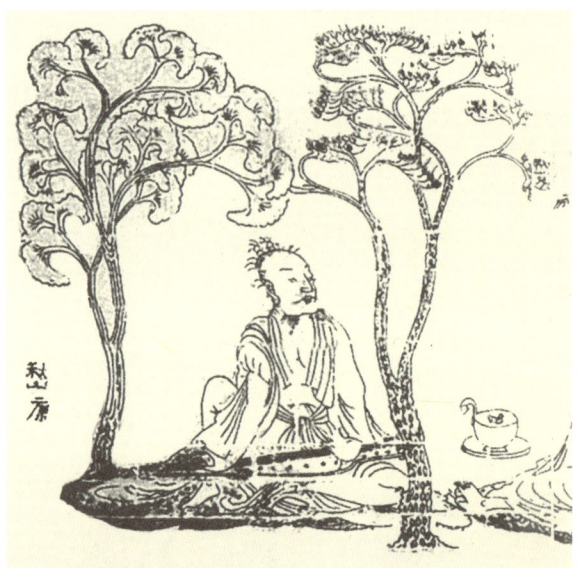

The mould-printed brick painting of the Southern Dynasty unearthed in Nanjing's Xishanqiao grave depicts seven dignitaries of Wei Kingdom and the Jin Dynasty who are also known as "seven wise scholars in the bamboo grove" in Chinese history. Ji Kang, sitting under a ginkgo tree, is playing the *qin* with his sleeves rolled up. His posture displays his self-possessed manner.

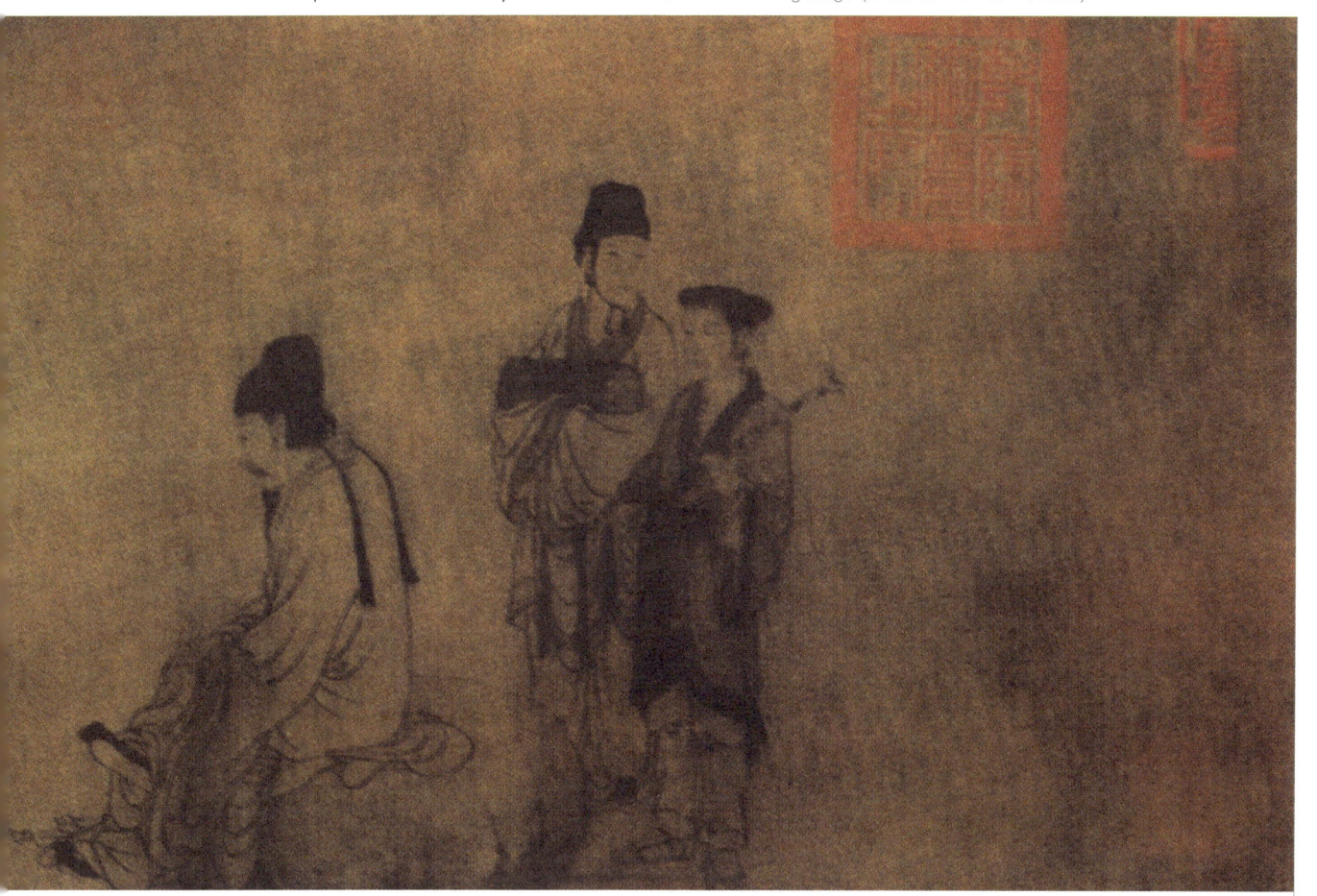

Zou Ji Remonstrates with the Duke of Qi by Talking about the Qin

Zou Ji lived in the Qi State during the Spring and Autumn Period and the Warring States Period. He was saddened to see the Duke of the Qi State wallow in drinking and womanizing and neglecting state affairs. One day, bringing his *qin* with him, Zou Ji presented himself before Emperor Wei. He said he would like to display his performing skill. Duke Wei of Qi told him to take a seat and start his performance. Zou Ji put the *qin* on the desk and made a show of his performance. But he did not pluck a single string. Impatiently, Duke Wei of Qi asked him for an explanation. Zou Ji said, "I know how to play the *qin*, and I also know how to make a *qin* and how one should play the *qin*." He still sat motionless. Duke Wei of Qi asked him to talk about how one should play the *qin*. Zou Ji rambled on about the method of making a *qin* and the way of playing the *qin* to cultivate oneself. He did not touch his *qin* while he spoke. Duke Wei of Qi lost his patience and said, "Your reasoning is sound, but too vague. If you don't play at all, how can I know whether your reasoning is significant and practical?" Then Zou Ji said seriously, "I compare the Qi State to a *qin*. Talking about how to govern our country without practical action won't do. Such is the case with me: talking about general principles without playing the *qin*. Your Majesty has been enthroned for nine years. You've talked a lot about the governance of the state, but you seldom take concrete measures. People are anxious for you to pull yourself together and start to handle state affairs again. I came here to talk about the *qin* instead of playing it. Isn't Your Majesty's practice the same as mine, that is, you don't govern the country you founded?" Tradition has it that after granting Zou Ji an audience, Duke Wei of Qi began to seek advice from all sides. By promoting what was beneficial and abolishing what was harmful, Duke Wei of Qi made his country strong and prosperous.

Age-old *Chiba*

Eight *chiba* (a type of flute) introduced from the Tang Dynasty are well preserved at the Nara Institute in Japan. They are of excellent workmanship with their surfaces carved with intricate patterns and figures. Instruments of this kind were used to perform court music in the imperial palace.

The instrument was named "chiba" (which in Chinese literally means the length of this variety of bamboo flute) during the Tang Dynasty. Tradition dictates that a musician called Lü Cai made this kind of flute as long as one *chi* (approximately 1.09 feet) and *ba* (eight) inches. This flute was also known as a "tune flute" because it was used to adjust the tune of the court music. Over time the *chiba* disappeared in most regions of China.

Rock Painting of *Baixi*

On this rock painting you can see a performance accompanied with mass *pangu* dancing and a bell and drum band depicted. The *pangu* dance was very popular in the Han Dynasty. The first row is composed of 5 female musicians who beat drums. The second row is composed of 5 male musicians with two *sheng*

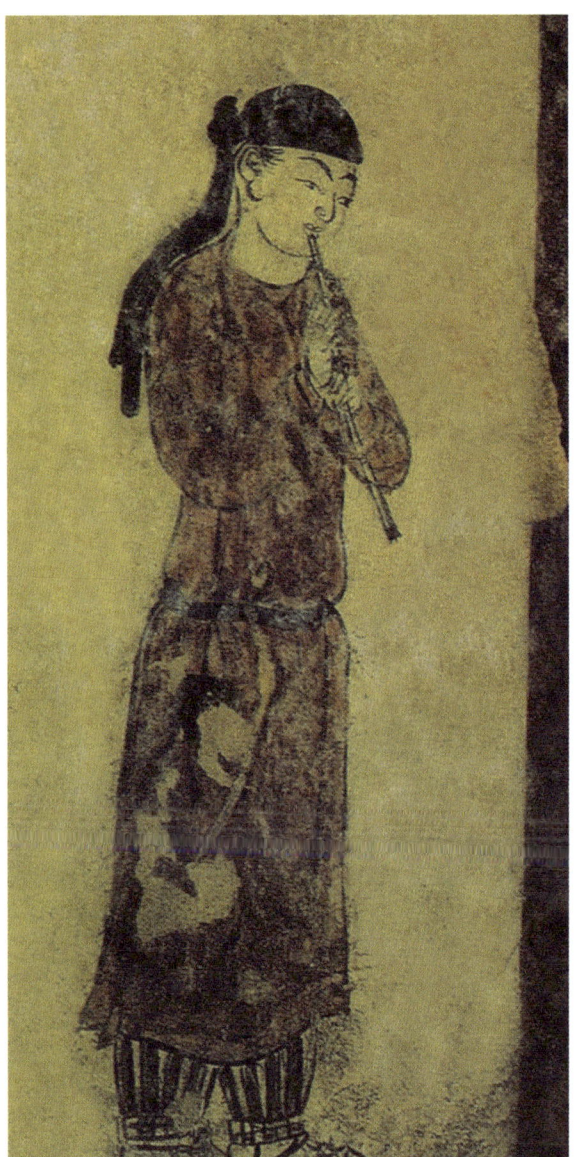

The *chiba* shown in the mural of Li Shuang's grave from the Tang Dynasty

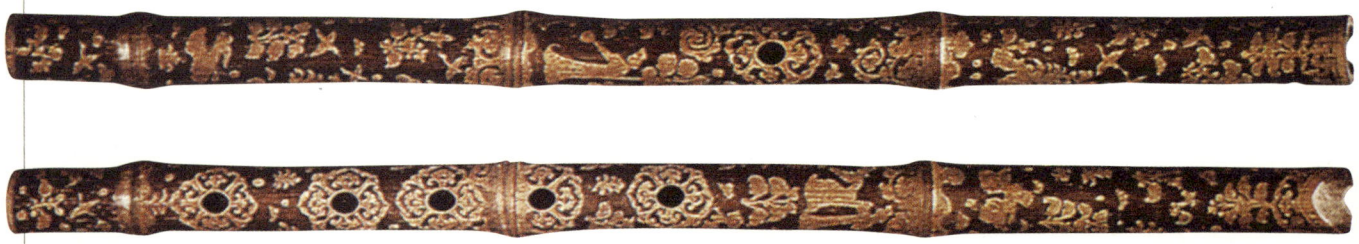

The *chiba* of the Tang Dynasty

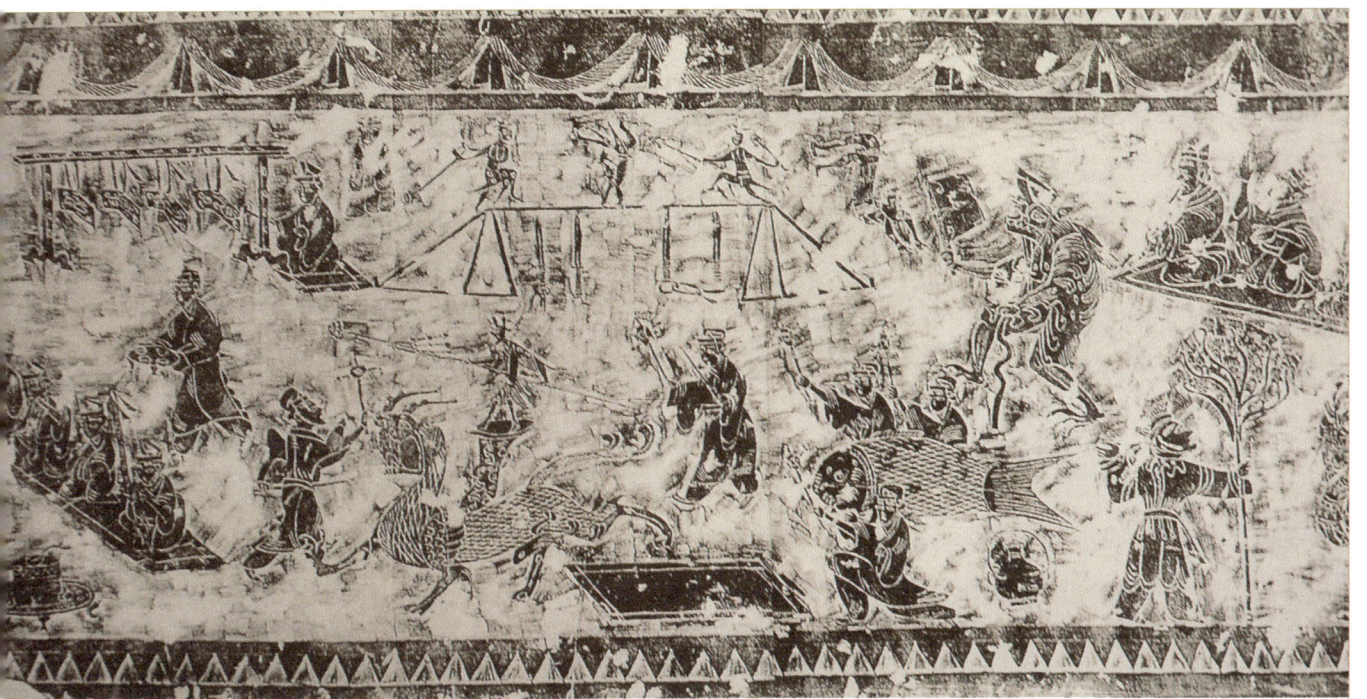

The rock painting of a *baixi* performance from the late Eastern Han Dynasty was unearthed at Yinan, Shandong Province. The three bands are shown to provide accompaniment to different acrobatic performances.

players, two *xiao* players and one percussionist. The next row is composed of 4 male musicians composed of one *yu* player, one *zhu* player, one *se* player and one beating either a *jiangu*, *bianzhong* and *bianqing*. This scene of a *baixi* performance is impressive in scope and the portrayal of performers is extremely accurate.

Cai Wenji and *Eighteen Passages of Hujia*

Cai Wenji, a daughter of the famous historian and musician Cai Yong, was herself a well-known musician during the last years of the Western Han Dynasty. During that period the whole country was thrown into disorder. While fleeing from her home, Cai Wenji was captured by the Southern Huns—an ancient nomadic people living in the north of China. Prince Zuoxian took her as his concubine and they had two children. During the twelve years when she lived among the Huns, Cai Wenji always missed her hometown. After he unified the north of China in 208 AD, Cao Cao sent an envoy to the Hun and bought her back after paying a big ransom. However, her two children were not allowed to accompany her. On her way back to her home, Cai Wenji played the tunes of *hujia* with her seven-stringed *qin*. In her sad and touching songs she expressed her longings for her native land and conveyed her sadness in parting from her children.

The *hujia* is a kind of wind instrument played by the ethnic groups in the west of ancient China. Its deep and resonant tone is suited to sad and melancholy tunes and expressing mixed sentimental emotions. The name of this composition means that it consists of 18 short passages. Cai Wenji's use of the Han designed *guqin*, was a great influence on future musical works.

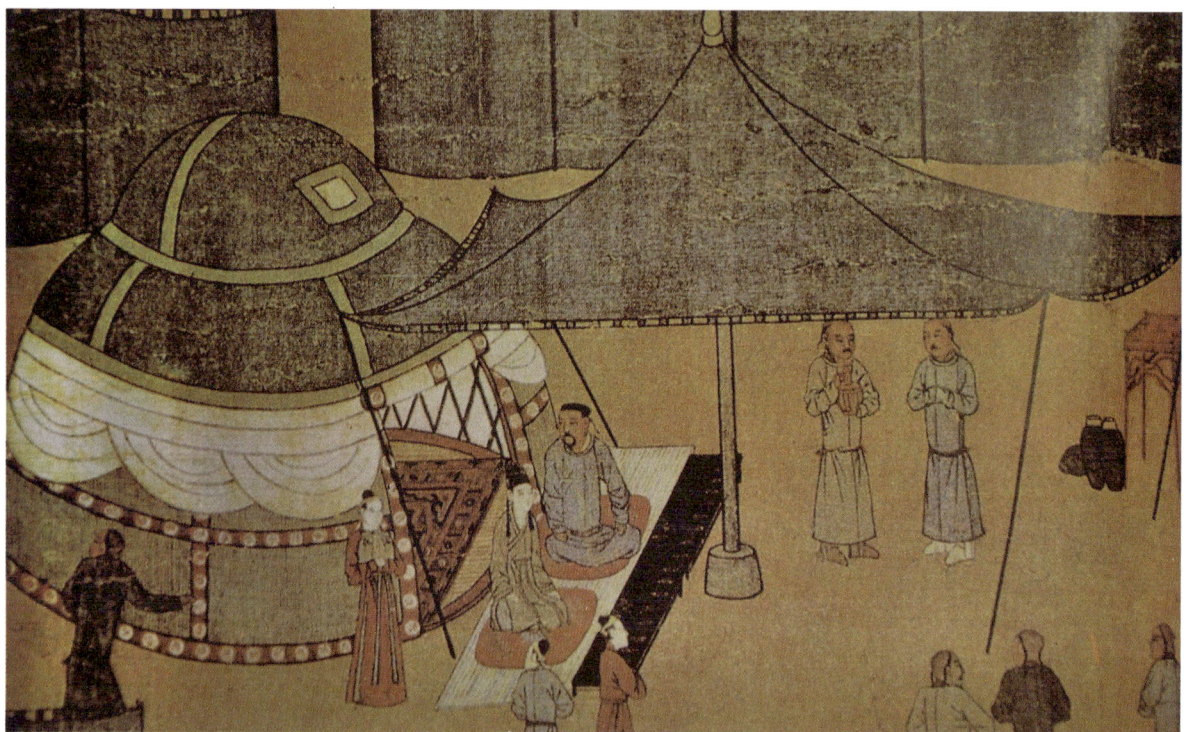
Copy from the Song Dynasty of *Eighteen Passges of Hujia* in Ming Dynasty

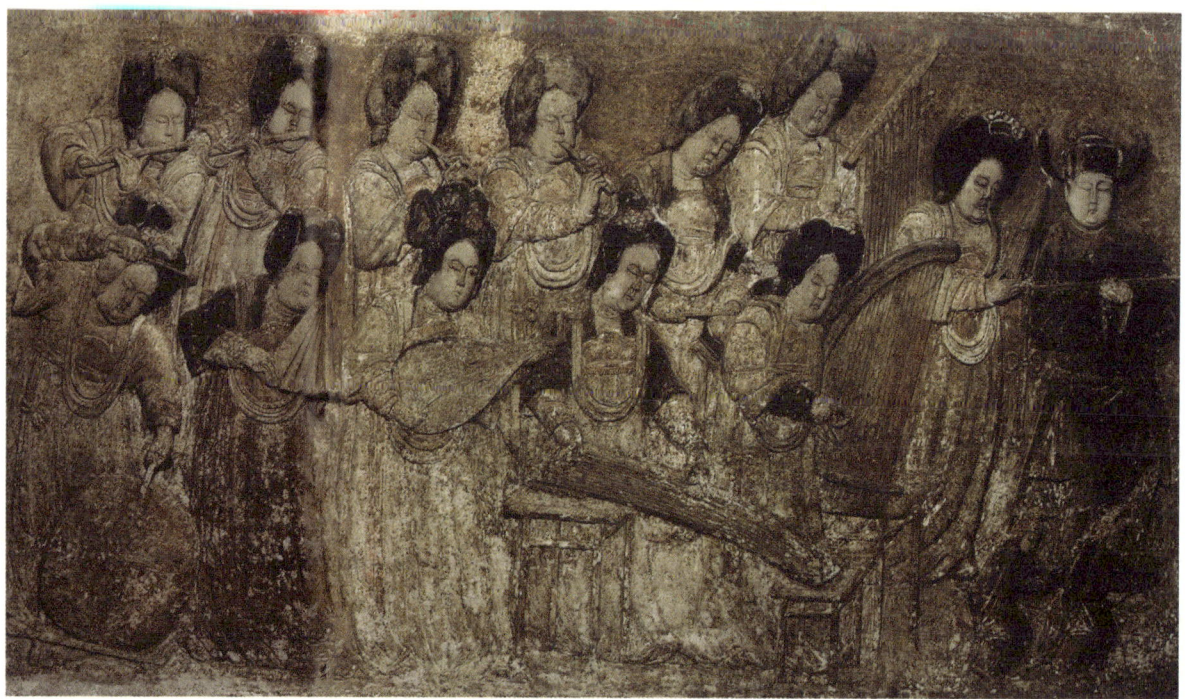
The Stone Carving of Self Amusement with Colored Painting of the Five Dynasties was unearthed in 1994 in Wang Chuzhi's grave at Quyang County, Hebei Province. Wang Chuzhi was a military governor during late Tang Dynasty and early Five Dynasties. The relief depicts a performance of *daqu*.

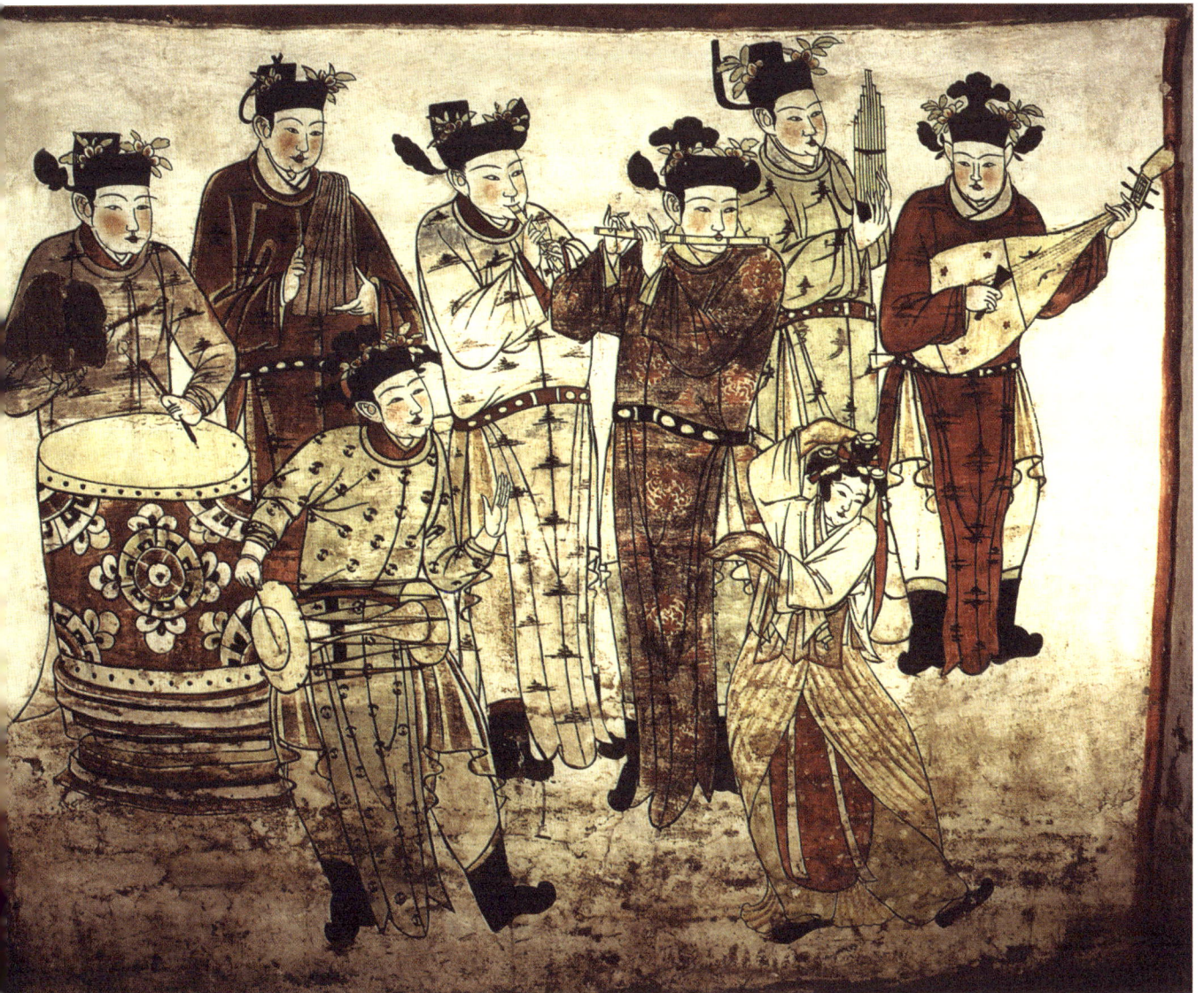

The *daqu* mural of the Liao Dynasty unearthed in Zhang's grave at Xuanhua, Hebei Province

Daqu of the Tang Dynasty

Daqu is the art of singing and dancing to the accompaniment of musical instruments. It inherited the Han tradition of combining the performance of a band with that of singing and dancing. It also incorporated the music of various ethnic groups such as the Xiliang, Qiuci, Shule and Gaochang, thus enriching the music style of the Tang Dynasty. According to historical records there were 121 compositions in the category of *daqu* and *Nishangyuyiqu* (which means "Melody of Colorful Garments") was its representative work. This was also considered a famous composition in religious music. This piece of *daqu* was composed by Li Longji, Emperor Xuanzong of the Tang Dynasty during the Kaiyuan years (712 – 741 AD).

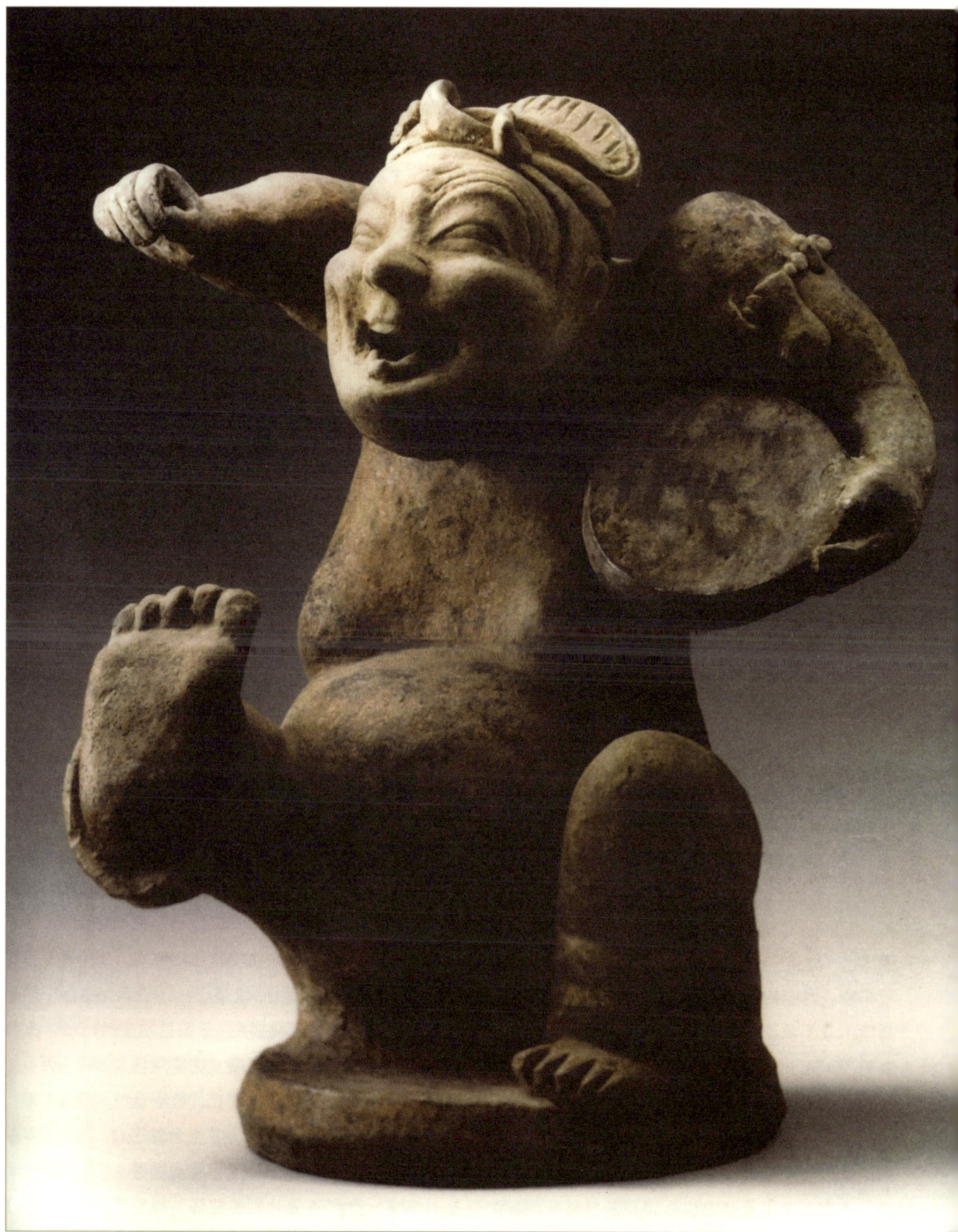

3 The Mature Stage
(From 960 to 1840 AD)

During these 800 years *quyi* (which means such Chinese folk art forms as ballad singing, storytelling, comic dialogues and clapper talks) and drama were vigorously developing. The solo or ensemble of musical performances reached artistic maturity. Collected works of *guqin* were published vigorously and studies on the aesthetics of music was becoming more popular.

The music in Chinese opera served as an accompaniment to the singing and spoken word in performances. The music conveyed the theme, plot and the conflict between characters. In addition, the musical language of Chinese drama served to connect plots and create an atmosphere. Different musical instruments were used respectively for different scenes in order to support the singing, acting or acrobatic fighting. It was the styles of music used that brought together the whole performance.

The music in Chinese drama is played by an ensemble. The musical accompaniment of the drama, which is called *changmian* in Chinese, was divided into the orchestra and the percussionists. The musical instruments used in the former were mainly the *huqin* (a type of 2 stringed violin), *dizi* (a type of flute), *guan* (a double reed wind instrument), *sheng* , *suona* (similar to an oboe) and *sanxian* (similar to a lute). Those used for percussion included the *bangu* (the single skin drum), *paiban* (a type of clapper), *bangzi* (a type of woodblock), *daluo* (a type of cymbals), *xiaoluo* (a type of gong), *naobo*, *qibo* (a type of cymbols) and *ling* (a type of chime).

The bowed stringed instruments were changing at this time due to the maturity of folk and dance music, and the emergence of new forms of dramatic art during the Song Dynasty. This laid the foundation of the final completion of Chinese ethnic music with four sections of wind, bowed, plucked, and percussion instruments. According to *The History of the Yuan Dynasty—Annals of Rites ands Music*, the *huqin* used at that time is similar to the present-day *huqin*. The Ming and Qing dynasties witnessed a further expansion of bowed stringed instruments amidst the development of dramatic music (*banhu* and *jinghu*), the spoken verse and lyrical songs (*sihu* and *zhuihu*) and the folk music (*erhu* and *gaohu*).

The spoken word and sung folk entertainment singing was popular during the Han Dynasty. The 2,000-year-old pottery figurine of an entertainer is speaking while beating the drum. Bare-chested and bare-footed, the entertainer is holding a drum under his left arm and a stick in his right hand. His performance is given in a funny and exaggerated manner. In the Han Dynasty men of low stature and unconventional looks usually acted as entertainers.

The *Qupai* of Chinese Dramatic Music

Qupai refers to the tunes used to enhance plot and create theatrical atmosphere. *Qupai* is divided into six categories: sacred music, banquet music, dance music, military music, wedding music and funeral music, e.g., *Xiaokaimen, Yeshenchen* and *Jiangershui*.

Each *qupai* has a specific name, structure and pattern and some *qupai* may also be only instrumental. The repetition of a tune is flexible in performance. According to some statistics, there are as many as a thousand different names for *qupai* and most of them are still used in various local operas, especially in such local operas as *kunqu* and *gaoqiang*. More than a hundred *qupai* are still used in the Beijing opera alone.

A Book of Music—an Encyclopedia of Chinese Folk Music

Chen Yang completed his *A Book of Music* in 1100 after over 40 years of research. The 200-volume book covers a wide range of subjects: the system of music, the theory of music, *bayin* (which means "musical sounds made by ancient instruments of eight categories of materials–metal, stone, string, bamboo, gourd, pottery, leather and wood), songs, local operas, and music for different rites. In addition to valuable historical records, there are a great number of precious illustrations. As the first encyclopedia

Story-telling with drum accompaniment was prevalent in the north of China. There was a woodblock Spring Festival picture published by Yangliuqing during the Qing Dynasty depicting a story told about the battle to capture Changsha. In the picture a female entertainer is beating the drum with a stick in her right hand while singing with clappers in her left hand. The two accompanists playing the *sihu* and *sanxian* respectively are sitting by her side. This is the typical scene of story telling prevalent in the north.

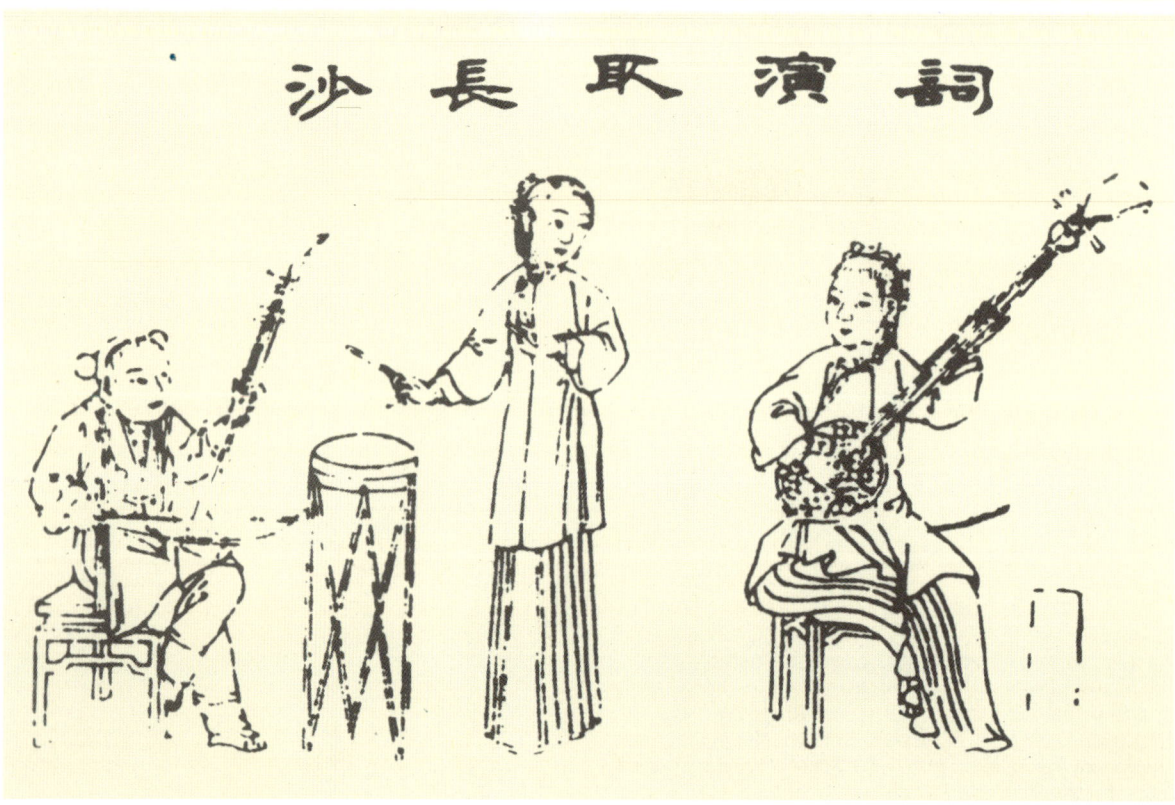

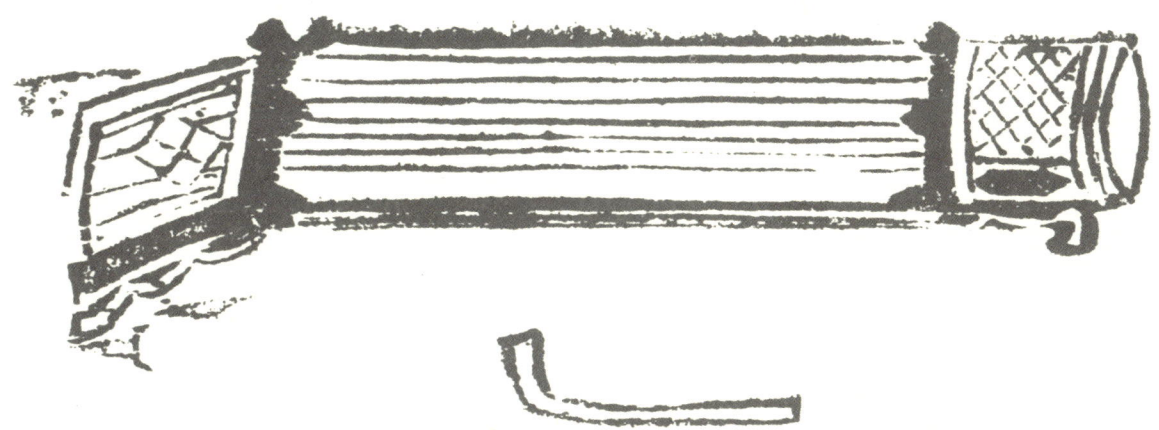

of traditional Chinese music it provides us with important historical documents about the culture and history of Chinese music before the Northern Song Dynasty.

This is a picture of the *yazheng* in *A Book of Music* by Chenyang of the Song Dynasty. The *yazheng* is a traditional musical instrument prevalent in Hebei, Henan, Jilin and Yanbian. It looks like the *zheng* and *se*. It is sounded by moving a thin bamboo strip across the strings.

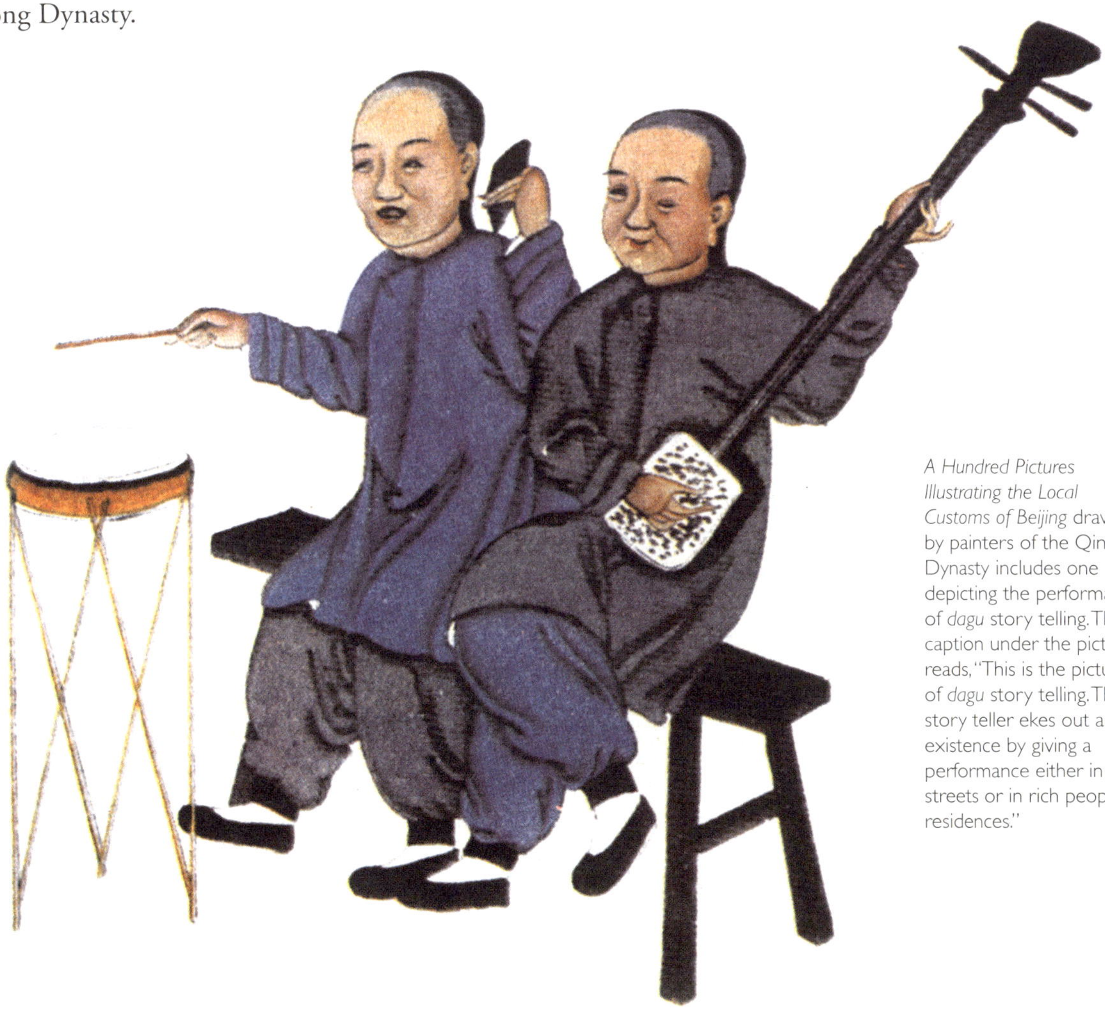

A Hundred Pictures Illustrating the Local Customs of Beijing drawn by painters of the Qing Dynasty includes one depicting the performance of *dagu* story telling. The caption under the picture reads, "This is the picture of *dagu* story telling. The story teller ekes out an existence by giving a performance either in the streets or in rich people's residences."

4 The Modern and Contemporary Stage
(From 1840 to present)

China is a country with many ethnic groups. All fifty-six ethnic groups have their own traditional musical instruments. Several thousand different types of instruments possess unique styles and features. A great variety of local ensembles exist in different ethnic regions and are capable of playing different genres of folk music with a variety of instruments, such as, wind and percussion instruments, traditional stringed and woodwind instruments, drum and wind instruments, stringed instruments and gongs and drums.

The traditional ensembles of stringed and woodwind instruments which are prevalent south of the Yangtze River are usually played by a small band in a courtyard. The music is known for its

This is *Painting of a Fair in Beijing* by a painter from the Qing Dynasty, which depicts a scene showing how percussion instruments were used in the social life of ancient China.

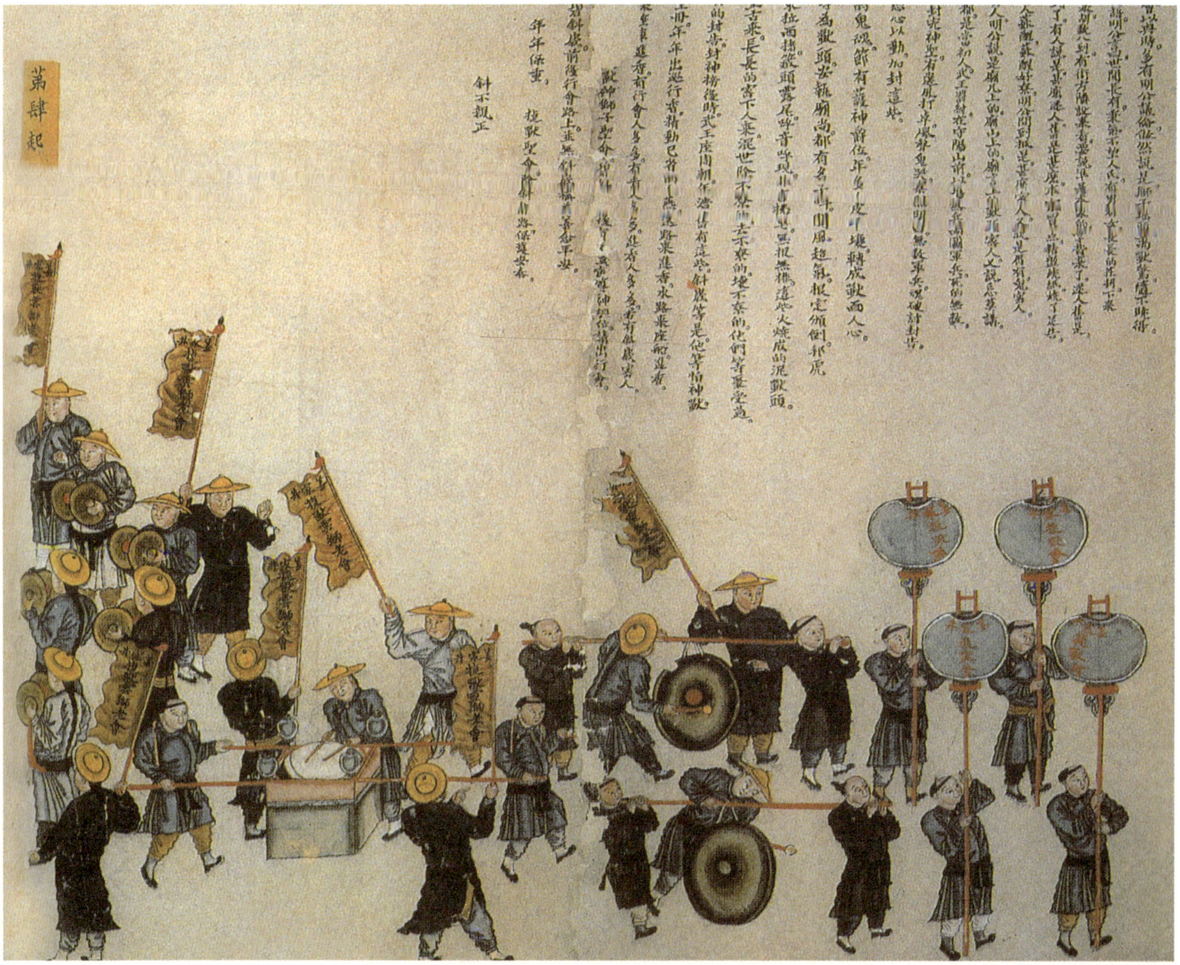

soft, melodious and exquisite tone. Ensembles of wind and percussion instruments, which are characterized as being rustic, straightforward and lively, are suited for a performance in a public square. Ensembles of drum and wind instruments with *suona* and *guan* as leading instruments were known for the flexibility and clarity of their performing style. Ensembles of stringed instruments including both the plucked and bowed stringed instruments were distinguished by their natural, refined and lyrical style. As the most common genre of traditional Chinese music, ensembles of gongs and drums are widely used to accompany dragon boat races, lion dances and dragon dances. Such performances mainly use copper percussion instruments and are usually given in a public square.

In modern times after 1840 Western music was introduced into China. Chinese folk orchestras were then formed and professional musical education came into being. At the beginning of the 20th century the famous Chinese musician Liu Tianhua established "The Chinese Music Promotion Society". He was engaged in writing new compositions and developing music for the *erhu* (similar to a violin) and *pipa*. He also devoted himself to the study of teaching of Chinese music. He made a great contribution to the improvement of Chinese instrumental music and created works such as *Guangmingxing*, *Kongshanniaoyu*, and *Liangxiao*. A group of talented folk artists represented by Hua Yanjun (known also as A' bing) also created such enduring works such as *Erquanyingyue* and *Tingsong* at this time.

After 1949 special attention was given to the following genres of folk music: Guangdong music, Hebei *Chuige*, Fujian *Nanyin*, Zhoushan *Luogu* and Jiangnan *Sizhu*. People of the music world collected and sorted out all the materials —the words, scores and tunes—necessary for these genres of music. Various bands and even orchestras of traditional Chinese instruments were set up throughout China.

Guangdong Music (Stringed and Woodwind Instruments)

Guangdong music took shape at the end of the 19th century and at the beginning of the 20th century by integrating folk tunes prevalent in the

Painting of Court Music Depicting the Times of Peace and Prosperity

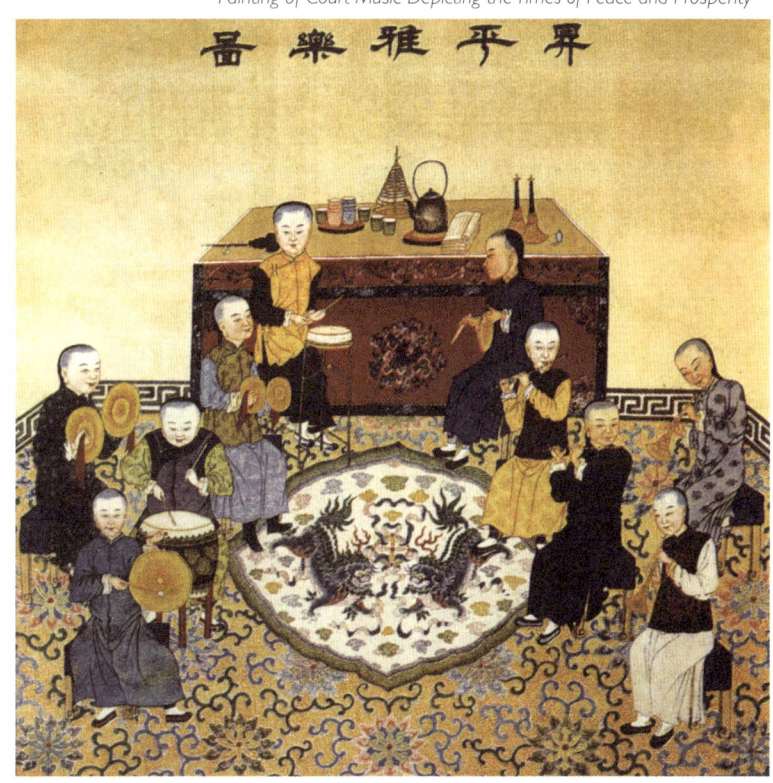

Zhujiang River Delta, Guangdong Province with Guangdong opera. Guangdong music is known for its crisp, bright and beautiful melodies. Due to its quick and joyful rhythm, Guangdong music consists of mostly short and single-mode pieces. Compositions of cyclic form are seldom heard.

Guangdong music was initially used to accompany the local opera or create an atmosphere for special occasions such as weddings and funerals. It is good at depicting the episodes of one's daily life, especially those of interest to the local people. Instead of showcasing serious themes about society and life, Guangdong music is composed to depict flowers, birds, fish, insects and natural scenes so as to please listeners' ears.

Jiangnan Sizhu (Stringed and Woodwind Instruments)

Jiangnan *Sizhu* is very popular south of the Yangtze River, especially in the south of Jiangsu Province, the west of Zhejiang Province and in Shanghai.

The ensemble is composed of mainly stringed and woodwind instruments. Very few percussion instruments are used. Its melodious, lively and joyful tunes are played in a smooth, exquisite and gorgeous style. As the music developed from the tunes people played for leisure, the tunes and words were originally improvised by the players themselves. In performances of this kind the musical skill is seen in the coordination of the musicians.

The China National Orchestra gave a Spring Festival concert at Vienna's Golden Hall in 1998. One item in the program was *Sanliu*—a famous composition of Jiangnan *Sizhu*. The ensemble of plucked stringed instruments was played without a conductor. As soon as they finished the impromptu performance, the audience, who marveled at the artistic appeal of the traditional Chinese music, broke into a deafening ovation and prolonged cheers.

Xi'an Guyue

Xi'an *Guyue*—an ensemble of traditional Chinese wind and percussion instruments with the *dizi* as the leading instrument—originated in the Tang and Song dynasties and assumed a fairly complete form in the Ming and Qing dynasties. Composed of *zuoyue* (music played by those in a sitting posture) and *xingyue* (music played by those in a moving status), this kind of music was often performed at fairs or in religious ceremonies held in temples. The art of *guyue* is still preserved by some Buddhist temples in Xi'an. The performers use the *di*, *sheng*, *guan*, *bangzi* and percussion instruments to create atmospheres for various occasions and depict different themes.

The *sheng*

Fujian *Nanyin*

Fujian *Nanyin*, prevalent in the south of Fujian Province, Taiwan and Southeast Asia, is known for its unaffected and refined melody. This kind of music has continued the tradition of the Tang and Song dynasties. Performances of *nanyin* can be seen in ancient paintings. Gu Hongzhong, a famous painter in the Southern Tang Dynasty of the Five Dynasties, depicts in his painting *The Night Revels of Han Xizai* a performance of court music at an official's banquet. The performance of the *paiban*, *pipa* and drums shown in the painting is almost the same as today. The instruments are arranged in two groups. One group consists of the *dongxiao* (a type

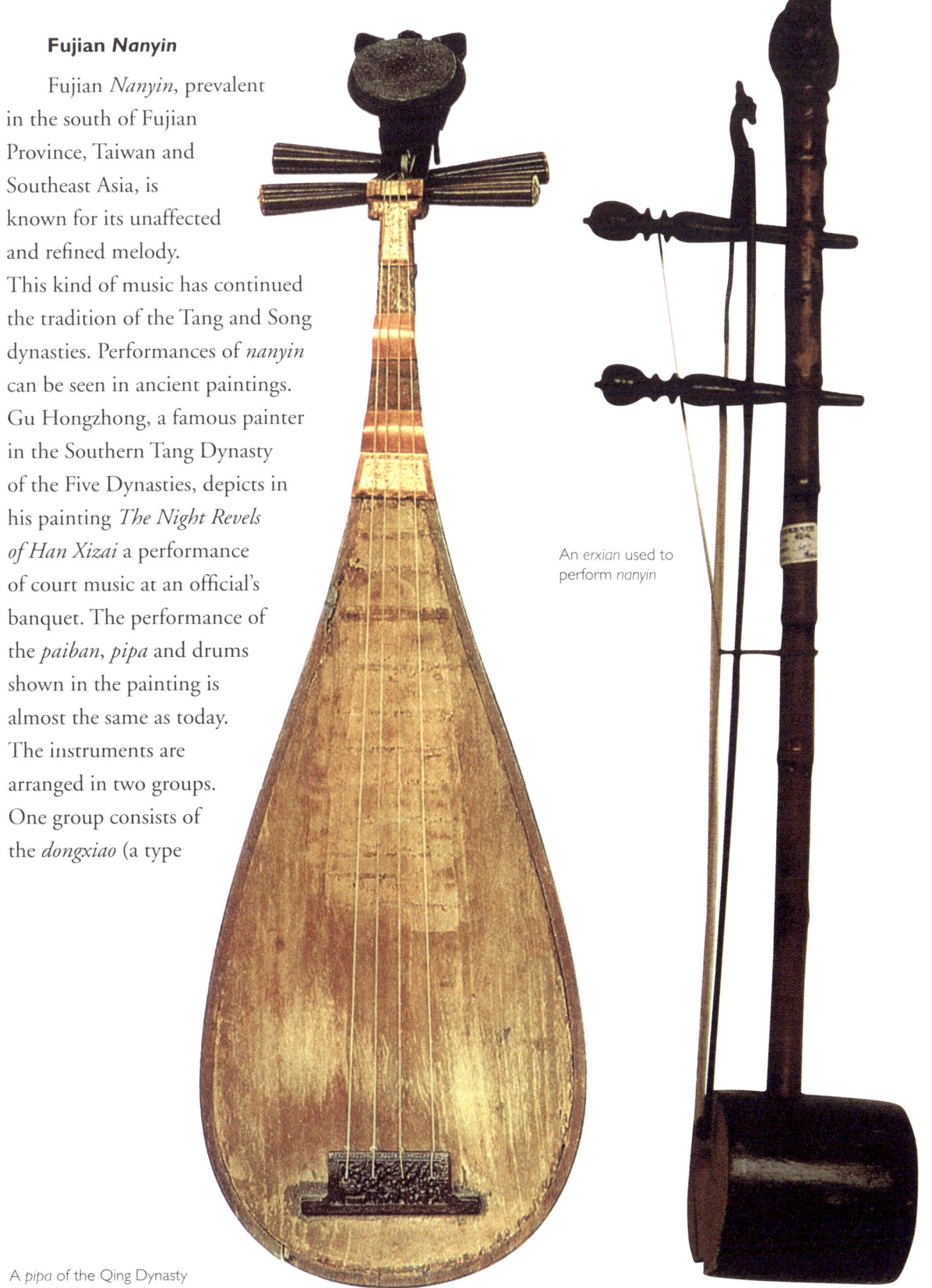

An *erxian* used to perform *nanyin*

A *pipa* of the Qing Dynasty

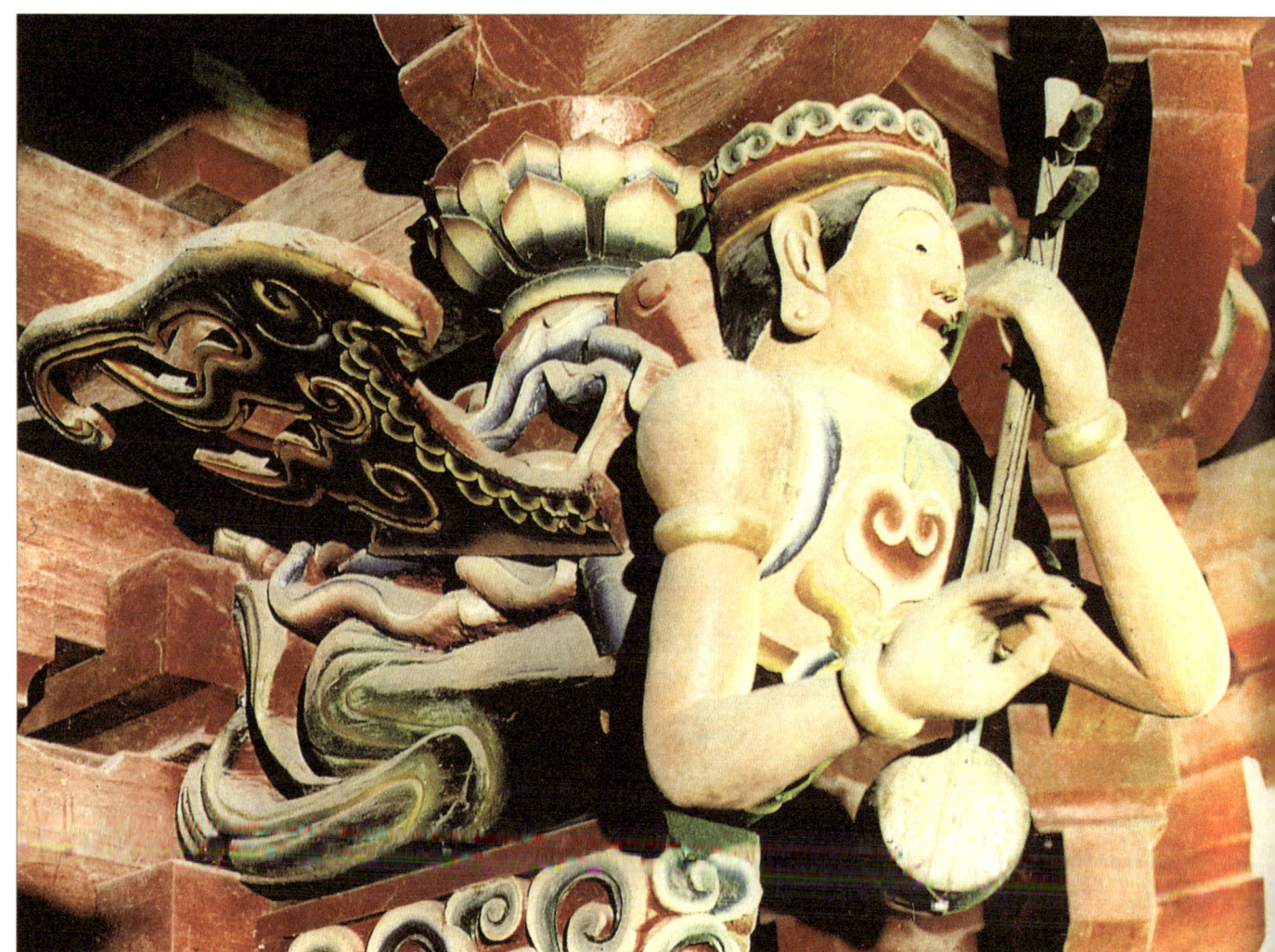

Flying musical entertainers, also known as "birds with a voice of gold", are woodcarvings supporting the roof of the main hall of Kaiyuan Temple in Quanzhou. The 24 birds with human heads are holding up the flitch beam with their heads and wings. Some are holding the *sheng*, *guan*, *xiao* and *di*; others are holding the four precious articles of the writing table (i.e., writing brush, ink stick, ink slab and paper); and still some others are holding treasures and mascots. Flying musical entertainers are regarded as a perfect combination of architecture, carving, religion and art.

of flute), *erxian* (a type of *huqin*), *pipa*, *sanxian* (a three-stringed type of lute) and *paiban* (a type of clapper) while the other group is composed of the *xiaosuona*, *pipa*, *sanxian*, *erxian* (two-stringed type of lute), *xiangzhan* (a miniature gong), *goujiao* (a small gong), *duo* (a large bel), *sibao* (a type of bamboo clappers), *tongling* (a type of handbell) and *biangu* (a type of drum).

Hebei *Chuige* (Ensemble of Pipe Instruments)

Hebei *Chuige*, prevalent in Hebei Province, originated from local folk songs and melodies from local operas. The players use pipe instruments to mimic vocal melodies. Some tunes succeed in portraying different characters. The representative tunes of Hebei *Chuige* include *Bangzidiao*, *Hebei bangzi*, *Shandong dagu* and *Xiaokaimen*.

Source of Oriental Style

In respect of the scale structure of Chinese music, the five-sound melodies are the fundamental feature of Chinese music because they reflect the unaffected, lively and smooth style of the tunes of Oriental music. Though techniques of expression are different in various genres of Chinese music (e.g., the smooth and melodious Jiangnan *Sizhu*, the unaffected and refined Guangdong music, and the rustic and unrestrained Northern *Guyue*), they share a common feature of adopting five-sound melodies to demonstrate their peculiar tones. This is considered the most fundamental feature of Chinese folk music.

Western music is distinguished by its seven-sound melodies based on twelve-tones of equal temperament. Importance is attached to aesthetic perception reflected by a good combination of harmony. The principal feature of Western music is its beautiful melody and perfect acoustics. However, Chinese music is based on the development of single-melody tunes. In addition, the kernel of Chinese music lies in its appeal of rhythms and the contextual beauty presented by its tunes.

Chinese Folk Orchestra

With the development of the ensemble of traditional Chinese instruments throughout China, people started to form Chinese folk orchestras by imitating the structure of the Western symphony orchestras and learning from their mode of composition. Stage performances gradually replaced the original style of performing on special occasions.

A Chinese folk orchestra is usually composed of four sections: wind, bowed, plucked and percussion instruments. The instruments prevalent among the Han form a large proportion. In order to meet the requirements of such an ensemble, many modified traditional instruments have been incorporated into the orchestra.

Dynasties in Chinese History

Xia Dynasty	2070 BC – 1600 BC
Shang Dynasty	1600 BC – 1046 BC
Zhou Dynasty	1046 BC – 256 BC
Western Zhou Dynasty	1046 BC – 771 BC
Eastern Zhou Dynasty	770 BC – 256 BC
Spring and Autumn Period	770 BC – 476 BC
Warring States Period	475 BC – 221 BC
Qin Dynasty	221 BC – 206 BC
Han Dynasty	206 BC – 220 AD
Western Han Dynasty	206 BC – 25 AD
Eastern Han Dynasty	25 AD – 220 AD
Three Kingdoms	220 AD – 280 AD
Wei	220 AD – 265 AD
Shu Han	221 AD – 263 AD
Wu	222 AD – 280 AD
Jin Dynasty	265 AD – 420 AD
Western Jin Dynasty	265 AD – 316 AD
Eastern Jin Dynasty	317 AD – 420 AD
Northern and Southern Dynasties	420 AD – 589 AD
Southern Dynasties	420 AD – 589 AD
Northern Dynasties	439 AD – 581 AD
Sui Dynasty	581 AD – 618 AD
Tang Dynasty	618 AD – 907 AD
Five Dynasties and Ten States	907 AD – 960 AD
Five Dynasties	907 AD – 960 AD
Ten States	902 AD – 979 AD
Song Dynasty	960 AD – 1279
Northern Song Dynasty	960 AD – 1127
Southern Song Dynasty	1127 – 1279
Liao Dynasty	916 AD – 1125
Jin Dynasty	1115 – 1234
Xixia Dynasty	1038 – 1227
Yuan Dynasty	1279 – 1368
Ming Dynasty	1368 – 1644
Qing Dynasty	1644 – 1911